Bakhtin and Theatre

What *did* Bakhtin think about the theatre? That it was outdated? That it 'stopped being a serious genre' after Shakespeare? Could a thinker to whose work ideas of theatricality, visuality and embodied activity were so central really have nothing to say about theatrical practice?

Bakhtin and Theatre is the first book to explore the relation between Bakhtin's ideas and the theatre practice of his time. In that time, Stanislavsky co-founded the Moscow Art Theatre in 1898 and continued to develop his ideas about theatre until his death in 1938. Stanislavsky's pupil Meyerhold embraced the Russian Revolution and created some stunningly revolutionary productions in the 1920s, breaking with the realism of his former teacher. Less than twenty years after Stanislavsky's death and Meyerhold's assassination, a young student called Grotowski was studying in Moscow, soon to break the mould with his Poor Theatre. All three directors challenged the prevailing notion of theatre, drawing on, disagreeing with and challenging each other's ideas. Bakhtin's early writings about action, character and authorship provide a revealing framework for understanding this dialogue between these three masters of twentieth-century theatre.

Dick McCaw is Senior Lecturer in Theatre and Performance at Royal Holloway, University of London.

Bakhtin and Theatre

Dialogues with Stanislavsky, Meyerhold and Grotowski

Dick McCaw

Routledge
Taylor & Francis Group
LONDON AND NEW YORK

First published 2016
by Routledge
2 Park Square, Milton Park, Abingdon, Oxon OX14 4RN

and by Routledge
711 Third Avenue, New York, NY 10017

Routledge is an imprint of the Taylor & Francis Group, an informa business

British Library Cataloging-in-Publication Data
A catalogue record for this book is available from the British Library

Library of Congress Cataloging-in-Publication Data
McCaw, Dick.
Bakhtin and theatre : dialogues with Stanislavsky, Meyerhold and Grotowski /
by Dick McCaw.
pages cm
1. Theater   Philosophy. 2. Theater   Production and direction. 3. Method
acting. 4. Stanislavsky, Konstantin, 1863 1938   Criticism and interpretation.
5. Meierkhold, V. E. (Vsevolod Emil'evich), 1874 1940   Criticism and
interpretation. 6. Grotowski, Jerzy, 1933 1999   Criticism and interpretation.
7. Bakhtin, M. M. (Mikhail Mikhailovich), 1895 1975   Influence. I. Title.
PN2039.M375 2015
792.01   dc23
2015003734

ISBN: 978-1-138-89144-9 (hbk)
ISBN: 978-1-138-89145-6 (pbk)
ISBN: 978-1-315-70965-9 (ebk)

Typeset in Baskerville
by Taylor & Francis Books

I dedicate this book to Carl Heap, who introduced me to theatre in 1974 and to the writings of Mikhail Bakhtin in 1982.

Contents

Preface

Bakhtin and theatre?

I was heartened to read in the preface to Ken Hirschkop's book *Mikhail Bakhtin: An Aesthetic for Democracy* that it took him many years to draw a book from his doctoral thesis. Mine has been exactly the same case: having completed and defended my thesis – *Bakhtin's Other Theatre* – in 2004, it has taken me ten years to arrive at a book that does the job that I had hoped the thesis might have done. The thesis followed the development of Bakhtin's ideas from the 1920s to the 1970s, and had chapters on Stanislavsky, Meyerhold, Grotowski, Materic and Vasiliev. When I started work on the thesis in 1997, I already had the title in mind: it punned on the word 'other', a key term in Bakhtin's thinking, and suggested that, while a certain rather old-fashioned image of theatre was important for him as a foil to help him articulate his ideas about the novel, his theory seemed to cast the shadow of a quite different, quite modern theatre. However, I found little meaningful connection between his theory and theatre practice.

A moment of illumination about character, novel and theatre came from a public discussion I had organised in the 1999 International Workshop Festival involving directors Mladen Materic and Anatoli Vasiliev. Materic argued that the notion of 'character' was a concept drawn from the nineteenth-century novel and had no bearing on contemporary theatre making. This fascinating claim both challenged and contextualised Bakhtin's ideas and I happily acknowledge a continuing debt to Materic.

I realised much later that the connection between Bakhtin and theatre was mainly autobiographical and dates back to 1982 when I was with the Medieval Players (1981–1992) – a touring theatre company that I created with director and actor Carl Heap. Our planned production for summer 1983 was an adaptation of Rabelais' *Gargantua* in Sir Thomas Urquhart's salty translation. While the idea of Rabelais appealed hugely, the reality of the novel posed problems: I did not find it funny and couldn't access its world. Carl suggested that I read a book by an eccentric Russian called Bakhtin which was a 'rambling and repetitious read' but might help me better understand Rabelais. He was right: *Rabelais and His World* made sense of the images and values in the novel, and gave me an appetite for Bakhtin's work which has been enduring. Gradually, more and more references to Bakhtin started to creep into the talks and workshops I used to give at schools and universities to drum up support for our performances. Bakhtin's vivid evocations of popular medieval and Renaissance culture were a sure means of gaining an audience's attention – he so brilliantly conveyed Rabelais' vital, vulgar, earthy, generous humour. As Bakhtin's books were translated throughout the 1980s so they fed into all subsequent talks that I gave. What began as a happy accident turned into a thirty-year fascination with this Russian thinker, but this in no way constituted a real connection between his thinking and theatre practice.

As I learned later, the Medieval Players was not the only theatre company to be inspired by *Rabelais and His World*. Wlodimierz Staniewski, director of the Polish Gardzienice Theatre Association; Georgian theatre director Robert Sturua; and Russian director Yuri Lyubimov are just three international figures who have been inspired by Bakhtin. Birgit Beumers describes how Bakhtin's ideas offered a solution to Pushkin's seemingly unstageable *Boris Godunov*:

> The carnival modality eliminated barriers between actors and audiences by suggesting a common shared space and aesthetic time unbroken by conventions; theatrical and sociopolitical constraints were ignored in this small universe in favour of open address.[1]

Paul Allain notes how Bakhtin influenced Gardzienice's artistic policy and practice.

> Staniewski was deeply inspired by Bakhtin's notions of carnival and the carnivalesque as detailed in *Rabelais and His World* and this book became central to Gardzienice's work. [...] Bakhtin's theories of carnival related to the Polish context on several levels and helped relate the theatre practice of Gardzienice to the political context.[2]

Allain goes on to explain how 'Physical elements were taken directly from Bakhtin. His description of the "grotesque" body and laughter that undermines authority were concrete enough for the company to physically interpret them'.[3] For example, they worked on how to 'develop the art of the belly laugh'. Staniewski 'turned laughter into a musical, rhythmic aesthetic form, that demands strict diaphragm control and physical looseness in allowing the body and the organs of the voice to release the sound'.[4] Although Allain argues that 'Gardzienice do[es] not literally interpret Bakhtin's writings', some of his descriptions are very literal. His observation that '[t]he body was the dominant instrument of communication with the mouth always open in song' teaches us little since most singing is done with an open mouth, and many acting styles – grotesque and non-grotesque – are body-based.[5] Interesting as this information is – and there is a study waiting to be written which will thoroughly document Bakhtin's considerable influence on contemporary theatre practitioners – it still did not get at the fundamental theoretical connection between his ideas and theatre practice.

I began to think again about Bakhtin and theatre in 2011 and spent two years thinking about how the doctoral thesis could become a book. It was only in 2013 when the notion that the argument could be organised around questions of theatre that the shape of the present book came into mind. This is exactly the key that brought Bakhtin's thinking and the thinking behind theatrical practice into a dynamic relation with each other. It soon became clear that the chapters of the thesis on Materic and Vasiliev had to go, and the focus had to tighten around a debate between Meyerhold, Grotowski and Stanislavsky. These three directors/pedagogues were constantly questioning themselves and each other about the nature of theatre and about the actor's work in theatre. The more I thought about the subject the more I realised that Bakhtin's writings – especially his early thinking – provided the ground for these questions. Although he applied these questions to a philosophical conception of the novel, it became clear that they could frame the enquiry of my chosen trio of theatre directors. The result is a book which is highly selective in its use of materials: I make little reference to the well-known texts by Bakhtin, and have chosen only certain aspects of his thinking. The same goes for writings by and about the theatre practitioners. Anything that did not help me to frame, answer and exhaust the potential of these questions of theatre had to be set aside. This book could have been bigger had I explored the dialogue about questions of theatre that was continued by Vakhtangov in Moscow, by Michael Chekhov first in Moscow, then England and the United States, and finally by Brecht in the German Democratic Republic after World War Two. Such discussion would fit into the frame of my argument, but it would take this book to an unacceptable length, so it will have to remain a project for the future.

Notes

1 Beumers (1997) 251.
2 Allain (1997) 33.
3 Allain (1997) 67.
4 Allain (1997) 67.
5 Allain (1997) 81.

Acknowledgments

Thanks to David Wiles who supervised my PhD thesis *Bakhtin's Other Theatre* (2004), the research for which forms the basis of the present book; to the late Vera Gottlieb who examined my thesis and encouraged me to make it into a book; thanks to Franc Chamberlain who, as ever, read early drafts of my work and offered helpful comments and advice; to Elaine Turner who read early drafts of this book and ever so tactfully steered me towards intelligibility; to Caryl Emerson who saw me through the latter stages of writing and gave me the strength to see the job through. Thanks also to Brian Roberts, to my parents and to Ali and Beth, whose love and support sees me through from project to project. Finally, thanks to my colleagues and friends at Royal Holloway, University of London with whom I am lucky enough to work.

A version of parts of Chapter 4 first appeared as an article entitled 'Paradoxes of Acting: Bakhtin and Stanislavsky' in *New Theatre Quarterly* 30(1): 29-39.

Abbreviations of works in the notes

Works by Bakhtin

Act	*Toward a Philosophy of the Act*
Hero	*Author and Hero in Aesthetic Activity*
Prehistory	'From the Prehistory of Novelistic Discourse'
Discourse	*Discourse in the Novel*
Chronotope	*Forms of Time and of the Chronotope*
Dostoevsky	*Problems of Dostoevsky's Poetics*
Rabelais	*Rabelais and His World*
Speech Genres	*Speech Genres and Other Late Essays*

Works by Voloshinov

Freudianism	*Freudianism: A Critical Sketch*
Philosophy of Language	*Marxism and the Philosophy of Language*
Discourse in Life	'Discourse in Life and Discourse in Art'

Works by Medvedev

Formal Method	*The Formal Method*

Works by Stanislavsky

Life	*My Life in Art*, Tr. Robbins (1967), Tr. Benedetti (2008)
Work	*An Actor's Work*, Tr. Benedetti (2008)
Role	*An Actor's Work on a Role*, Tr. Benedetti (2010)

Works by Grotowski

I quote from three English translations of articles that were informally distributed to visitors to Grotowski's Centre in Pontedera and which have now been published in *Il Teatro Laboratorium di Jerzy Grotowski 1959–1969* (Pontedera: Fondazione Pontedera Teatro, 2001)

'Exercises' (pp.184–204)
'That Which Was' (pp.225–240)
'The Director as Professional Spectator' (pp.241–257)

Introduction

Methodology: questions, images and dialogue

If you are going to write a book about theatre, the last person from whom you would seek help is someone who regards the genre as outdated. Such is the case with Mikhail Mikhailovich Bakhtin (1895–1975). Although Bakhtin mentions Konstantin Stanislavsky (1863–1938), his books make no reference to either Vsevelod Meyerhold (1879–1940) or Jerzy Grotowski (1933–1999), the three theatre practitioners who will be examined in this study, and in turn none of them mention Bakhtin.[1] All three figures revolutionised how theatre was conceived and practiced in their lifetimes. All three wrote about the inspirations and detractions that fuelled and informed their vision of a new theatre. This book sets up a dialogue between their writings about theatre and those of Bakhtin, a dialogue deeply rooted in the thinking and assumptions behind their practice and theory.

There is a continuing controversy about what Bakhtin actually wrote. The works listed in the bibliography under the names of Valentin Voloshinov (1895–1936) and Pavel Medvedev (1892–1938), some commentators claim were authored by Bakhtin. Voloshinov, Medvedev and several others were all part of a philosophical group that met regularly in the 1910s and 1920s and is now known as the Bakhtin Circle. That there is a community of concerns linking the thinkers is without question. As to who authored certain works is not a question that will be discussed here simply because it has no bearing on my argument.

Roland Barthes chose to call a collection of his essays *L'obvie et l'obtus* (1982) (*The Obvious and the Obtuse*) – a provocative title, and one which also describes the approach I intend to take, because, apart from meaning 'stupid', the word 'obtuse' also accurately describes the oblique angle of attack I intend to take with the writings of Bakhtin. Here I am following Bakhtin, who takes a similarly oblique approach to his arguments. The greater part of my argument is drawn from concerns raised in his early work which is least known to readers. This consists of two unfinished manuscripts which have been given the editorial titles: *Toward a Philosophy of the Act* and *Author and Hero in Aesthetic Activity*. In a move that might appear obtuse, there will be little discussion of carnival, the carnivalesque or dialogism – the concepts for which he is best known. His early work is philosophically dense and approaches questions of human relationship at a very basic, one could say almost obvious, level. In most of his books Bakhtin's approach was to use a literary work as the point of departure for a more broadly philosophical discussion: an angle of attack that was anything but narrow. In *Problems of Dostoevsky's Poetics* he declares his interest in types 'of artistic thinking' whose 'significance extends far beyond the limits of the novel' and which touch 'upon several basic principles of European aesthetics'.[2] My interest is precisely in these different 'types of artistic thinking': how do practitioners describe and defend their approach to theatre making? How do these types of artistic thinking connect with those of the Bakhtin Circle? The notion of 'artistic thinking' invites us to consider the different kinds of theory being written by Bakhtin and our chosen theatre practitioners.

Caryl Emerson takes the relation between philosophy and artistic thinking a stage further by arguing that not only does Bakhtin 'fail to distinguish; he outrightly insists that techniques of art, to be aesthetically legitimate, must be capable of extending and refining philosophical problems that can't be resolved – that cannot be even conceptualised – in any other way'. Thus does this philosopher-critic's notion of polyphony, and later his idea of the novel as a genre, become 'philosophy by another means'.[3] It is precisely my aim to demonstrate that 'techniques of art' (in this case theatre) can extend and refine philosophical problems raised in Bakhtin's writings. It is with this notion of doing 'philosophy by another means' that I shall address questions about character, about empathy, about learning and development and about kinds of knowing, and the conditions under which they take place.

Posing 'questions' and problems is at the heart of the methodology of the Bakhtin Circle. Valentin Voloshinov explains why he uses the word *vopros* which translates as 'question' or 'problem':

> It is sometimes extremely important to expose some familiar and seemingly already well-studied phenomenon to fresh illumination by reformulating it as a problem, i.e., to illuminate new aspects of it with the aid of a set of questions that have a special bearing upon it.[4]

The titles of four of Bakhtin's works include the word *vopros*. Late in his career Bakhtin explained the methodological importance of questions:[5]

> With meaning I give answers to questions. Anything that does not answer a question is devoid of sense for us. […] Meaning always responds to particular questions. Anything that does not respond to something seems meaningless to us; it is removed from dialogue.[6]

Bakhtin sets the bar high with his injunction that '[a]nything that does not answer a question is devoid of sense for us', but it does support my decision to focus on questions of theatre throughout this book. This is the primary methodological filter throughout my argument: however interesting Bakhtin's ideas might be, I have limited myself to those which illuminate *questions of theatre*. I will argue in this book that there is a range of questions or problems that pertain to theatre as a genre; by answering such questions we can better understand the vision or aspiration of a particular theatre maker, indeed one can characterise an approach to theatre by the questions he or she asks and answers. Stanislavsky, Meyerhold and Grotowski sometimes offer different answers to the same question, at other times they frame completely different questions. 'Questions of theatre' could also be understood in the sense of putting theatre into question, in the way that Bakhtin constantly does when he argues that the novel is a genre that is more apt than drama to answer the aesthetic and philosophical questions that interest him.

My chosen questions of theatre may seem obvious. Bakhtin argues that the situation of one's body in time and space affects how one sees and knows the world. Does Bakhtin's sense of situation have a connection with Stanislavsky's concept of given circumstances? More broadly how does the space and time of a theatre performance affect its meaning? Bakhtin's interest was in how our situation affects our understanding of ourselves and others. He then developed this into an examination of the relation between the author and a character. To illustrate his point he asks whether an actor could be considered an author of a character. His argument hinges on the degree to which an actor empathises with their character.

For all the references he makes to theatre, Bakhtin never asks questions about theatre or examines how it functions as an artistic form, as distinct from the novel. He draws on it as a source of metaphor in order to frame philosophical questions about and through the novel. If he asks few questions of theatre because he considers that, along with epic and lyric, it is an old genre that has been superseded by the novel, then this flies in the face of the facts. Russia was in the vanguard of theatrical practice and experiment from 1895 to the early 1930s; Russian theatre was in its ascendancy, and had in no way been superseded by the novel. But if it *is* superannuated then why did he make so many references to theatre, references which indicate some considerable familiarity with the form? At the very least we can ask why he never devoted a study to comparing theatre and novel as distinct artistic forms.

The dates of Bakhtin's life (1895–1975) provide the historical frame of this study. 1895–1917 were the final twenty-two years of the Czars and marked a time of rigorous censorship. After the Revolution (1917–1921) followed nearly a decade of passionate debate and struggle as the new socialist state sought to find its identity, a debate that was finally extinguished in 1934 with the declaration of an official state artistic policy: Socialist Realism. 1956 saw the beginning of a cultural thaw with Kruschev's policy of de-Stalinisation, the same year that Soviet forces brutally supressed the Hungarian uprising and Vwadislwav Gromulka began a political and cultural 'thaw' in Poland. In terms of theatre our period begins three years before Konstantin Stanislavsky and Vladimir Nemirovich-Danchenko established the Moscow Art Theatre in 1898 and continues through the restless experimentation and then political struggles of Vsevelod Meyerhold which led to his execution in February 1940. The year 1956 saw Grotowski engaging in the political and cultural events of that year and our period ends with the first two phases of his creative career, the Theatre of Productions (1959–1969) and his Theatre of Participation which culminated in his 1975 University of Research of the Theatre of Nations.

The first forty years of our history contain a wealth of debate about the nature and function of theatre. Stanislavsky demanded that his actors forget all habits of showmanship and theatricality and live rather than play their parts. Less than twenty years later his protégé Meyerhold proposed a return to precisely the theatricality Stanislavsky had rejected, and embraced the Russian Revolution which at first offered little place for the older director. This seeming opposition between the two men changed in the mid-1930s when Stanislavsky began to develop his Method of Physical Actions, and ultimately appointed Meyerhold as his successor at the Opera Studio, not least to protect him from the increasingly shrill criticisms of the socialist authorities. With the declaration in the mid-1930s of Socialist Realism as state artistic policy there was no further need for debate about aesthetics: the matter was officially resolved.

The debate initiated by Stanislavsky and Meyerhold was rekindled in the writings of Grotowski, who had studied Theatre Direction at the GITIS institute in Moscow. One of his first productions was Mayakovsky's *Mystery-Bouffe*, first produced by Meyerhold in 1918, the heyday of his 'theatrical revolution'. Grotowski also returned to Stanislavsky's later approach to acting, the Method of Physical Actions, which became a central part of his teaching. Grotowski's revolution in theatre was both progressive and backward looking: in an age of ever greater technological sophistication in television and film, he demanded a return to the basic element of theatre – the encounter (or could one call it a dialogue?) of the actor and the audience. Once again, theatre as a genre is reinvented by being put into question. By 1975 he had left theatre altogether in search of another form of dialogue with the public. All three men are linked in their pursuit of the fundamental question: what is theatre?

This book could be called an interdisciplinary study but a phrase often used by Bakhtin describes it better: it is 'Janus-faced'. Janus was a domestic god with two faces who would be found at the threshold of Roman houses, one face looking out from the house, one looking in. The themes of looking and of position – points of view – and of time and space are centrally important to Bakhtin's early thinking, as is the theme of doubleness in his later writings. My proposal to examine some of Bakhtin's key concepts by considering them in relation to theatre, and key questions of theatre in the light of some of Bakhtin's writings is in this sense Janus-faced. In one of his early writings Bakhtin mentions Janus in relation to the worlds of culture and the world of life.

> The act of our activity, of our experience, like the two-faced Janus, looks in different directions: at the objective whole of the realm of culture and at the unrepeatable uniqueness of experienced life, but there is no single and unitary plane where both aspects could mutually define one another in relation to a single, unique unity.[7]

This rather dense quotation from *Toward a Philosophy of the Act* requires some explanation. There are many distinctions being made here, ones that will resonate throughout Bakhtin's career. The first is the difference between two kinds of knowledge, one that is cognitive and whose value is independent of time or place, the other a subjective, embodied meaning event that takes place at a particular time and place. Stanislavsky and Grotowski place great emphasis on these two kinds of knowing. The distinction between repeatability and uniqueness takes us to a fundamental question about theatre (and indeed any) performance: how can a performance have the feeling of being a unique event even though the same set of lines and actions is being repeated?

Another methodological element to this book is Bakhtin's notion of dialogue, a concept that he began to formulate in his 1929 *Problems of Dostoevsky's Art*, with the notion of polyphony, and further developed in his book-length essay *Discourse in the Novel* (1934). Once again, he defines this as a quintessentially novelistic concept: it is therefore not a dramatic dialogue broken into statement-and-response, 'but that special type of novelistic dialogue that realises itself *within the boundaries* of constructions that *externally* resemble monologue'.[8] In French a *faux ami* (false friend) is a word that seems to be the same in English, but is in fact different. Dialogue is such a term in Bakhtin's theory: in his eyes it categorically does not refer to theatre.

The relations between the three directors in this study can be understood in terms of what Bakhtin would call dialogical voicing. In the early days of the Revolution Stanislavsky's writings about constructivism, though not directly mentioning his protégé, most probably had him in mind; and on the other side Meyerhold developed his revolutionary theatre in reaction to his former teacher's realism. At this point each defined their own work as being unlike the other's. In other words, their own artistic approach was made with the other person in mind, even though they weren't being directly named or cited. This dialogue changed when Stanislavsky began to explore his Method of Physical Actions and thus came closer to Meyerhold's more movement-based theatre, even as the younger director was moving towards a more realistic kind of theatre. Certainly Meyerhold considered their approaches coming together:

> The basic problem of the contemporary theatre is that of preserving the element of improvisation in the actor's art within the complex and exact form the director has found for a production. [...] I recently spoke with Konstantin [Sergeyevich]. He also thinks about that. We are approaching the solution of the same problem like builders of a tunnel under the Alps. He is moving from one side, and I from the other. And inevitably, somewhere in the middle we must meet.[9]

The same dialogical interpenetration is true of Grotowski, whose writings carry the unspoken (and sometimes explicit) memory of both Meyerhold (especially in his early work) and Stanislavsky. In *Towards a Poor Theatre* he admits:

> I was brought up on Stanislavski; his persistent study, his systematic renewal of the methods of observation, and his dialectical relationship to his own earlier work make him my personal ideal. Stanislavski asked key methodological questions. Our solutions however, differ widely from his – sometimes we reach opposite conclusions.[10]

Grotowski makes two points that are very pertinent to this argument. The first is his very detailed description of Stanislavsky's ceaseless self-questioning, a process that Grotowski amplified in the various phases of his career (two of which are covered in this book). The second is the more obvious point that while he and Stanislavsky might agree on what the 'key methodological questions' are, their answers are quite different.

Throughout this section I have talked about the 'questions' shared by both philosophers and theatre practitioners, but one could just as easily consider these as themes or preoccupations which are then put into question. Although there is an overall chronological vector to this book, the argument is held together just as strongly by themes which cross between Bakhtin and Stanislavsky and then on to Meyerhold and Grotowski. These questions are the warp threads around which a history of theatre in Eastern Europe between 1895 and 1975 is woven.

Themes

Time and space, body and image

Bakhtin argues that we have two perspectives on being a human in the world, the first is the subjective and embodied centre – the *I* – from which we perceive the world; the second is our perspective of *other* people and their activity in the world. These perspectives are roughly equivalent to subjective and objective modes of knowing (feeling and thinking). This offers common territory for both Bakhtin and Stanislavsky who share underlying assumptions about the convincing-ness of embodied over cognitive knowledge. Both men similarly place great importance on the faculty of empathy which enables one to move from one perspective to the other. Empathy is a process which begins with you seeing the situation of another person and because you feel sympathy for their plight, you put yourself in their place so that you can feel what they are feeling. Put in Bakhtin's terms, you perceive an *other* and (you imagine) experiencing this person as an *I*: you move from a visually apprehended image into a physical experience.

Bakhtin's early theory of ethical and aesthetic activity is rooted in the tempo-spatial situation described above. Your position in time and space is your unique and given perspective on the world, and it is your ethical responsibility to answer from it. The place and time of this meaning is here and now, it is immediate, personal and uncommunicable; but this results in the problem that the act-performing *I* alone can know their lives in terms of these brilliant but short-lived moments. Bakhtin's tying of two kinds of meaning to their positions in time and space results in a categorical distinction between what an *I* and what an *other* can know: I can only know myself as an *I*, and others as *other*. Furthermore, he asks us to accept that because I cannot see myself *therefore* I cannot write my own story (or draw my own portrait). I cannot know myself as a whole in the way that I can see others around me as complete wholes. This tempo-spatial situation leads to Bakhtin's theory of aesthetic obligation: just as I must respond to an ethical 'ought' with an action, so it is my aesthetic responsibility to respond to another's need for what one could call 'narrative completion'. At one level his theory is utterly true of our existence as embodied beings, but I shall question Bakhtin's insistence that I cannot imagine or represent myself, that is, create a narrative by which I can make sense of my actions, and thereby plan my future. I will argue that a discussion of Stanislavsky's actor training will very usefully illuminate this seeming dichotomy between moment and narrative.

Bakhtin soon moved away from time and space as a physical situation and in *Forms of Time and of the Chronotope* (1937–1938) Bakhtin tracked the evolution of a certain mode of representation where the individual consciousness is involved in a living engagement with the historical environment. The 'chronotope' is a concept borrowed from biology and refers to when an individual organism co-evolves with its environment. He further developed this conception of body, time and space in his study of Rabelais (1965). So, although he wrote about this subject in very different ways across his career, the theme remains a constant within his writings. The point of connection with theatre is obvious since all theatre performances take place at a particular time in a particular venue and are performed by actors whose movements and groupings in space are grasped as moving images which evoke a kinaesthetic response in the audience. The difference is that Bakhtin is writing about a symbolic language while in theatre time and space signify directly: they are experienced as being significant by both the actor and the audience.

Let us now consider how time and space are 'doubled' in the theatre. Firstly there is the time and place in which a play is set. Secondly there is the performance of the play, both the duration – 'the two hours' traffic on the stage' – and the physical space of the stage, staging, furniture and properties. While still being in the world of the play, a member of the audience can remain sensitive to the duration of performance and where it drags or races. Stanislavsky's early revolution in theatre demanded that his actors focus their entire attention on the represented world of the stage on their side of the proscenium arch and ignore the audience's presence on the other side: to play to or for the audience was an example of 'theatricality'. Meyerhold embraced such theatricality and adapted the stage to come closer to the audience: he removed the proscenium frame and extended the stage action into the auditorium by means of an apron stage. The acting style of Meyerhold's constructivist productions lay in the rhythmic timing of the actions and the sculptural mass of the staging, as well as the opportunities this offered the actor to move. No longer was the stage a representation of another place but a constructed space with elevated walkways, chutes and treadmills that demanded actors who were acrobatic in their stage skills: space is grasped in its plastic reality, time in its rhythmic possibilities. As with the shift from representation to abstraction in painting, the stage space and its lighting is Meyerhold's reality: there is nothing behind it or before it. Grotowski's later productions – from *Kordian* (1962) to *Akropolis* (1965) – erased the division between stage and auditorium even further with the audience seated in the midst of the action.

From the above discussion one can notice the very obvious difference of focus between how Bakhtin and theatre practitioners consider the themes of time, space and body. Actors have to be both *I* and *other*, both a living and reacting 'self' *and* an image; their own flesh and bones are the sculptural material from which they create a moving image of the character. In the same way, time and space are the materials with which actor, director, lighting designer and set designer create the production: they are primary semiotic materials. While Bakhtin might write about a real, embodied meaning, this remains at the level of philosophical theory; for the actor it is a question of practice and a supremely pragmatic question involving training and constant experiment. Bakhtin's early theory offers no possibility for the individual to learn or develop since the *I* is effectively disembodied and static. I will argue that his own approach to body, space and time, and indeed to the experience of being an *I* and my experience of other people, is very limited, and that a comparison with theatre will reveal a much richer and more dynamic account of this fundamental human activity of making meaning. Framing the practical strategies of Stanislavsky within Bakhtin's philosophical concerns and concepts allows one to imagine a dynamic form of meaning making that is centred upon embodied experience. Although none of the three director/pedagogues have any pretention to writing philosophy, I aim to show how their writings about theatre practice can illuminate Bakhtin's fundamental questions about how humans make sense of themselves and each other, and how this relates to questions of character and acting.

Character and author, body and image

The centrality of this theme to Bakhtin's early thinking can be gleaned from the editorial title given to the longer of his two early manuscripts – *Author and Hero in Aesthetic Activity*. Although Bakhtin's thinking about character had changed by the time he published his *Problems of Dostoevsky's Art* in 1929, his early thinking provokes a very fruitful series of questions about the relationship between author and hero. The first question concerns how the creation of heroes relates to our relations with people in our everyday lives. We have already seen that it is impossible for an *I* to grasp him- or herself as an image: they cannot see themselves from the outside, a perspective which can only come from a loving *other*. *I* am incapable of seeing or knowing myself as a finished image, therefore *I* need the redemptive activity of a loving *other* to offer me completion. They have to be loving, otherwise why would they engage in such an exercise, and why would you (as an *I*) invite them to? It is this redemptive love that distinguishes Bakhtin's lower case *other* from the post-modern Other, that figure which indicates total difference from me. Far from being a threat to one's identity, his lower-case *other* offers the open-ended *I* a sense of completion. Everyone is both an *I* (for myself) and an *other* (for every other *I*), and though I cannot create a convincing image of myself, I can, in an act of friend-ship, do this for another. There is a major question (one that Bakhtin didn't pose) concerning this sense of completion which returns us to time and space. True, an *other* can offer us completion as a spatially grasped image, but this process takes place in time, and because the image is finished, it cuts short my open-ended existence. Effectively, it kills me as a being that has the capacity to change or develop. In short, Bakhtin offers a spatial solution to a temporal problem; he fails to acknowledge the categorical difference between a finished character, whose meaning is fixed, and a living person who retains the capacity (Bakhtin calls it a 'loophole') to change and develop in the future. Open-endedness is very much Janus-faced. On the one hand it may well generate anguish at the contingency of our existence, but on the other it is also the very index of our being alive and able to change ourselves and make a new future.

Another major question concerns the parallel that Bakhtin creates between the relationship of *I* to *other* and author to hero. In mathematics this is called a homology, where the structure of relations between A and B is the same as that between C and D. Bakhtin seems to suggest that all characters have to be based on real people, which is an idea that bears little scrutiny. Aren't most characters drawn from aspects of real people that are assembled as a composite in the author's imagination? The question of how characters relate to people in everyday life is one that will be much discussed in the chapters on Bakhtin and Stanislavsky, both of whom believed that characters were real people. I would go so far as to say that it is the analogy between the character and the human being which guarantees the truth of the representation.

A second question following from Bakhtin's early theory is the degree to which aesthetic activity involves the author being outside the hero and the degree to which one needs to empathise with (to enter into) the hero. One can legitimately read this question in the light of Stanislavsky's demand that actors identify with their characters, and Brecht's that they maintain a distance from them (very crudely put). Rather than expressing it as an alternative between distantiation and empathy, one could ask – as Bakhtin does – what degrees of distance and empathy are required to create a character. The answer is that you need both: in the process of creating a character there is an empathetic stage where the author enters into the life of the subject-to-be-a-hero in order to gather information about what it feels like to be in that situation, to see things through the eyes of the hero. The following phase of composition – selecting and sequencing this information – takes place at a distance from the 'hero'. This final return to one's own position outside the hero – 'outside-ness' – is central to Bakhtin's theory of aesthetic creation, and seemingly puts him at odds with Stanislavsky. This question of empathy and outside-ness will be discussed in Chapter 4.

There is much common territory between Bakhtin and Stanislavsky, but ultimately they ask quite different questions and describe different creative processes. Where the philosopher is interested in rendering a human being intelligible as a character, the theatre director is helping actors to render an existing character as a living human being. Bakhtin's ideas about authorship (in the novel) oblige us to rethink the relationship between actor and character in theatre. A character isn't given but has to be created – by the author and by the actor. The work of the actor as described by Stanislavsky requires much training, and it is precisely this practical engagement that is lacking in Bakhtin, and which can help illuminate questions of embodiment, even of judging degrees of empathy and aesthetic distance. Just as in the section above I argue that time and space in theatre possess a quantifiable materiality, so the body is not just an image, it is the material by means of which the actor conveys a character. And that transformation – literally, a changing of the way the actor's body moves in space – takes years of work to achieve.

The most important thing upon which both men agree is that there is such a thing as an author and such a thing as a character. The early Bakhtin considers the character as the image of a living human known to the author; Stanislavsky considers the character as a human whom the actor must bring to life in performance. However different their modes, both agree that what makes the representation of the character real is this analogy with a human being, an analogy based on the assumption that because a character is a human being, *therefore* truthful acting is about being true to life. This analogy is a cornerstone of realism, and one that Nick Worrall questions in his book on the Moscow Art Theatre. He argues that '[i]t is ironic that, almost at the precise historical moment that modernist artists were moving away from a view of human character imagined "individualistically", or conceived as ontologically "real", Stanislavsky attempted to resuscitate the notion of a meaningful human psychology and a humanly knowable "truth"'.[11]

Many of these assumptions – about realism, about degrees of identification and aesthetic distance, about the very nature of a character – are questioned in the practice and theories of Meyerhold and Grotowski, neither of whom subscribed to the notion that the truth of characterisation lay in the actor identifying with the character. Meyerhold argues that a character is much more of a mask than a living person, and turned to the very same mask-characters from Commedia dell'Arte that feature in Bakhtin's essays on the novel of the 1930s, and in *Rabelais and His World* (1965). From his Symbolist experiments to his later Commedia dell'Arte and constructivist productions, Meyerhold takes an external movement-based approach to character. The movement of the actor's body is expressive, theatrical, almost musical, and has little to do with the realist representation of another person's behaviour. In no way did he share Bakhtin and Stanislavsky's notion of character as a person.

Grotowski's approach to character differs from both the earlier directors, and yet also retains elements of their notions of character and acting. Stanislavsky planned a two-part work on actor training, the first entitled *An Actor's Work on Him- or Herself* (which he left unfinished) and *An Actor's Work on a Role* (for which he left some sketches). Grotowski reverses the thrust of this approach and argues that work on a role is a means by which actors can work on themselves as people. Grotowski's approach is intensely personal but it is not in the service of a representational kind of acting. In this respect he is much closer to Meyerhold when he proposes that the actor's job is to create a score of sounds and movements which it is the audience's job to interpret. There is no longer an assumption that the audience and the actor share the same experience during a performance.

Another area of contention was the 'psychological' approach to character. Stanislavsky describes the excitement at reading a script and meeting the characters for the first time. For him the character is a person and has a mind that it is the actor's job to understand. Stanislavsky's 'psychology' is based on this assumption about character. Although he did read a number of psychologists – Freud not being among them – this was to confirm rather than question his assumptions about human nature. We have already seen that Meyerhold's notion of acting is more to do with stylised gesture and movement and involves little discussion of the inner mental state of either character or actor. The psychologist Ivan Pavlov (1849–1936) provided a model of human behaviour that fitted well with his notion of acting. Following Pavlov, Meyerhold argued that if an actor made a particular gesture it would elicit a particular emotion in the audience. Grotowski's notion of character draws on neither of these kinds of psychology and has everything to do with a negotiation with cultural images and values that he feels need to be questioned through our acts of theatre. Although many of his plays drew on the repertoire of Polish Romantic writers like Wyspianski, Mickiewicz and Slowacki, he put into question the actions of nationalist heroes like Wyspianski's *Kordian*. Their heroes are a point of departure for an investigation rather than a celebration of cultural values like Polish nationalism.

At no point in Bakhtin's career were his theories about character underpinned or paralleled by psychology. In his early writings he took a phenomenological approach which took mental experience as a self-evident phenomenon that required no further explanation or discussion. The only connection with psychology lies in Franz Brentano's definition of phenomenology as 'descriptive psychology'.[12] It is not that he doesn't address the question of psychology; rather he dismisses its validity as a means of explicating the problems that interest him. For this reason he rejects the psychology of both Freud and Pavlov. I shall examine two distinct kinds of psychology: the first is the non-faculty sense in which Stanislavsky uses the word in relation to character. It is that unacknowledged set of assumptions and principles that allows us to talk about believable characters, about their behaviour being logical, about them being well-drawn. In other words it is the psychology of realist literature. The second psychology concerns the scientific claims and theories of figures like Freud and Pavlov, and I shall examine how these theories have changed or informed the notion of character and the nature of acting.

Realism and revolution

The themes of realism and revolution criss-cross in a very interesting way throughout the period of Bakhtin's lifetime. In 1898 Stanislavsky was championing his version of realistic acting as a 'revolution' in theatre. As Worrall has already pointed out, modernism (a very different revolution) was emerging across Europe and by 1917 had already found distinctly Russian forms when the Revolution overthrew the Czarist regime. For a short period the Russian Revolution and the cultural revolution of modernism found common cause, this despite the conservative artistic taste of Lenin, and the attempt in 1923 of his cultural commissar Lunacharsky to take theatre 'back to Ostrovsky' (i.e. to a more realist approach to art). Meyerhold was in the vanguard of a revolutionary experiment – cultural and political – which rejected the assumptions and techniques of Stanislavsky's realist theatre and acting. After Lenin's death, modernist experiment fell increasingly out of favour with the state authorities, and by 1934 Socialist Realism was declared to be the official cultural policy and a version of Stanislavsky's approach to acting and theatre production was adopted as part of this policy. This debate concerned the very nature of theatre and acting: what is the content of theatre, who is it for and how can it be performed?

Stanislavsky wrote the Russian version of his autobiography *My Life in Art* in 1928 and chose to describe his 'revolution' in theatre as the removal of all theatricality and convention from the stage. Given the political and cultural context, one has to wonder at his choice of the word 'revolution', more especially since he was writing thirty years after the event.

> In our destructive and revolutionary aims, in order to rejuvenate the art, we declared war on all the conventionalities of the theatre wherever they may occur – in the acting, in the properties, in the scenery, the costumes, the interpretation of the play, the curtain, or anywhere else in the play or the theatre. All that was new and that violated the usual customs of the theatre seemed beautiful and useful to us.[13]

Key words in this argument are 'new', 'conventionalities' and 'customs'. In one sense his approach was very evidently no longer 'new', since it was challenged by Futurism and constructivism; but for him these experiments were superficial novelties and did not convey a deeper sense of the 'new', as in that which is lived and real. This key distinction between convention and the 'real' – that which is lived and experienced – runs through Stanislavsky's reflections and is taken up again by Grotowski in his theatrical and post-theatrical activities. Two questions follow from this distinction. Firstly, can theatre operate without conventions or form? Bakhtin (and even more emphatically, members of the Circle) would argue against, while Stanislavsky and Grotowski argue for the case. Secondly, is this sense of the 'real' an aesthetic experience or a grasping of a truth about the world?

Worrall notes that Stanislavsky's 'religion of realism' was a reaction against 'the obsessional aspects of naturalistic disclosure', by which he means 'the reductionist perspectives of naturalism's faith in the absolutely material, against its belief in physiological and environmental determinants which reduce spirit to matter and desire to mere appetite in a spiritless universe'.[14] Can the human spirit be understood or expressed materially, i.e. through linguistic form? Stanislavsky (and Grotowski after him) rejected the notion that humans are in any way a product of or determined by their environment; he rejected the notion that the human spirit, that consciousness, could only be understood through material expression in signs. At a philosophical level he rejects a materialist explanation of a spiritual question. At a theatrical level this meant clearing the stage of unnecessary props and scenery and allowing the play to communicate through acting rather than setting. Although coming from a very different intellectual tradition, Bakhtin's early writings locate the 'real' in physical feeling (in my body, here and now) rather than in cognition which (as stated above) can be anywhere and at any time. Here Bakhtin is presenting the real as a phenomenal category rather than realism as a genre. Grotowski will argue that this bodily sensation is more authentic than anything that is mediated through culture.

The experimental Ukrainian director Les Kurbas embraced the challenge of the times, and declared: 'Away with art for art's sake.' Kurbas and his followers formally repudiated their former servitude to 'beauty'; they deliberately forgot that they had created 'art not for partisan aims but as an aim in itself'. Now they declared in their statute that 'the theatre is a means of agitation and propaganda'. This was their passport for continued life and for the possibility of further developing the modern Ukrainian theatre.[15]

One of the big questions for the revolutionary regime was how to create a culture for a new society, one that acknowledged and addressed the needs and interests of the working people. Meyerhold, like Kurbas, created pieces of agitprop theatre, promoting the aims and ideals of the Revolution. Their aim was to educate and engage the proletarian audience. This challenge was echoed in every aspect of cultural and social life. It is hard to imagine such an extraordinary situation where artists can tear up the cultural rule book and start again, but this time creating work for all members of society and not just a privileged elite.

For Meyerhold this political engagement meant creating a different kind of theatre, both in the sense of the genre and its place of performance: Benedetti gives an idea of the sweep of this intellectual and cultural movement.

> [Meyerhold's] insistence that theatre should be theatrical received support particularly among the younger members of the intelligentsia including, in time, Vakhtangov and members of the First Studio. A work of art should not attempt to present itself as 'natural', but should reveal itself as a human construct, as an artefact, making its means of communication evident. This aesthetic found its theoretical formulation in the work of Viktor [Shklovsky], who developed the notion of [*ostranjeni*], making strange, the precursor of Brecht's *Verfremdung*. By the 1920s the movement had emerged as Formalism.[16]

Many questions and points follow from this passage. The word 'nature' is central to Stanislavsky's understanding of truth and believability in acting. Many of his pronouncements include appeals to a 'human nature' which he argues is universal across all peoples and times. While Stanislavsky might argue that this is 'how things are', revolutionaries would argue that it was the 'status quo', the present state of affairs, that had to be changed.

As Benedetti states, Viktor Shklovsky, one of the founders of Russian formalism, saw the problem as one of cultural habituation – readers and audiences had simply become desensitised to the literary word. In 'Art as Technique' he argues '[i]f we start to examine the general laws of perception, we see that as perception becomes habitual, it becomes automatic'. He continues,

> art exists that one may recover the sensation of life; it exists to make one feel things, to make the stone *stony*. The purpose of art is to impart the sensation of things as they are perceived and not as they are known. The technique of art is to make objects 'unfamiliar', to make forms difficult, to increase the

difficulty and length of perception because the process of perception is an aesthetic end in itself and must be prolonged.[17]

It is precisely this accent on sensation as opposed to cognition ('things as they are *perceived* and not as they are *known*') that was challenged by Bakhtin, Medvedev and, as Stanley Mitchell explains, by Brecht.[18,19]

> [...] while Shklovsky's *ostranjeni* was a purely aesthetic concept, concerned with renewal of perception, Brecht's *Verfremdung* had a social aim: if the world could be shown differently, i.e., as having different possibilities, could it not be differently made? Brecht wished not to strike at perceptions, but at the consciousness of his spectators. Shklovsky expressly denied the cognitive function of art: 'the aim of art', he wrote, 'is to give sensation of a thing as something known.'[20]

Brecht criticised Dadaists and Surrealists who 'used alienation-effects of the most extreme kind' precisely because 'their objects do not return from alienation'. Just as Shklovsky aimed for pure sensation so Dadaist art 'ends in an amusement'; there was no cognitive and no political function in either approaches to art.[21] Brecht's alienation was not purely an effect, it was a means by which the audience could be brought to a new way of thinking about the social world and to realising that we do actually have choices, because the sequence of events is not inevitable. Theatre is about sensation, experiencing and cognition. As Worrall puts it,

> Brecht's main arguments against narrow versions of 'realism' were based on the tendency of realistic methods to underwrite the 'status quo' and reinscribe the contours of a 'given' reality within the consciousness of the perceiver, rather than to awaken new ways of seeing and interpreting social reality, or challenge accepted orthodoxies.[22]

Shklovsky, Meyerhold and Brecht all argued that we could see and feel the world in a different way by considering the forms by which it is represented – be it how literature is written or how plays are acted and staged. The 'revolution' that was modernism provided techniques and vocabulary for Russian artists to engage in the cultural and political revolution. Gradually these questions about what is art and theatre started to be answered by party members as they tried to establish an official cultural policy. Where in the early days of the Revolution Meyerhold was given an official post within the government, soon the decision making about what theatre is and who it is for shifted from the pens and mouths of practicing artists to those of party members. As early as 1923 there was a tension between artist and official, which soon translated into a division between an experimental and a more conservative, realist approach. Bradshaw interprets Lunacharsky's call, 'back to Ostrovsky', as meaning a return to

> psychological fullness and the application of this realism to contemporary themes. The slogan was in effect an official call for a return to nineteenth-century

realism as the proper mode for a socialist theatre. A parallel movement was noted in literature and the other arts.[23]

Whyman notes how in the 12th Party Congress in 1923 'Lenin was negative about innovation' and 'it was also stated that the theatre style of the MAT could be more readily available to mass tastes, in preference to some of the experimental work going on in other theatres, if subtlety and psychological nuances (the main value of MAT) could be avoided'.[24] Thus by the late 1920s realism, Stanislavsky and MAT were back in political favour with the authorities: Worrall writes about the 'appropriation of the Moscow Art Theatre as a cultural instrument of the one-party state and the canonisation of its exemplary realist methods'.[25] Whereas before the Revolution realism had a non-explicit political role in supporting the status quo (the political was presented as the 'natural'), now the Soviet state's 'espousal of Stanislavskian versions of realism were devices used to underpin an orthodox promulgation of that state's self-image'.[26] Autant-Mathieu argues that the MAT's thirtieth birthday in 1928 was celebrated in style because their artistic policy of psychological realism 'was less offensive to the political leaders of the time, who had been born in the nineteenth century and had received a conventional education, than the daring and provocative productions of the avant-garde and left-wing theatres'.[27] Once again, we see realist theatre supporting the status quo, only now it is in the name of the proletariat and not the bourgeoisie.

Before dismissing the entire project of a theatre for the people let us remember Rolland Romain's provocative question in his 1903 *The People's Theatre*: 'You want an art of the people? Then do something to have a people.' He then continues, '[w]e had to wait for the 1917 Revolution to see such a people emerge in the USSR'.[28] When the American critic Norris Houghton visited the Soviet Union in 1934, he observed:

> I was to go to the theatre ninety times in Russia and not more than a dozen times was I to see a vacant chair. […] This is a theatre for the common man, and not the bourgeois elite. Theatre is part of their life. Life is not some abstraction that is to be represented.[29]

The questions raised in this section are not easily answered, but will be posed throughout this book: do popular theatre and experimental theatre have to be mutually exclusive? Is avant-garde theatre always for a bourgeois audience? Was the artistic vision of Mayakovsky, Meyerhold and other leftist theatre makers doomed to failure? Is realism (which has a history of not more than two centuries) some kind of default mode for how we represent the world to ourselves?

This books ends in the 1960s and early 1970s in Poland. In 1959 Grotowski joined Ludwig Flaszen to work in a small theatre in Opole. Although his name is now associated with theatre, Grotowski was first known in politics 'as a national-level activist of a revisionist Communist youth organisation, the Union of Socialist Youth – Political Centre of the Academic Left'.[30] His first writings engage with the events of the Warsaw October where Gromulka had taken power and ushered in a more tolerant regime, but one that did not excite the military response that the Soviet Union had made in Hungary earlier that year. Grotowski's revolution in theatre was at once forward and backward looking. Although he staged classics from the Polish Romantic repertoire, his pared-down versions are not in the tradition of nineteenth-century realism. But neither are they in the vanguard of techno-logical experiment since he argued that in order to survive as a medium, theatre needs to be what film and television are not: a live and unrepeatable encounter with an audience. Anything that compromises that communion must be removed – hence his theatre was called 'Poor'. Then, at the height of his fame as a theatre maker he turned to creating para-theatrical meetings – communions with an audience that involved no attempt at artistic representation or acting. These meetings come to a climax in Wroclaw where he created an International University of the Nations in 1975, the year Bakhtin died.

Art and life

This theme is closely linked to realism and revolution and follows from Houghton's question about the relation between art and life in the theatre that he saw in Moscow (see p.15). An underlying assumption of realism is that the artifice of art must be invisible so that the life being represented can come through as clearly as possible. Language and form have to be transparent, like a window on the world. Since artifice is deception this is quite as much an ethical as an aesthetic matter. The focus has to be on the (represented) truth and not on the (representing) untruth which conveys it. The actor Mikhail Shchepkin (1788–1863), a huge influence on Stanislavsky, expresses it as a distinction between the simplicity of real life and playing: 'I felt that I had spoken some words simply – so simply that, had they been uttered in life rather than in a play, I would have said them in just that way.'[31] Nikolai Gorchakov explains how Stanislavsky approached the matter: 'He understood that artistic truth lies beyond the theatre walls, in ordinary life. And he thirsted to know ordinary life, with its real people, rather than shadows that uttered long and bombastic monologues.'[32] This distinction is central to the thinking of Stanislavsky and Grotowski for whom a 'simplicity' of theatrical means becomes the foundation of his 'Poor Theatre'. In the light of the above discussion on political engagement how does one interpret this commitment to being 'true to life'? What exactly is this 'life' if not a status quo, an affirmation of how things are and will always be?

Worrall argues that the construction of a character is a means by which we protect ourselves from the meaninglessness of life. Oscar Wilde considers a character as a thing we construct to present ourselves to others (in Bakhtin's terms, we present *I* as *other*). Worrall compares this with Luigi Pirandello who 'suggested that any human construct, such as personality or a philosophical system, was an inherently self-deceiving device developed in order to shield ourselves from the terrors which life itself constitutes as a destructive force on a par with the forces of nature'.[33] Extending this argument one can state that it is more honest to admit the categorical difference between art and life, than to pretend that art can be life. Worrall then turns to the realist Stanislavsky who 'seems seriously to have considered it possible to convert Life permanently into Art'.

> Hence the need arose for a working method, a 'system' which could attempt to convert (in an almost religious sense) raw human nature, inert matter and consciousness, into another superior form of existence – a Life as (or in) Art.[34]

It is for this reason that Stanislavsky discouraged the audience disrupting the semi-religious ritual of a performance with applause. (Grotowski also actively discouraged applause during or after a performance.)

Mel Gordon takes this argument about life and art further by noting that Stanislavsky's 'troupe declared that since they hated the falsehood of the stage, they equally opposed the hypocrisies of life. An actor could not create truthfully in the theatre without incorporating a sense of truth and simplicity into his everyday life'.[35] Allied with this distrust of art is a belief in the truth of nature as opposed to the city. Stanislavsky's First Studio of 1905 was a converted barn in the country where the actors took part in cultivating the land. (There is an underlying set of oppositions here between nature and culture, the instinctual and the intellectual, body and mind.) Grotowski continued this belief in the ethical work of the actor, and indeed of the value of working in the countryside. These then are the main themes that will be examined through the book. In the next section I shall explain how they are put together.

How this book works

The book is broken into six chapters, the first providing an overview of Bakhtin's thinking from 1919 to 1975; the next three chapters examine the questions of theatre that arise from a dialogue between the early writings of Bakhtin and Stanislavsky; the final two chapters explore how these questions are developed, reframed and answered by Meyerhold and Grotowski. The Conclusion develops the central questions and themes of the book.

Part I – Bakhtin and theatre (Chapter 1)

One can think of this as a long chapter or as seven short essays with an introduction and conclusion. After considering Bakhtin's direct involvement in theatre, each essay plots the chronological development of his thinking, highlighting the key concepts associated with each period. The first deals with his early manuscripts which will provide much of the conceptual material for the whole book; next comes the work of Voloshinov and Medvedev (leading members of the Bakhtin Circle), which marks a shift away from Bakhtin's early phenomenology and focuses on a sociological approach to language. The central four essays deal with the works by which Bakhtin is best known: his study of Dostoevsky, then his essay *Discourse in the Novel*, his essay on the chronotope, and finally his book on Rabelais. The final essay looks at his last works.

Part II – Bakhtin and Stanislavsky (Chapters 2–4)

These three chapters set out the field of argument that will then be further developed in the chapters on Meyerhold and Grotowski and the Conclusion. In *Author and Hero* Bakhtin sets out to answer three questions:

1   How is an action and its space experienced in the act-performer's self-consciousness?
2   How is the action of the other experienced by me?
3   On what plane of consciousness is its aesthetic value located?[36]

Chapter 2 deals with the first question – how 'an action and its space' are experienced by the person performing the action – and Chapter 4 tackles the second and third questions of how another's action is experienced by me, and which of us can give aesthetic value to this action. Chapter 2 – Time and space in the novel and in theatre – draws mostly on Bakhtin's *Philosophy of the Act*. Chapter 4 – Authoring a character – draws on *Author and Hero*, which examines how and why one should author a hero and invites an examination of how and when the actor can be considered as an author of their character. Where Bakhtin's process starts with a real-life human being and aims to create a literary hero, Stanislavsky's acting process starts with an already written hero and aims to create a living human being. Chapter 3 – Psychophysical acting – examines how Stanislavsky's approach to actor training can inform Bakhtin's ideas about embodied action.

Because this book takes a mostly thematic approach I will not follow the chronology of Stanislavsky's writings, but begin with a study of his later Method of Physical Actions because of its correspondence with concerns of *Philosophy of the Act*. Stanislavsky's development will be traced twice; firstly in a study of his approach to staging at the end of Chapter 2, and then in his approach to Embodiment, Psychology and the Psycho-physical in Chapter 3 – Psychophysical acting.

Chapter 2 – Time and space in the novel and in theatre – broadly deals with time, space and meaning in Bakhtin's and Stanislavsky's theories. The first section – Acting from the centre – considers the act-performer's experience of space. Both Bakhtin and Stanislavsky write about us being at the centre of our worlds, a centre which constitutes a unique place in the world, offering a unique perspective on the world, and from which we answer the world with our actions. It is our moral obligation to answer from this actual place. The third section – Given and created – develops Bakhtin's notion of ethical obligation, arguing that neither meanings nor our own being can be experienced other than through the performance of an act. Meaning and being are active rather than passive. This leads to the fourth section – Value, sense, meaning – which examines Bakhtin's idea that living and felt meaning can only be experienced as true if it is situated in time and space. Far from being abstract categories for organising sensation, time and space are what allow meaning to become a personal event. The section Acts and tasks develops the idea that meanings can only be created through the performance of once-and-for-all acts. A summary of these four major concepts points out connections with

Stanislavsky's theory of acting which are then analysed more fully in the three following sections: Acts and tasks; Time and timing in performance; Theatrical space.

The biggest contrast between Bakhtin and Stanislavsky comes when considering the body and the mind – the matter of Chapter 3. Stanislavsky describes his approach to acting as Psycho-Physical, that is, it depends on the mind and body working together. What wasn't clear from Hapgood's translations of *An Actor Prepares* and *Building a Character* was that Stanislavsky's *An Actor's Work* was divided into two parts, the first called Experiencing, and the second Embodying [the role]. In other words, the very conception of his account of the system was psycho-physical. For all Bakhtin's insistence upon the 'concrete' as opposed to the abstract or theoretical, his was still a theoretical approach, one, to repeat Holquist's excellent phrase, where he 'continually seeks to generalize about uniqueness'.[37] One could say that he is trying to lay the philosophical foundations for an understanding of the individual and of individual experience. But the thrust of Bakhtin's argument will always be that a person *should* take account of the body in a discussion of how we as humans make meaning from our experience of the world. He isn't interested in questions of how or why our experiences occur, that is, whether they are a response to psychological or sociological factors. Taking, as he does, a phenomenological approach his only concern is to establish that these experiences actually take place. Although Clark and Holquist note his interest in psycho-physical researches in Petersburg, in these manuscripts Bakhtin shows little interested in psychology. Similarly, he takes the body's agency for granted – it is in the world and it generates sensation, and that is sufficient for his philosophical purposes. As for the relation between the mind and body – this is not even a topic for discussion.

Bakhtin's interest in the body (and this carries through to his later study of Rabelais) is in how it is seen, felt and valued. It is not the body *per se* that is of interest, but the experience and the image of the body when performing an act. Echoing Stanislavsky's concept of circles of attention, Bakhtin insists that the act-performer must focus solely on the task in hand, on what lies before one, and not engage in any imaging of oneself because such self-consciousness would detract from the successful performance. In this way we will see Bakhtin distinguish between the inner and outer body as they are experienced. Both are known through act-performing, the first concerns how it feels to act, the second what it looks like and what effect that act has had. This distinction between an inner and outer body leads us back to the question of value. One of Bakhtin's most problematic assertions is that we can neither give value to nor understand the meaning or even the nature of our own bodies and their actions. This evaluative (one could also use the word 'axiological') perspective comes from outside, from the other who gives us an image of ourselves. He gives the example of how it is that a mother both names and gives value to the baby's body, who thus learns about what to call hands and fingers, and to know that they are or could be loved and valued. Through our dialogue with others we learn to know ourselves as bodies, as embodied beings. This argument about how we see ourselves through the eyes of others, leads to the argument of Chapter 3 which is about how this act of imaging leads on to the more sustained act of authoring heroes.

Stanislavsky's explicitly practical approach means that he is seeking to answer questions about *how* the actor can use their body to achieve a convincing performance. Much of Chapter 3 is therefore concerned with Stanislavsky's very pragmatic researches into how he could draw on a variety of techniques and disciplines to help the actor live their roles more fully. As concerns the mental aspect he mixes romantic notions of the creative subconscious with contemporary researches in psychology – from Ribot's affective memory to Pavlov's reflexology. Apart from trying to understand the nature and source of creativity, he was equally concerned with how to develop the actor's attention on the task of acting. His approach to the physical aspect begins with a response to his own body; it was very tall and, according to him, resistantly stiff. We follow the descriptions in his autobiography of how he struggled with his body – hence the section's title, The resistant body and the image of the body – Stanislavsky's resistant body – to find what he called a quality of stillness on stage. This is a detailed account of how Stanislavsky created his own very syncretic training to develop an actor's body. This training enabled him to move from his 'given' to a 'created' *and* a creative body. Bakhtin's body remains little more than a site of action, its activity taken for granted. Stanislavsky explains how this active, acting body and mind can be developed.

Chapter 4 deals with Bakhtin's theory of how a character is authored and begins with a more thorough discussion of *I* and *other*. This picks up on the argument about the two perspectives on the body. While his conception of an *I* does correspond to a first-person, internal experience, he argues that as a state of being it is existentially incomplete. Indeed it is precisely not a 'state' but an ongoing process of being. I cannot envisage or encompass myself as a 'whole' in the way that I can see other people as complete and finished entities in space. I can never think of myself as finished in time, my life always tends towards the yet-to-be, and consists of plans and contingencies whose unknown and unknowable outcomes will shape my future; it is thus not possible for me to grasp the objective meaning or value of these actions while they remain unfinished business. Only an *other* can – indeed, it is their responsibility to – provide this finished image from their outside perspective, and what motivates them is that they value this observed person. As Morson and Emerson put it, I need the *other* 'as a necessary witness to what I do'.[38] The dialogue between the act-performer and the observer is described as a meaning event: one person completes the action of another by giving it meaning and value. While the moment of experiencing the other's life is achieved through empathy, putting oneself in the other person's place, the aesthetic work of authoring the hero must take place in one's own place outside of the hero. Bakhtin's categorical insistence on the return to one's own place to undertake the aesthetic work opens a discussion of the role of empathy in the actor's work. Diderot calls this argument the Paradox of the Actor, which questions the degree to which actors should empathise with or maintain an aesthetic distance from their characters. Another way of putting the argument is to ask whether the actor merges with the character, or maintains a double existence.

The chapter will conclude by addressing broader questions raised during the discussion. What is the relation between a character in a play and in a novel? To what degree does Bakhtin's notion of an event as an unrepeatable moment of meaning-creating have relevance for theatre, which is a peculiar mixture of repetition (the same play performed every night) and utter uniqueness (no audience and no performance is ever the same)? This notion of event leads to the last question about the sense of truthfulness or realism that both men insisted upon in the representation of human experience.

Part III – Meyerhold (Chapter 5)

When Stanislavsky was revising *My Life in Art* for the 1928 Russian edition he squared up to the criticisms from Meyerhold and his fellow constructivists. A note that he made while preparing the Russian edition reads: 'In the Chapter on the Revolution say that constructivism is a good thing, but they didn't make very good use of it and it was discarded.' He then continues, '[p]redict that the actor's art is on the decline. In the chapter on the Revolution state that this is the result of all that affected stylisation'.[39] Meyerhold followed his idol Wagner in wanting to create a *Gesamtkunstwerk* or Total Theatre, which involved all available media – film, projections, recorded sound, live music, circus skills, constructivist sets and lighting. Meyerhold was a stage auteur who, to the frustration of writing partners like Tretyakov, created stage montages from all available means, text being considered as one of many. The whole in his Total Theatre was the stage production not the written play – the piece was created for the spectator not written for a reader. His answer to the question, 'What is theatre?' is quite different from that of either Stanislavsky or Grotowski.

To make this point about the proximity of his politics and his theatre, let us compare his experiments with the staging with those of two contemporaries. Adolphe Appia (1862–1928) conceived of the open-stage *Festspielhaus* at Hellerau (near Dresden) as a place where the audience and the performer came together in festive activity (as the name *Festspielhaus* suggests). Edward Gordon Craig's (1872–1966) very similar conception of an open stage shorn of 'realist' backdrops and a proscenium arch was motivated by an aesthetic vision, a new kind of theatre consisting of light and movement. Meyerhold's design for a multi-purpose theatre was designed in great part for political reasons – it was to take the stage argument into the auditorium. An auditorium that contained a new proletarian audience that he demanded would be engaged in the argument of the play.

To put Meyerhold and Stanislavsky into opposing camps is too reductive. When Stanislavsky created a studio in 1905 it was given to Meyerhold for his experiments, and when the old director was dying he appointed the younger director as his successor at the Opera Studio. Both men championed Symbolist playwrights. But there were differences, and these were most evident in the 1910s and 1920s. Probably the biggest bone of contention was theatricality, an acknowledgement that what was happening on stage was theatre and not real life – an obvious problem for Stanislavsky who tried to create Life on stage in a totally artless (un-artificial) way. Rather than deny the artifice, Meyerhold wanted to emphasise this, whether it was in his early Symbolist productions, his Commedia dell'Arte inspired productions, or his masterly re-imagining of Gogol's *The Government Inspector* of 1926.

Once Meyerhold came across the theatrical vocabulary of Commedia dell'Arte he found the perfect model for his gestural, political and decidedly non-realistic form of acting. Looking at photographs and reading accounts of his productions it is clear that they involved great spectacle. The sets weren't in any way realistic pictures, but structures that offered the actor unlimited opportunities for movement throughout the stage space. Such theatre demands a very particular kind of actor, and therefore of actor training, which he called biomechanics. This in turn owed a debt to Pavlov's emerging psychology, behaviourism which gave Meyerhold the courage and licence to believe that specific types of movement would elicit corresponding emotions in the audience. The truth was in external bodily movement and not in the actor's inner psyche. Although it appears that we have created the greatest distance possible from Stanislavsky, we should remember that by the late 1930s the old master was making his own experiments with a method based on the qualities of Physical Actions. This focus on how movement creates meaning is a theme which links the later Stanislavsky, Meyerhold and Grotowski who returned to work on the notion of Physical Action. Once again, we are invited to consider how human movement can be a way of communication and a form of knowledge that is independent from language. Meyerhold's biomechanical theory also points to a more materialist relationship between body and mind than that offered by Stanislavsky. In Part II we will have already seen how an autonomously moving bodily self is absent in Bakhtin's conception of the *I*, and the discussion of Meyerhold's biomechanics takes the argument further. For Bakhtin, meaning was a literary, a verbal, phenomenon; the body was only intelligible when seen.

The connection between Bakhtin and Meyerhold comes in the vocabulary of Commedia dell'Arte. It was Commedia dell'Arte that took Meyerhold away from his very static Symbolist productions, and it was the same stock of popular images that took Bakhtin away from a dense philosophical discourse, to his more accessible studies of the novel and of Rabelais. Once again, the idea of character masks brings us to our guiding theme – character. Bakhtin demonstrates how the figure of the fool can help us to understand the role of the author within prose fiction. In his master-work on Rabelais he plunders the same images as Meyerhold to recreate the world of *Gargantua and Pantagruel*. His notion of 'a theatre without footlights' again echoes the practice of Meyerhold who, along with Appia and Craig, tore out the footlights. Although there is this wealth of local connections between Bakhtin's writings of the 1930s, we have to look to the larger context in order to continue our examination of character.

Grotowski (Chapter 6)

Grotowski describes how at the beginning of his career he was a devoted follower of Stanislavsky. A look at his 1960 production of Mayakovsky's *Mystery-Bouffe* shows the debt that he also owed to Meyerhold's notion of Total Theatre. From his beginnings in Opole, where in the first season of 1959–1960 he produced three productions, he gradually reduced the number of productions per year and the lavishness of the theatrical means. In 1969 he produced a piece that used only two large lights, no costumes, no properties, no set and often no seating for the audience. In an early manifesto Grotowski was very clear that theatre should not try and compete with either film or television since its technology would always be inferior but should focus on that event of co-being between the actor and the audience. If he began with Meyerhold's Total Theatre, he ended with a theatre of the Total Act – a Poor Theatre. Grotowski demanded a meaning event that occurred in real time and place, rather like the one imagined by the early Bakhtin.

Grotowski continued Meyerhold's compositional approach in the intricate montages that he created from texts that were often but not exclusively taken from the Polish Romantic repertoire. Quite obliquely, Grotowski seemed to be asking questions about Polish nationality (Gromulka's political changes of 1956 turned out to change little, and Poland was still under the political authority of the Soviet Union) and the relevance of art in a country which had witnessed the atrocity of Auschwitz. Where Meyerhold was keen on promoting debate and disagreement within the audience, Grotowski's engagement was at once raw and yet distant in that the audience were complicit but not actually participating. His stage setting and his montage of texts set up a tension between the social myth and present reality lived by the audience. Those universal and eternal truths that Stanislavsky assumed would be shared by playwright, actor and audience are put into question by Grotowski. This not only influenced his stage setting and script editing but also his approach to acting. The score that helps the actor to create successive performances is not shared with the audience. Grotowski's notion of acting operates on an acceptance that the audience and the actor will experience different emotions throughout the play, even though the entire event is set up as a dialogue between them. It is a dialogue that is structured around the meanings of the play and not on empathetic engagement with the character. It is for this reason that I have suggested that this is a post-modern approach to characterisation. The actor's work is to create something that will affect the audience. It does aim to achieve an emotional response, though an emotion not shared by the actor.

Conclusion

In the spirit of this book, I shall return to the questions of theatre that I have set out above. The aim will be to come to some provisional answers while at the same time opening their frame of reference. For example, *I* and *other* will be considered in the light of Martin Buber's *I* and *thou*, and Bakhtin's theory of the image will be compared with that of the early Sartre. The debate between Stanislavsky and Meyerhold about the nature of psycho-physical acting will be considered in the light of contemporary writings on neurophysiology. I hope that this book offers a new way of thinking of theory and practice.

Notes

1 According to Duvakin, Bakhtin and he met (2014) n.p.
2 *Dostoevsky* 3.

3 Emerson (1997) 81.
4 *Philosophy of Language* 112.
5 *Problems of Form, Content and Material* (first published 1924), *Problems of Dostoevsky's Art* (first published 1929 then as *Problems of Dostoevsky's Poetics* in 1963), *Problems of Literature and Aesthetics* (*Voprosy literatury i estetiki*, 1975), *The Problem of Text* (an editorial title given to a collection of his late notes), in *Speech Genres* (1986) pp.103–128.
6 *Speech Genres* 145.
7 *Act* 2.
8 *Discourse* 320 (my italics).
9 In Gladkov (1997) 167.
10 Grotowski (1991) 15–16.
11 Worrall (1996) 11.
12 Moran (2000) 25.
13 *Life* (1967) 319.
14 Worrall (1996) 6.
15 In Bradshaw (1954) 281.
16 Benedetti (1988) 228.
17 Shklovsky in Lemon and Reis (1965) 11, 12.
18 In *The Problem of Content, Material, and Form in Verbal Art* (1924).
19 In *The Formal Method* (1928).
20 Mitchell (1974) 74.
21 Brecht in Brewster (1974) 96.
22 Worrall (1996) 6.
23 Bradshaw (1954) xiii.
24 Whyman (2008) 236.
25 Worrall (1996) 4.
26 Worrall (1996) 6.
27 Autant-Mathieu (2003) 73.
28 In Komissarzhevsky (1959) 9.
29 Houghton (1962) 23.
30 Cioffi (1996) 82.
31 Gorchakov (1957) 66.
32 Gorchakov (1957) 66.
33 Worrall (1996) 184.
34 Worrall (1996) 184–185.
35 Gordon (1987) 18–19.
36 *Hero* 42.
37 Holquist (1990) xx.
38 Morson and Emerson (1990) 75.
39 Senelick (2008) ix.

Part I

Bakhtin and theatre

1 Bakhtin and theatre

Introduction

Throughout his career, Bakhtin used drama and theatre as a means of explaining his ideas about the novel. He used references to plays and to the situation of the actor in three ways. In his early manuscripts he compares how a writer and an actor author their characters. This is the only instance of him actually engaging in the creative process of the actor, and this engagement is in most part a rhetorical device to explain the creative process of the writer. More frequently Bakhtin refers to drama as being one of the older genres along with epic and lyric, all of which have been overtaken by the more multi-dimensional and open-structured novel. Although these references to drama as a fixed and old-fashioned art form are very general, even so Bakhtin does provoke the student of theatre to consider the differences between drama and theatre and the novel, and how both generate meaning within the reader/spectator's imagination. His third set of references are to specific character masks or roles from theatre – for example, from Atellan farce or Commedia dell'Arte – which are used as a means of exploring and explaining different kinds of authorial activity in novelistic discourse. In other words, this last use of theatre reference returns us to the first one where he explores the activity of the author relative to the characters in a novel. Because Bakhtin used theatre as a constant point of reference, it is possible to offer an overview of his principal concepts while at the same time discussing his field of theatrical reference. Janus-faced to the last, my argument will be a reading against the gradient of Bakhtin's arguments about drama and theatre.

Bakhtin's involvement with theatre

Clark and Holquist's biography indicates that Bakhtin showed an early interest in theatre. His German governess organised him and his brother Nikolai 'in dramatic renderings, such as acting out scenes from the *Iliad*. The boys continued to put on dramatic performances long after the governess had gone, and Mikhail was still involved with theatre in Nevel after his university days'.[1] They go on to note that in the 1920s he and Lev Pumpiansky (a member of the Bakhtin Circle) 'together produced an open-air production of *Oedipus at Colonnus*, using a cast of over 500 pupils from local schools'.[2] They also refer to two lecture series that he gave 'for the Artists' Trade Union, on theatrical production and the history of literature'.[3] From this biography it appears that Bakhtin maintained an academic interest in theatre throughout his career: 'For years he also ran a seminar on aesthetics and the history of the theatre at the Mordovia Theatre for Music and Drama, as he had in Nevel and Vitebsk.'[4] Clark and Holquist also refer to a broader theatricality both in the conduct of Bakhtin and other members of the Circle. Later they note members of the Circle were

> all verbal and contentious. None could have been called a passive disciple. Moreover, the thread of theatricality bound them all, from Pumpiansky's tendency to dress in costumes, to the entire group's love of charades and word games, to Medvedev's close involvement with the theatre itself.[5]

This is a reference to Medvedev's active involvement in Gaideburov and Skarskaia's Travelling Theatre and his writings for their journal.[6] A final portrait of Bakhtin and the Circle seems to be a back-projection of the carnivalesque that is described in *Rabelais and His World*:

> Another idiosyncrasy was Bakhtin's love of eccentricity, peculiar people, and recherché jokes. In those turbulent, post-Revolutionary years, Bakhtin forged bonds with people who had a common flair for theatricality, disguises and pranks. These qualities permitted them to transcend the restrictions that ordinarily close people off from one another and to create a kind of community of the spirit that rendered immaterial, if only briefly, the differences between commissar, actor, philosopher, and musician.[7]

Was this suspension of differences, and the transcendence of barriers between the members of the Circle, really characteristic of their behaviour, or a projection of Bakhtin's later theory onto his early life? In all events, this anecdotal evidence of Bakhtin's theatricality in no way helps us to understand the more substantial questions of theatre that arise from reading his works.

Secondary material

One of the first commentators to write about Bakhtin and theatre was Tzvetan Todorov. In *The Dialogical Principle* (1984) he cites a text by Goethe (though co-signed with Schiller) from 1797 called 'On Epic and Dramatic Poetry' where, as suggested by the title, the epic is opposed not to the novel but to *drama*: 'The epic poet relates the event as *perfectly past*, while the playwright represents it as *perfectly present*.' The opposition between epic and drama is clearly rooted here in the dichotomy of 'relating' and 'representing' (which in turn refers back to the opposition of *diegesis* and *mimesis*).[8] But, he concludes, 'we never find (unless it is in the unpublished materials) the confrontation we await, between the novel and drama'.[9] There is a reason why there is not and could not be such a confrontation: Bakhtin never specifies what he means by the words 'drama' and 'theatre' as either a genre or a medium. His interest extends only in so far as it illuminates, positively or negatively, the nature and function of verbal creation or the novel. Drama and theatre are never the primary subjects of enquiry.

Another early commentator was Julia Kristeva, whom Marvin Carlson cites as a proponent of what he calls a 'theatre within language'.

> She speaks of carnival and dialogism under the operations of performance and dramatic action. She speaks of carnival as a mise en scène in which 'language escapes linearity (law) to live as drama in three dimensions. At a deeper level, this also signifies the contrary: drama becomes located in language. A major principle thus emerges: all poetic discourse is a dramatisation, dramatic permutation (in a mathematical sense) of words.'[10]

The phrase 'drama becomes located in language' could also describe how Bakhtin uses figures from the Commedia dell'Arte to explain the discursive activity of the author in the novel. Kristeva echoes a passage cited by both Todorov and David Lodge where Bakhtin argues that 'every writer (even the purest lyric poet)' is 'a "playwright" insofar as he distributes all the discourses among alien voices, including that of the "image of the author" (as well as the author's other *personae*)'.[11,12] Once again, theatre is not the subject of enquiry but a source of metaphor.

In his 1993 article 'On the Borders of Bakhtin' Graham Pechey contends that drama is the master genre for understanding the distinction between voices: 'Without that dramatic model of individuation constantly before them, the voices of novelistic prose would scarcely be formed.'[13] In a much nuanced discussion of Brecht he not only returns to Todorov's distinction between narration and imitation (*diegesis* and *mimesis*), but also between epic and drama. Very often in Brecht's plays the characters are 'actor-narrators' as well as being embodied characters in the action; Pechey underlines the playwright's insistence that he was interested in characterisation, and cites Galileo and Courage as examples of fully drawn characters.[14] Precisely because of this mix of the diegetic and the mimetic, Brecht's drama is 'open' and challenges Bakhtin's argument that 'drama' is a closed genre. Pechey goes on to argue that Bakhtin can help us to understand Brecht's 'non-dramatic dialogism':

> with Bakhtin's help we can see that what Brecht projects and seeks to realise in epic theatre is nothing less than a (non-)dramatic dialogism; that it is called 'epic' precisely because its every word and movement is not only 'shown' but *told*, inwardly divided between 'dramatic' actualisation and an 'epic' retrospection which both ironises them and hypothesises alternatives.[15]

The key point that Pechey makes in the context of this study is that these distinctions are often made when drama is reduced to the written text, to literature: 'Drama is perhaps not so much monological in essence as *monologised* by being read as "literature" rather than theatre.'[16] He also makes an excellent point about theatricality: in Renaissance tragedies the drama parodies the theatrical pomp of royal ceremony and procession: 'the "power" of theatre we might say lies in its formal parody of the "theatre" of power.'[17] Pechey opens two lines of enquiry that cannot be answered in this study, but are worthy of future research: that drama can appear monological when read as literature and that Brecht's Epic Theatre (there is a reference to Brecht on page 46 of *Rabelais and His World*) demonstrates the open-ness that Bakhtin claimed for the novel.

Pechey has also suggested that Bakhtin's ideas could be applied to a broader notion of theatre. Once again, this reverses the thrust of Bakhtin's argument that the novel had overtaken older genres like the epic, lyric and dramatic. Pechey argues that theatrical modes of 'semioticity inhabit in our time a multitude of institutional sites besides theatre', and points to an 'exponential growth of the dramatic' in contemporary culture.

> We have only to look at the field of metaphor upon which the general Bakhtinian theory of discourse draws its earlier formulations to see that a materialist semiotics of theatre is wholly compatible with that theory. The utterance is a 'speech performance'; discourse is the 'scenario' of the event; it relies on the 'chorus support' of other voices: a semiotics of this kind is positively encouraged by these explicitly theatrical metaphors that Bakhtin's theory uses to establish its materialist credentials.[18]

Bakhtin and other members of the Bakhtin Circle most certainly did make use of theatre as a field of metaphor to illustrate the different ways in which language is used both in speech and writing. Although the greater part of this study will look at how Bakhtin's theory of literary composition can be applied to more practical questions of theatre, in this chapter I shall follow Pechey in demonstrating how theatre provides metaphors to illuminate the dynamics of literary and social discourse.

In *The Bakhtin Circle* Craig Brandist introduces the German critic Spielhagen, who opens out further the questions of drama and novel, and *mimesis* and *diegesis*. Brandist explains how Bakhtin was influenced by Friedrich Spielhagen (1829–1911) who

> advocated a minimalisation of direct narrative intervention in the novelistic text and the maximisation of dramatic dialogue to allow the hero to reveal his or her own distinct view on the world. The narrator should *show* rather than *narrate* characterisation, and this leads to a new type of literary objectivity – a quality that Bakhtin repeatedly attributes to the work of Dostoevsky.[19]

Brian Poole devotes a long article to explaining how Spielhagen influenced Bakhtin. He notes Spielhagen's insistence that the modern novel should be dramatic, that is, exclude any direct authorial voice. There is not sufficient space to follow the full intricacy of Poole's argument (which traces Spielhagen's notion of dramatic narrative back to Aristotle), but I will offer a brief overview.

In *Discourse in the Novel* Bakhtin notes when a novel can become bad drama:

> The novel, when torn out of authentic linguistic speech diversity, emerges in most cases as a 'closet drama' with detailed, fully developed and 'artistically worked out' stage directions (it is, of course, bad drama). In such a novel,

divested of its linguistic diversity, authorial language inevitably ends up in the awkward and absurd position of the language of stage directions in plays.[20]

Poole explains that these 'stage directions' are where an all-knowing, all-seeing author sets the scene, or describes a character. Bakhtin acknowledges the influence of Spielhagen in a note on the quotation above: 'In his well-known works on the theory and technique of the novel, Spielhagen focuses on precisely such unnovelistic novels.'[21] Poole's article traces Spielhagen's aesthetic back to Aristotle, through Lessing, Schiller and Humboldt, and it is in relation to the latter that he returns us to the distinction between *mimesis* and *diegesis*:

> Humboldt's discussion of narrative methods not only helped Spielhagen to differentiate between *showing* character action and *narrating* character description; it also implied an aesthetic judgment related to the purported superiority of the former technique and to the limitations of the latter.[22]

The dramatic is that which delivers the character to the reader with greater immediacy than the narrated. This discussion of dramatic narrative (and that, in essence, is the subject of Poole's long article on Spielhagen) leads to a fundamental question about the degree to which terms like 'drama', 'dramatic', 'theatre' and 'theatrical' are being used metaphorically.

Spielhagen's central thesis is that 'the novel is a stage upon which the author presents acting characters behind which the author himself disappears entirely'.[23] Poole gives an example of this metaphor at work: 'The dramatist', he writes,

> has no other task than to lay bare the souls of his figures, the actor provides the body. He stands physically before us, demonstrates to us his existence *ad oculos* and *ad aures*, thundering it, lisping it, smiling it, weeping it into our hearts.[24]

(Poole doesn't comment on the role of the actor, but presumably it is the reader who must bring the characters to life in their imagination.) Poole warns against too literal a reading of Spielhagen, but argues that if

> we accept the heuristic function of Spielhagen's analogies, we find that his critique of narrative techniques is aimed at reducing the consummating function of the author – to the advantage of the autonomous interaction of the characters amongst themselves. In his obviously metaphoric use of the 'stage' and the 'dramatic illusion', Spielhagen rarely speaks in favour of a complete dramatic illusion, but often against the presence of a 'director' appearing on stage in the middle of a dramatic scene.[25]

Poole explains how Spielhagen describes such authorial interference as either 'directorial business' (*Regisseurgeshäfte*) or 'director's work' (*Regisseurarbeit*) which 'not only interrupts the drama; it also introduces the author's narrative discourse in a form that *persecutes* the characters and passes judgment upon them by revealing their private life *indiscreetly*, in a manner unknown to the characters themselves'.[26]

Already we have all the figures involved in theatrical work: the playwright, the director, the actor and, by implication, the audience. It is telling in the context of this study of three director-pedagogues that Spielhagen uses the stage director as a figure for the over-intrusive author.

In the conclusion to this section, Poole describes the work of the director as the one who provides a monological 'reading' from all the potential meanings of a work. But a director can be like an over-intrusive author who 'continually describes the physical appearance and thoughts of his characters', which means that 'the only perspective we have of the characters is the author's own perspective: by comparison with drama, it's a one man show'.[27] Spielhagen offers a very pungent metaphor for such invasiveness, arguing that the author should not 'affix a character to his heroes like labels stuck to the outside of wine bottles' because such external labelling 'contravenes the very nature of character as an open-ended and non-objectifiable quality of every human being'.[28] This opens the central question of the ethical and aesthetic relationship between author and character, and the related question of who it is that authors a character in theatre: playwright, director, actor or audience? We will return to this question of the authorship of a character in Chapter 4.

Early manuscripts

The references to theatre in Bakhtin's early and unpublished manuscripts are quite different in character to those in his later, published works. Whereas in later writings he refers to a variety of plays and types of theatre (from Atellan farce to medieval morality plays to Commedia dell'Arte), in his early manuscripts he addresses the creative work of the actor. He actively imagines what the actor sees and does when on the stage. Indeed, the actor's work becomes a figure for the work of any of us in our everyday lives trying to understand the experience of another person. But Bakhtin goes further than wanting to understand another person. His task is to represent that other person *as a character*. He uses the figure of the actor to explain how authoring a character involves more than empathy – putting oneself in the place of the other person – it also requires that one returns to one's own place outside of the other person in order to create an image of them as a character.

The actor's work on a character, according to Bakhtin, can only be considered aesthetic work when

> he produces and shapes *from outside* the image of the hero into whom he will later 'reincarnate' himself, that is, when he creates the hero as a distinct whole and creates this whole not in isolation, but as a constituent in the whole of a drama. In other words, the actor is aesthetically creative only when he is an author – or to be exact: a co-author, a stage director, and an active spectator of the portrayed hero and of the whole play.[29]

The last sentence complicates matters by introducing both the stage director and the active spectator. Elsewhere Bakhtin argues that playing 'begins really to approach art – namely, dramatic action – only when a new, non-intervening participant makes his appearance, namely a spectator'.[30] But here he is writing about a child rather than an actor playing, and this 'life event' is being contemplated 'in an aesthetically active manner' by this observer who 'in part, *creates* it (as an aesthetically valid whole, by transposing it to a new plane – the aesthetic plane).'[31] From these two quotations it is clear that Bakhtin's primary interest is in neither the theatre nor even the work of the actor, but rather a kind of creative observation that requires this 'non-intervening participant'. The ethical strivings of the hero become the content of the aesthetically created image of their life: Bakhtin insists upon the distinction between the ethical action in real life, and the aesthetic image of that life in verbal creation. His thinking about authorship balances on this fine line between participation and observation, about the visual image that is given to the observer, and the aesthetic image that is created by the author.

Bakhtin's early theory of authorship is almost classical in its insistence upon an aesthetic distance between the author and the hero. By way of explaining this, Bakhtin argues why it is impossible to adapt Dostoevsky for the stage.

> Dostoevsky involves us in the world of the hero, and we do not see the hero from outside. [...] That is why Dostoevsky's heroes on stage produce an entirely different impression from one they produce when we are reading. It is in principle impossible to represent the specificity of Dostoevsky's world on stage. [...] There is no independent and neutral place for us; an objective seeing of the hero is impossible. That is why the footlights destroy a proper apprehension of Dostoevsky's works. Their theatrical effect is – a dark stage with voices, and nothing more.[32]

Once again, Bakhtin is either unaware of or uninterested in the history of theatrical productions since Dostoevsky must be one of the most adapted novelists on the Russian stage. He must surely have known of the Moscow Art Theatre's adaptations from Dostoevsky: *The Possessed* (1913) or the *Village of Stepanchikovo* (1917)? How is it that Bakhtin, who had had at least one experience of producing a play (*Oedipus at Colonnus* 1918) and in 1919 gave 'two lecture series on theatrical production', could write something that makes so little sense in terms of theatrical production?[33,34] We should note in passing the reference to the footlights which would 'destroy a proper apprehension of Dostoevsky's works'. I shall discuss the image of footlights more fully in the section which deals with carnival and theatre, and only mention it here to note this early use of the figure. One might wonder whether this rather quaint nineteenth-century image of theatre was how he actually conceived of the stage.

Why is it only in his early writings that Bakhtin draws on the figure of the actor? It might very well be because at this stage of his thinking he conceives of the relationship between author and hero in terms of actually bodied beings, people who see and are seen in real time and space. Bakhtin dramatises the situation of *I* and *other*, presenting them as two figures facing each other and looking at each other. His early thinking is theatrical in the sense that we spend our lives observing (and being observed) in time and space: *theasthai* in ancient Greek meant to behold or view, *theatron* was a place for viewing.

The writings of the Bakhtin Circle

Graham Pechey has already highlighted the phrases 'speech performance' and the 'scenario' and they are characteristic of the terminology found in Voloshinov's *Freudianism, A Marxist Critique* (1927) and *Marxism and the Philosophy of Language* (1929), and Medvedev's *The Formal Method* (1928), along with a number of articles written by both men. Rather than being concerned with questions of characterisation or forms of experience, the authors focus on the social situation of the speaker. We are no longer dealing with two consciousnesses – *I* and *other* – but a much larger social grouping, all of them contesting their case through speech performances. The action is now verbal, and the scenario is therefore understood as a place of linguistic exchange; it is a typical speaking situation, one where words are laden with the meanings of former speakers.

In *Marxism and the Philosophy of Language* Voloshinov argues against Ferdinand de Saussure's approach to studying language. Saussure distinguished between *langue* (the underlying system of a given language at any one time) and *parole* (speech, or language as it is used) and insisted that one cannot study language at the level of *parole* because it would lack any methodological coherence. Voloshinov argues that language only exists as utterances (or what Searle would later call Speech Acts), as words uttered in a particular social and historical context. Pechey is right to see this approach to discourse as being inherently dramatic, since language is being considered in terms of utterance and its context. One cannot think of language without thinking of the speaker, the listener and the time and place of the utterance, which explains why Pechey singled out the theatrical term 'scenario'. Voloshinov uses the term throughout his writings: in *Freudianism* he describes discourse as being 'like a "scenario" of the immediate act of communication' and that in order to understand this scenario, 'it is essential to reconstruct all those complex social inter-relations of which the given utterance is the ideological refraction'.[35] In *Philosophy of Language* he states that each word we utter 'is a little arena for the clash and criss-crossing of differently oriented social accents. A word in the mouth of a particular individual person is a product of the living interaction of social forces'.[36] In the essay he restates his thesis that verbal discourse is 'like a "scenario" of a certain event' in order to explain how it is that we interpret such a discourse: 'A viable understanding of the whole import of discourse must reproduce this event of the mutual relationship between speakers, must, as it were, re-enact it, with the person wishing to understand taking upon himself the role of the listener.'[37] Like an actor, the reader or listener has to 'reproduce the event' of the original debate. Later he argues that 'competent artistic perception' involves the reader who 're-enacts it, sensitively surmising from the words and the forms of their organisation the specific, living, inter-relations of the author with the world he depicts and entering into those inter-relations as a third participant (the listener's role)'.[38]

Voloshinov gives an example of such a scenario involving a one-word utterance: two people are sitting in a room, both silent.

> Then one of them says, 'well'. The other does not respond. At the time the colloquy took place, both interlocutors looked up at the window and saw that

it had begun to snow; both knew that it was already May and that it was high time for spring to come; finally, both were sick and tired of the protracted winter. [...] Now that we have been let in on the 'assumed', that is, now that we know the shared spatial and ideational purview, the whole sense of the utterance 'well' is perfectly clear to us and we also understand its intonation.[39]

This could be a scene from a play or short story by Anton Chekhov. Voloshinov explains that both speakers understand the utterance because they both share the same 'spatial and ideational purview', i.e. the given circumstances of their situation. It could be an example used by Stanislavsky to explain how the given circumstances help an actor with the delivery of a particular line or gesture. Far from the abstract and non-historical approach taken by Saussure,

> this fundamentally social phenomenon is completely objective; it consists, above all, of *the material unity of world that enters the speaker's purview* (in our example, the room, the snow outside, the window, and so on) and of *the unity of the real conditions of life* that generate *a community of value judgements* – the speaker's belonging to the same family, period or other social group.[40]

As Voloshinov explains, values are the meanings that prompt us to perform actions in the world. Thus 'behavioural utterances' like the one above 'actively continue and develop a situation, adumbrate a plan for future action, and organise that action'.[41]

Voloshinov goes further by explaining the social dimension to an utterance. Even if the utterance concerns the basic need of hunger, how, or even whether it is delivered 'depends upon the hungry person's general social standing as well as upon the immediate circumstances' because these are 'the circumstances that determine in what evaluative context, within what social purview, the experience will be apprehended'.[42] Voloshinov broadens the concept of given circumstances to include the 'immediate social context' for it is this which will determine 'possible addressees, friends or foes' and even the speaker's own reaction to being hungry: 'dissatisfaction with cruel nature, with oneself, with society, with a specific group within society, with a specific person, and so on.'[43] He goes on to give examples of how different groups would articulate their hunger: the fatalistic resignation of beggars or peasants contrasts with that of organised workers whose experience of hunger 'will be marked predominantly by overtones of active and self-confident protest'.[44] The tendency towards objectivity and a sociological method indicates quite a profound methodological shift from Bakhtin's early manuscripts. Whether Voloshinov and Medvedev helped Bakhtin to think beyond his early phenomenology is a matter for debate, but certainly his later work was rooted in an analysis of spoken word, and used a historical and sociological methodology.

Theatre provides a vivid metaphor for this situation of verbal exchange. Take, for example, the one-word utterances cited above. One can understand their meaning contextually, but that meaning is conveyed through intonation, through how a word is delivered. Voloshinov explains that intonation 'always lies on the border of the verbal and non-verbal, the said and the unsaid. In intonation, discourse comes directly into contact with life'.[45] Intonation establishes 'an active attitude toward the referent, toward the object of the utterance, an attitude of a kind verging on *apostrophe* to that object', and it is precisely this buttonholing approach which co-opts the listener '*as witness and ally*'.[46] Voloshinov quotes a passage from Dostoevsky's *Diary of a Writer* to demonstrate how expressive intonation can change the meaning of a swear word. Six drunk artisans are having a heated discussion and each one uses the word to express a completely different theme: for example, the second drunk repeats the 'very same noun in response to the first fellow, but now in an altogether different tone and sense – to wit, in the sense that he fully doubted the veracity of the first fellow's denial'.[47] Again, one can imagine such an exercise being used in actor training.

Voloshinov draws a major generalisation from his analysis: 'no utterance at all, whether scientific, philosophical or literary, is possible without something being implied.'[48] In other words, every statement implies some community of values which shares the same ideological purview, 'be that of the family, clan, nation, class and many encompass days or years or whole epochs'.[49] Elsewhere Voloshinov uses a more theatrical term: 'The participants in the situation, whose presence is so very obviously essential, we shall term the audience of the utterance.'[50] He then fully evokes the sense of a public or theatrical address to an audience:

> Any utterance, public speech, lecture, etc. is intended for a listener, i.e. to be *understood* and *responded to* by him. […] The utterance looks for this *agreement* or *disagreement*, in other words for a *critical reception* on the part of the listener ('the audience'). Any experienced speaker or lecturer takes full account of this dialogic aspect of his speech. The attentive listeners do not face him like an indifferent, inert, immobile mass of people apathetically following his words. No, he is confronted by a lively, multi-faceted interlocutor. Any movement by a listener, the way he sits, the expression on his face, a cough or change of position, all this is a clear and expressive reaction that provides a constant accompaniment to his speech, as any professional speaker knows.[51]

Although Voloshinov is writing about those attending a public speech or lecture, the emphasis on an engaged, un-indifferent, audience echoes the kind of live participation that Meyerhold (and Brecht) sought from the audience in their theatres. Indeed this live interaction with the spectator is a defining feature of theatre. It is telling that neither Bakhtin nor members of the Circle made much mention of contemporary theatre practice, predominantly holding to a conventional, realist account of theatre. Voloshinov describes the active and urgent political debates that one imagines took place in the 1920s, cultural and political debates in which the theatre of Meyerhold and Mayakovsky took a very active role.

The latter part of Voloshinov's *Marxism and the Philosophy of Language* is taken up with a description of different ways of reporting another's speech. To explain two very different approaches, he borrows a distinction from Heinrich Wölfflin's *Principles of Art History*:

If we wish to reduce the difference between the art of Dürer and the art of Rembrandt to its most general formulation, we saw that Dürer was a draughtsman and Rembrandt a painter. [...] They are two conceptions of the world, differently orientated in taste and their interest in the world, and yet each capable of giving a perfect picture of visible things.[52]

From this Voloshinov distinguishes between a linear style where there is no interest in the 'colour' of the speech, it is simply a bald reporting. 'The basic tendency of linear style is to construct clear-cut, external contours for reported speech, whose own internal individuality is minimised.' There is a 'stylish homogeneity' 'in which the author and his characters all speak exactly the same language'. In what he calls the pictorial style there is a lot of interference between speeches: 'Its tendency is to obliterate the precise, external contours of reported speech; at the same time, the reported speech is individualised to a much greater degree – the tangibility of the various facets of an utterance may be subtly differentiated.'[53] There is a correspondence between linear and pictorial styles and dialogue in drama and dialogue in the novel, and this is a distinction we shall see Bakhtin making in his later writings. The clear-cut 'lines' of drama are very different to the character zones in novels where indirect reported speech – what is now called 'free indirect speech' – results in a mixture of the author's (reporting) and the character's (reported) voice. David Lodge gives a useful definition of this:

This technique [...] consists of reporting the thoughts of a character in language that approximates, more or less, closely to their own idiolect and deleting the introductory tags, such as 'he thought', 'she wondered', 'he said to himself' and the like, that grammar would normally require in the well-formed sentence. Free indirect speech [...] allows the novelist to give the reader intimate access to a character's thoughts without totally surrendering control of the discourse to that character (as in the epistolary novel).[54]

This ability to have the voices of author and hero merging within one utterance became the proof for Bakhtin that the novel was superior to theatre as an artistic genre. Where Spielhagen demands the removal of the author to allow for characters to present themselves, this marks a similar foregrounding of the character's speech by removing 'stage directions' like 'she wondered', but 'without totally surrendering control of the discourse to that character'. Novelistic dialogue within the utterance lies in this overlapping of the voices of author and character. This discussion of the voice (or vision) of the author and character continues in the next section about Bakhtin's book on Dostoevsky.

Dostoevsky

Bakhtin and Dostoevsky

Dostoevsky was a constant focus of Bakhtin's attention from the beginning to the end of his career. In a letter of 18 January 1922 Bakhtin announced he was writing a work on Dostoevsky which he hoped 'to complete in no time at all'. By November of that year its publication was 'announced as forthcoming in the Petrograd journal *Life and Art*, but for unknown reasons the book did not appear'.[55] When *Problems of Dostoevsky's Art* was published in 1929 it marked a distinct shift in emphasis in his approach to how the author related to the hero. Poole explains that in *Author and Hero* '[n]othing escapes the author's omniscient vision, not even that which comes later temporally, and in this sense the hero must be dead to be represented'. In Dostoevsky's novel, however, the author has no 'evaluation of his own' and the 'narrator has no surplus of vision, no perspective'; 'authorial discourse cannot encompass the hero and his word on all sides, cannot lock in and finalise him from without'.[56] Very much in the spirit of Spielhagen's aesthetic, Dostoevsky allows his characters to reveal themselves through their dialogue, thoughts and actions. Poole comments:

> Every reader of Dostoevsky's *The Idiot* will recall how difficult it is to piece together the early life of Prince Myshkin. Both characterisation and the self-revelation of intimate biographical details are often deferred until they may function as part of the dramatic action.[57]

If Bakhtin's first book on Dostoevsky marked a break with his early thinking about authorship, the second edition – *Problems of Dostoevsky's Poetics* – attempted to include material on laughter and *menippea* that might have been better in another work. Poole notes 'a fundamental contradiction' between Bakhtin's early emphasis on 'objective' narration in Dostoevsky's works and the 'later attempt to interpret Dostoevsky's novels in a tradition of laughter and carnivalesque forms'. He argues that this 'shift in focus allowed Bakhtin to interpolate ideas from his study of Rabelais he despaired of publishing elsewhere. (Bakhtin did not believe that *Rabelais and His World* would make it through the press.)'[58]

This sense of Bakhtin having to smuggle material into his studies of Dostoevsky is developed in a conversation with Sergei Bocharov where Bakhtin, aged seventy-seven, argues that his work on the writer was 'morally flawed'. He explains that 'beneath this unfree sky' he could not 'speak directly about the main questions', those that 'Dostoevsky agonised about all his life – the existence of God. In the book I was constantly forced to prevaricate, to dodge back and forward'.[59] Bocharov wonders whether this inability to write frankly about religious issues didn't have a positive side, because it obliged Bakhtin to engage in the form of dialogue:

> Bakhtin's consistent detachment from the upper layer of content – from the *dialogues* of the heroes and their *ideas* – enabled him to isolate the object under consideration in its purest form (the aesthetic object in his methodology) and thus to discover *dialogue* as the inner form of the novel and the placement of *ideas* in the dialogue. Surely we don't need to regret this achievement.[60]

Bakhtin's theory of dialogue is most certainly one of his enduring achievements, being at the heart of his conception of character, of meaning and of the novel as an art form. As ever, the dialogue of drama – a monological form – is used as a figure to illustrate the more complex dynamics of the novel – a dialogical form.

Dostoevsky and theatre

According to his biographer Joseph Frank, the connection between Dostoevsky and theatre is unambiguous:

> Dostoevsky's passion for the theatre unquestionably sprang from a deep personal inclination that did not need any external stimulus. He had, after all, initiated his literary career as a young man by writing poetic tragedy; and on taking up his pen once more in Siberia after prison camp, he had begun to write a play.[61]

Frank also notes that the account in *The House of the Dead* of the production of the popular vaudeville *Filatka and Miroshka the Rivals* and *Kedril the Glutton* is based on fact – Dostoevsky actually did stage them in the prison camp. A lesser-known fact about Dostoevsky is that he also took part – along with Turgenev – in a celebrity production of Gogol's *The Government Inspector* in February and March 1863. Theatre impresario Pyotr Veinberg gives an account of how Dostoevsky, '[w]ithout any hesitation', agreed to play the role of Shpekin, the post office director.

> The theatre lovers of St. Petersburg already knew Dostoevsky as a good literary elocutionist who could give superb readings of his own literary works. Here, Dostoevsky also displayed a gift for acting. I think that no one who knew Fyodor Mikhailovich during the last years of his life could have imagined him as a good comic actor. Yet, he was not merely an actor, but a very good one, who could make the audience laugh in a very Gogolean manner. In fact, Dostoevsky-Shpekin was an actor above reproach.[62]

The association with theatre went further when on 20 January 1872, Dostoevsky wrote a letter to Princess Obolenskaya 'about staging *Crime and Punishment* in Russian theatres'.[63] This intriguing reference opens up the possibility that Dostoevsky also considered that his novels could be staged. An equally tantalising connection with theatre is revealed in Ignat Avsey's introduction to *The Village of Stepanchikovo* when the fact that it was 'initially conceived as a play was revealed by Dostoevsky's widow in conversation with Konstantin Stanislavsky when the latter was planning to adapt it for the stage in 1891'. However the difficulty in getting 'the requisite public performance certificate from the censor' persuaded him 'to revert to the genre of the novel'.[64,65]

When describing the 'fundamental category in Dostoevsky's visualising' Bakhtin argues that he 'saw and conceived his world primarily in terms of space, not time', in terms of '*coexistence* and *interaction*' (his italics). 'Hence his deep affinity for the dramatic form.'[66] (Though he qualifies this statement in a note: 'But, as we have said, without the dramatic prerequisite of a unified monologic world.'[67]) Put another way, many of Dostoevsky's novels include (but do not conclude with) incredible melodramatic set pieces or catastrophes – moments when characters are brought together for a socially embarrassing debacle. In these scenes characters are exposed to public scrutiny, shaming or ridicule that is often excruciatingly painful to read. Such climaxes include the vigil over the stinking corpse of the Holy Father Zossima in *The Brothers Karamazov*, the 'literary quadrille' in *The Devils*, or Nastasia Filipovna's birthday party in *The Idiot*. It is such moments of extreme humiliation that push characters to a degree of self-consciousness near to madness and constitute 'new kinds of authorial provocations to dialogue' rather than opportunities for *catharsis*.[68] For all the influence of Spielhagen's Aristotelian drama, these catastrophes offer no resolution to the different points of view, but 'on the contrary, reveals their incapability of resolution under earthly conditions; catastrophe sweeps them all away without having resolved them. Catastrophe is the opposite of triumph and apotheosis. By its very essence it is denied even elements of catharsis'.[69] These 'extraordinary situations' induce heightened consciousness and self-discovery, their function being to 'cleanse the word of all of life's automatism and objectness' and 'force a person to reveal the deepest layers of his personality and thought', thereby discovering the 'man in man'; they do not offer the aesthetic analgesia or the resolution of Aristotelian catharsis; catastrophe, like dialogism, has no resolution.[70]

The hero in Dostoevsky

Brian Poole has already noted the difference between the aesthetically 'finished' image of the hero in Bakhtin's early manuscripts and the open-ended character in his Dostoevsky study who is more of a living voice. Bakhtin explains that 'the hero interests Dostoevsky as a particular point of view on the world and on oneself, as the position enabling a person to interpret and evaluate his own self and his surrounding reality'.[71] The hero now becomes 'the author of a fully weighted ideological conception of his own, and not as the object of Dostoevsky's finalising artistic vision'.[72] Bakhtin argues that

> [w]hat the author used to do is now done by the hero, who illuminates himself from all possible points of view, the author no longer illuminates the hero's reality but the hero's self-consciousness, as a reality of the second order.[73]

Is it because Dostoevsky's characters talk so much about themselves and about others that they seem so readily to adapt to the stage?

Possibly the most surprising reference to theatre in Bakhtin's writings is where he compares the way that the dramatist Racine and the novelist Dostoevsky give form to their characters. He argues that both writers have found a form that perfectly matches their conception of character:

> This comparison sounds like a paradox, for the material out of which each realises a whole and adequate art is indeed far too diverse. Racine's hero is all objective existence, stable and fixed, like plastic sculpture. Dostoevsky's hero is all self-consciousness. Racine's hero is an immobile and finite substance;

Dostoevsky's hero is infinite function. Racine's hero is equal to himself; Dostoevsky's hero never for an instant coincides with himself. But artistically, Dostoevsky's hero is just as precise as Racine's.[74]

Here we have the perfect opposites: Racine's characters whose meaning is finished and closed to further interpretation and Dostoevsky's who are endlessly open. This should remind us that Bakhtin's book on Dostoevsky was about the poetic structure of his novels, about dialogical relations, about the portrayal of subjectivity rather than about the subject matter. The reference to Racine not only reflects the breadth of Bakhtin's knowledge of theatre, but the subtlety of his conception of literary form.

A more predictable reference to theatre is his description of the 'philosophical drama' of Raskolnikov's inner speech in *Crime and Punishment* (1866) (he could just as easily have chosen the tortured inner dialogues of the Underground Man in *Notes from Underground* (1864)). Bakhtin describes how every person whom he sees or who comes into his mind 'touches a sore point in him and assumes a firm role in his inner speech'. In his (in their) febrile imagination Raskolnikov forces 'them to answer one another, to echo each other's words or to expose one another'. As a result his inner speech unfolds like a philosophical drama, where the dramatis personae are embodied points of view on life and on the world, realised in living situations.[75] But it is 'like' a philosophical drama, and is not something that could be staged. Once again in Bakhtin's mind the nature of novelistic discourse resists any possibility of reduction to drama.

Dialogue in the novel, theatre and life

In Chapter 1 of *Problems of Dostoevsky's Poetics* Bakhtin takes two contemporary critics to task for muddling the dialogue specific to drama with the new 'dialogism' or polyphony of Dostoevsky's novels. Anatoly Lunacharsky compares Dostoevsky's polyphony to that in Shakespeare (and Balzac), an imputation that Bakhtin argues is premature because drama *as a genre* cannot be polyphonic since its dialogue – like dialectics – resolves into one world-view, one set of values (his definition of a monological genre).[76] Yes, Bakhtin argues, the *social discourse* of Shakespeare is multi-languaged – reflecting the different registers at play in sixteenth-century England – but the *generic construction* of his plays tends towards ideological closure. Emerson and Morson support Bakhtin's argument by warning that heteroglossia mustn't be confused with dialogism/polyphony:

> Polyphony is not even roughly synonymous with heteroglossia. The latter term describes the diversity of speech styles in a language, the former has to do with the position of the author in a text.[77]

Once again, the argument revolves around the relation between author and hero.

In the same chapter Bakhtin criticises Leonid Grossman for understanding 'dialogue in Dostoevsky's novel as a dramatic form, and even dialogisation as necessarily a dramatisation'.[78] Bakhtin counters that

> [t]he whole concept of a dramatic action, as that which resolves all dialogic oppositions, is purely monologic.[79]

> The characters come together dialogically in the unified field of author, director and audience, against the clearly defined background of a single-tiered world.[80]

Again and again he returns to the fact that 'dramatic dialogue in drama and the dramatised dialogue in the narrative forms are always encased in a firm and stable monologic framework'.[81] Returning to the opposition between finished and unfinished dialogue he argues that drama as an art form is incapable of supporting several unmerged worlds – it cannot accept the co-existence of voices which remain unresolved. Bakhtin is not just talking about dialogue in literature – novel or drama – but as a philosophical principle in life: 'Two voices is the minimum for life, the minimum for existence.'[82] This is quite as much an ethical injunction of how to live together as it is how to address each other.

> [D]ialogic relationships are a much broader phenomenon than mere rejoinders in a dialogue, laid out compositionally in the text; they are an almost universal phenomenon, permeating all human speech and all relationships and manifestations of human life – in general, everything that has meaning and significance.[83]

This is as categorical a statement of the difference between dialogue in the novel and drama (and indeed in everyday life) as one can get.

The mystery play and menippea

Bakhtin doesn't only use theatre as an example of what the novel is *not* – he also uses certain kinds of theatre as a means of describing how the author interacts with the hero. Still retaining some of the spatial sense of his earlier theory, he describes the author's movement within and around the zone of the character. He argues that the medieval 'mystery play' can help us to understand Dostoevsky's approach to his characters. To make an obscure connection even more complex, he sees a similarity between the Roman satirical form of the *menippea* and 'the mystery play. The Mystery Play is, after all, nothing other than a modified medieval dramatic variant of the *menippea*'.[84] For instance, he takes Dostoevsky's early short story 'The Double' as an example of such theatralisation:

> What results is a peculiar sort of mystery play, or rather morality play, in which the actors are not whole people but rather the spiritual forces battling within them, a morality play, however, stripped of any formalism or abstract allegorising.[85]

Bakhtin plays fast and loose with his definitions: the single morality play (for example, *Mankinde* or *Everyman*) is quite a different kind of drama to the cycles of mystery plays performed in York, Chester or Wakefield. Morality plays were often allegorical where the mysteries were dramatisations of Old and New Testament stories. Typically, Bakhtin rejects their tendency to monological 'formalism or abstract allegorising'.

On one hand, the *menippea* and morality play are both characterised by their mixture of high and low speech (what he elsewhere calls heteroglossia), a vertical range that is also reflected in the staging. For example in *Mankinde* there is a Hell's Mouth from which the devil Titivillus appears, a platform stage in the middle representing Earth and a raised area representing Heaven. This explains how Dostoevsky's words ring out 'before heaven and before earth, that is, before the entire world':[86]

> In fact it is the universal sweep of the Medieval play, indeed of the dream poems, of any genre which allows a non-naturalistic account of the universe: 'The Dream of a Ridiculous Man' presents us with a full and complete synthesis of the universalism of the menippea – a genre of ultimate questions of worldview – with the universalism of the medieval mystery play portraying the fate of mankind: earthly paradise, the Fall, redemption.[87]

Such a reference both returns us to Bakhtin's earlier religious preoccupations and opens up a further theatrical dimension to his thinking. The figurative spaces that Bakhtin takes to describe the speech activity of his characters and authors are the puppet booth, the hawker's cart, and the booth and trestle stage of the morality play, all of which are set up in the marketplace, the medieval equivalent of the Greek *agora*. These are all stages, large and small, from which his eclectic dramatis personae deliver their speeches. Although Bakhtin may be critical of the closure of drama as a genre, he looks to the popular theatre as a figure for the staging of social dialogue.

Bakhtin also draws on how some morality plays (like *Mankinde*) are dramatisations of a struggle within the conscience of a character. Although Bakhtin doesn't mention it, the generic roots of this theatre lie in a dialogue written by Prudentius (348–405) called the *Psychomachia* where the voices of good and evil struggle within the Christian psyche. Holquist describes it well:

> Bakhtin translates Dostoevsky's dictum that the heart of man is a battle-ground between good and evil into the proposition that the mind of man is a theatre in which the war between the centripetal impulses of cognition and the centrifugal forces of the world is fought out.[88]

The superscription to *Mankinde* is *Vita hominis militia super terram est* – man's life on earth is a battle. Bakhtin calls this 'microdialogue', which he defines as 'the intra-atomic counterpoint of voices, their combination solely within the bounds of a single dismantled consciousness'.[89] The Underground Man in *Notes from Underground* and Raskolnikov from *Crime and Punishment* both shun face-to-face dialogue, preferring to engage in internal debate, that is, thinking about rather than speaking to their interlocutors. Underground Man sustains an obsessive internal 'dialogue' which at once replays and then attempts to downplay his dependency on other people's opinion of him. This, then, is a theatre of dialogue – one that is internal and unfinalised.

Dialogue in the novel and in theatre

The essays 'Epic and Novel' and 'From the Prehistory of Novelistic Discourse', and the book-length study *Discourse in the Novel* (1934–1935) all come from a volume whose English title is *The Dialogic Imagination* (1981) and whose Russian title was *Questions of Literature and Aesthetics* (*Voprosy literatury i estetiki*, 1975). I mention this difference of title because it reminds us of Bakhtin's preference for problems and questions, for an open exploration, and avoids the suggestion that the essays explore one particular thing, even if it is his multiform notion of novelistic dialogue. One significant difference between Bakhtin's writings and those of Voloshinov and Medvedev is his theory of comedy. He insists that comic and low languages are used in the novel to unbalance the serious and high official languages. In 'From the Prehistory of Novelistic Discourse' he shows how mimicry and parody reveal the direct and serious word to be 'one-sided, bounded, incapable of exhausting the object', later adding that they reveal 'its limitations and insufficiencies'.[90] Where the serious deals in distance and hierarchy, the comic brings things and people together.

In these essays Bakhtin develops his theory of how the author relates to the hero. His metaphor is, as before, spatial, thus he writes of a character in a novel always having 'a zone of his own, his own sphere of influence on the authorial context surrounding him'. He then goes on to describe this zone in a novel being

> stylistically profoundly idiosyncratic: the most varied hybrid constructions hold sway in it, and it is always, to one degree or another, dialogised; inside this area a dialogue is played out between the author and his characters – not a dramatic dialogue broken up into statement-and-response, but that special type of novelistic dialogue that realises itself within the boundaries of constructions that externally resemble monologues.[91]

Before the discussion of free indirect discourse the voices of author and character were being merged, now Bakhtin goes further by writing about the merging of the voices of different characters. This is a classic example of Bakhtin's formulation of the difference between dialogue in the novel and dialogue in the theatre: 'In drama there is no all-encompassing language that addresses itself dialogically to separate languages, there is no second all-encompassing plotless (nondramatic) dialogue outside that of the (nondramatic) plot.'[92] Indeed, if there is no 'second representing consciousness, if there is no second representing language-intention, then what results is not an image (*obraz*) of language but merely a sample (*obrazec*) of some other person's language, whether authentic or fabricated'.[93] The argument is still about how an author can find the correct place (an evaluative not a spatial standpoint) from which they can frame an image of a character's speech.

In these essays Bakhtin develops his thinking about the relation between popular theatre and the novel, suggesting that the 'durable popular masks' of the Atellan farces of the first century CE and the Commedia dell'Arte had a 'great influence on the novelistic image of man during the most important stages of the novel's development'.[94] Returning to the contrast of comic and serious, he contrasts the flexibility of the comic mask with the fixed role assigned to a hero in an epic – who 'cannot become the hero of another destiny or another plot'.

> On the contrary, popular masks – Maccus, Pulcinello, Harlequin – are able to assume any destiny and can figure into any situation (they often do so within the limits of a single play), but they cannot exhaust their possibilities by those situations alone: they always retain, in any situation and in any destiny, a happy surplus of their own, their own rudimentary but inexhaustible human face.[95]

In *Author and Hero* Bakhtin emphasised the aesthetic value of finalisation and fixed position; here he chooses images that allow for open possibility and change of position. Bakhtin doesn't fully develop these references (to Maccus from Atellan farce, Pulcinello and Harlequin from Commedia dell'Arte), and only later does he explain that their 'happy surplus' stems from the fact that they 'are heroes of free improvisation and not heroes of tradition, heroes of a life process that is imperishable and forever renewing itself'.[96] The reason for mentioning these masks has little to do with theatre as a genre and everything to do with their 'enormous influence on the development of the novelistic image of man'.[97] While he is still focusing on an aesthetic image (*obraz*) now he is suggesting that such images are part of a popular patrimony which extends back centuries and is a generic resource for the realist novel.

Just as the market square is the place where many languages are allowed to be spoken, so Commedia dell'Arte is an artistic model of heteroglossia: 'Italian dialects were knit together with the specific types and masks of the comedy. In this respect one might even call the commedia dell'Arte a comedy of dialects. It was an intentional dialectological hybrid.'[98] Bakhtin will continue to make this claim in his 1963 revision of his 1929 book on Dostoevsky, and in his 1940 thesis on Rabelais. Each time he rehearses his theory, among a wealth of recondite parodies from ancient through to medieval times, he makes reference to Atellan farce and Commedia dell'Arte.

Having discussed the relation between author and hero, Bakhtin then turns to his theory of utterance. Like Voloshinov before him, he is interested in the dynamics of the spoken word. He observes that

> in real life people talk most of all about what others talk about – they transmit, recall, weigh and pass judgement on other people's words, opinions, assertions, information; people are upset by others' words, or agree with them, contest them, refer to them and so forth.

He calls this 'living hermeneutics' before concluding that the 'majority of our information and opinions is usually not communicated in direct form as our own, but with reference to some indefinite and general source: "I heard", "It's generally held that" [...] and so forth'.[99] When a person decides to speak of a certain thing they enter into an 'arena' of already existing evaluations and opinions about that thing, there is already a dialogising 'background that [...] complicates the path of any word toward its object'.[100] This is very far from Shklovsky's aim of getting back to a direct connection between word and thing — to feel directly the stoniness of a stone. Bakhtin's language-world is an echo-chamber of previous evaluations, conflicting and concurring, about that stone. He explains how within 'almost every utterance an intense interaction and struggle between one's own and another's word is being waged, a process in which they oppose or dialogically interanimate each other'.[101] This explains why an utterance is a 'considerably more complex and dynamic organism than it appears when construed simply as a thing that articulates the intention of the person uttering it, which is to see the utterance as direct, single-voiced vehicle for expression'.[102] He concludes by noting that this is why such 'novelistic double-voicedness cannot be unfolded into logical contradictions or into purely dramatic contrasts'.[103]

Dramatic dialogue cannot represent heteroglossia because, 'it cannot ultimately be fitted into the frame of any manifest dialogue, into the frame of a mere conversation between persons; it is not ultimately divisible into verbal exchanges possessing precisely marked boundaries'.[104] In a footnote he adds that the 'more consistent and unitary the language, the more acute, dramatic and "finished" such exchanges are'.[105] In his eyes, the difference is between the single and closed dialogue of drama and the plural and open dialogism of the novel: one could compare it to the single line of a melody and the chordal layering of harmony. One is bound to ask whether Bakhtin is justified in arguing that '[p]ure drama strives toward a unitary language, one that is individualised merely through dramatic personae who speak it'.[106] What is this 'pure' drama? Aware that he is making a sweeping generalisation, he explains in a footnote: 'We are speaking, to be sure, of pure classical drama as expressing the ideal extreme of the genre. Contemporary realistic social drama may, of course, be heteroglot and multi-languaged.'[107] While this is a concession to the drama of Bakhtin's times, he doesn't explain what he means by 'realistic social drama' or how it might be heteroglot. These concessions are something of a sop thrown to theatre, but do not indicate any serious engagement with it as an artistic form. His narrative is that popular theatre provided the images and sense of play that were necessary for the development of the novel which then superseded the earlier genre. Later we will see him state that theatre stopped being a serious genre after Shakespeare. The fact that Meyerhold, Tairov and Vakhtangov all took considerable inspiration from the popular theatre of Commedia dell'Arte is not mentioned by Bakhtin. Nor does he seem to have considered the possibility that the actor's performance of a character can be considered as dialogical, since there is always a degree of authorial consciousness (i.e. the actor's) present in any characterisation.

Time, space and the chronotope in the novel and in theatre

In his book-length study *Forms of Time and of the Chronotope* Bakhtin charts the historical development of the literary forms by means of which time and space are represented in the novel. As so often with the work of Bakhtin, it is difficult to judge the scope of his argument: do these forms apply only to the novel, or to any form of artistic expression – like theatre? Even if Bakhtin had answered 'yes' to all, the task still remains to explore the application or relevance of the concept of the chronotope to theatre. The subtitle to Bakhtin's essay is 'Notes Towards an Historical Poetics', a history that stops at the end of the nineteenth century (as do his historical surveys in *Author and Hero* and *Discourse in the Novel*). Bakhtin is silent about the challenge to realist art and literature that emerged at the beginning of the twentieth century and equally silent about the flowering of theatrical experiment which happened in the 1910s and 1920s. One cannot comment on what Bakhtin did not write about, and can only guess at why he chose to be silent.

Bakhtin's *Chronotope* essay chronicles the development of the novel's representation of time and space leading to the realist novel of the late nineteenth century which achieves an unparalleled ability to represent human consciousness. In his 1973 introduction to the essay he explains that time and space in the novel are not being discussed as 'transcendental' categories 'but as forms of the most immediate reality. We shall attempt to show the role these forms play in the process of concrete artistic cognition (artistic visualisation) under conditions obtaining in the genre of the novel'.[108] Unlike philosophy (Bakhtin is writing about Kant in this passage) or science, the novel deals with embodied and concrete realities. In the novel 'time thickens, takes on flesh, become artistically visible; likewise, space becomes charged and responsive to the movements of time, plot and history'.[109] He is using a set of familiar distinctions: cognitive versus embodied knowledge, artistic versus scientific and, as ever, what constitutes an artistic image. Towards the end of his study he explains how the information about an event 'can be communicated but without the chronotope it cannot become an image [*obraz*], that is, an artistic means of representation'.[110] The theme of the image runs throughout Bakhtin's writings early to late, and always it is about moving from the merely factual to an 'artistic means of representation'. This sense of vital meaning is amplified in a footnote where Bakhtin explains he had attended a lecture given by A.A. Ukhtomskii 'on the chronotope in biology' which also touched upon 'questions of aesthetics'.[111] Bakhtin is not just writing about the represented time of 'plot', but about time-based processes of organic development, and invites us to compare how organisms develop in a responsive dialogue with their environment with how human beings develop images of their existence in time and space. Although Bakhtin would not make the point, we should remember the very obvious fact that theatre is a matter of actual bodies, present to other living bodies who share the same time and space of a performance.

To get a flavour of his argument let us follow how he charts the development of our present sense of private space and interiority. He argues that while there was no sense of the privateness of individual experience in third-century Hellenic narratives, it was starting to develop as a result of a growing ability to distinguish between inner and outer space, of domestic space and of the landscape outside.

> Landscape is born, that is, nature conceived of as horizon (what a man sees) and as the environment (the background, the setting) for a completely private, singular individual who does not interact with it.[112]

He notes that 'numerous petty details of private life begin to take on an importance; in them, the individual feels himself "at home", his private sense of self begins to take its bearings from these petty details'.[113] To put Bakhtin's argument about private space into the context of theatre, think of the number of plays since 1880 that have been set in a living room, kitchen or a similarly recognisable domestic space. Compare the space of the naturalist plays of Ibsen (*Ghosts*, *The Wild Duck*, *Hedda Gabler*) and his early and late symbolic plays (*Peer Gynt*, *When We Dead Awaken*): he moves from the cosmic to the domestic and back to the cosmic. Or think of Chekhov's *Three Sisters*, *Uncle Vanya* or *The Cherry Orchard*, which are all set in rooms in which his characters think about the spaces and time beyond and before them: a future in Moscow for the three sisters, the grinding work-filled future of doing the accounts for the estate, or a future without either the cherry orchard or the family house for the Ranevsky family. Are these examples of the 'realistic social drama' about which Bakhtin was writing? The indoor place of these plays allows for a certain kind of reflection upon and of the world in which the character lives.

As ever, in his *Chronotope* essay Bakhtin makes a wealth of references to theatre, but not simply as a negative foil for the novel: as in *Discourse* he uses figures from popular theatre to explain the discursive dynamics of the novel. The references in *Chronotope* are similar to those of *Discourse in the Novel* and his Dostoevsky book: the popular traditions of theatre and masks and portable stages that would be erected in the marketplace for their performance. Of the many quotations Bakhtin makes from Pushkin, one focuses on the need for contemporary theatre to return to its popular roots in the marketplace.

> When Pushkin said that the art of the theatre was 'born in the public square', the square he had in mind was that of 'the common people', the square of bazaars, puppet theatres, taverns, that is the square of European cities in the thirteenth, fourteenth and subsequent centuries.[114]

In a footnote he offers the full quotation from Pushkin:

> We saw that national tragedy was born in the public square, that it developed there, and only later was called to aristocratic society. [...] How can our tragedy, written on the Racinian model, unaccustom itself to aristocratic habits? How is it to shift from its measured, pompous and fastidious conversation to the crude frankness of folk [*narodnaja*] passions, to the license that is granted statements on the public square?[115]

Whereas Bakhtin will use the marketplace as a figurative place in which a plurality of languages co-exist, Pushkin is being more literal: it is a place of performance to which theatre makers should return, rather than continuing with Racine's outdated and aristocratic theatre. It is a place to which Meyerhold did return. Pushkin is writing about two very different theatrical chronotopes, two very different ways of representing time and space on stage. Racine's theatre – possibly the classic theatre Bakhtin was referring to – has a fixed stage which represents classical tales in a formally rigid style; Pushkin's romantic notion demands a form of theatre that acknowledges a very different acting style and audience.

Masks of the rogue, the clown and the fool

The question about Bakhtin's use of theatre as metaphor is never more pertinent than when Bakhtin introduces the 'masks' of the rogue, clown and fool which 'carry with them into literature first a vital connection with the theatrical trappings of the public square, with the mask of the public spectacle'. He goes to explain that 'the very being of these figures does not have a direct, but rather a metaphorical significance'.[116] Bakhtin is making an incredibly subtle argument about the use of a form. The popular theatre practice of the Renaissance is taken as a metaphor to explain the relation between an author and the world and characters of a novel. A mask is a character (in the case of Commedia dell'Arte, a language) which the actor takes on when it is worn on his or her face; it is a repertoire of movements, of speeches, of attitudes and of actions. Bakhtin argues that they are not real people, 'their being coincides with their role, and outside this role they simply do not exist'. These three masks (rogue, clown, fool)

> insist on their right to be 'other' in this world, the right not to make common cause with any single one of the existing categories that life makes available; none of these categories quite suits them, they see the underside and the falseness of every situation.[117]

This metaphor of popular theatre may have taken us some distance from the more philosophical discourse of *Author and Hero*, but the concerns are similar. He is still concerned by the positioning of the author vis-à-vis the hero, but now it is about finding room to manoeuvre rather than simply aesthetic outside-ness.

In his earlier manuscript outside-ness was an aesthetic, perspectival necessity for an objective and truthful finalised image of the hero. In this later work distance is equated with the parody or irony that allows the author to maintain a 'position' on the subject. The mask is a device by means of which the author can write about things without giving away his or her true identity. Masks help to bring things out into the open, they are on the surface, they externalise things: 'This creates that distinctive means for externalising a human being, via parodic laughter' (parody and laughter are themes that will be developed in his Rabelais book).[118] Bakhtin is writing about different kinds and uses of space: at one level there is the historical place of the market square, but Bakhtin sees symbolic significance in this real space: in this square, thoughts and feelings are externalised, they are brought out into the open, and from outside-ness he draws two further distinctions: between the internal, private realm of psychology, and the external public realm of discourse, and between the horizontal dimension of equal interaction, and the vertical dimension of hierarchy and authority.

In some of Bakhtin's more rhapsodic passages he delights in the many meanings of masking.

> In the struggle against conventions, and against the inadequacy of all available life-slots to fit an authentic human being, these masks take on an extraordinary significance. They grant the right *not* to understand, the right to confuse, to tease, to hyperbolise life; the right to parody others while talking, to not be taken literally, not 'to be oneself'; the right to live a life in the chronotope of the entr'acte, the chronotope of theatrical space, the right to act life as a comedy and to treat others as actors, to rip off masks […].[119]

This passage works at so many levels. He begins with the social and existential demand that an authentic human being cannot be fitted into any of the available life-slots that are on offer in society. Here he returns to his insistence on our potential for becoming, that existential surplus (the 'loophole') which means that we can always be more, can always exceed any one particular slot for being. Not to have a loophole is to have no future, no capacity to change and develop. Masks help us to negotiate these mismatches and overlaps. Here his concerns are ethical rather than aesthetic.

What are we to understand by the 'chronotope of the entr'acte' and 'the chronotope of theatrical space'? What does he mean by treating other people 'as actors'? Later in his essay he refers to these masks in the novel as a kind of 'prosaic allegorisation', or 'prosaic metaphor' and admits to the difficulty of finding terms that adequately reflect this artistic process. With Rabelais' *Gargantua and Pantagruel* or Sterne's *Tristram Shandy* he argues that 'a special complexity and multi-layeredness entered the novel; "intervallic" chronotopes appeared, such as, for example, the chronotope of the theatre'.[120] He later explains that '[a]t the heart of *Tristram Shandy* lies the intervallic chronotope of the puppet theatre, in disguised form. Sterneanism is the style of a wooden puppet directed and commented upon by the author himself'.[121] (The Russian puppet theatre, or *Balagan*, was hugely important to Meyerhold.) A possible meaning for these theatrical chronotopes is that they are transitional kinds of form:

> Indeed, what matters here is the allegoricised being of the whole man, up to and including his world view, something that in no way coincides with his playing the role of the actor (although there is a point of intersection).[122]

These theatrical notions of time and place offer the novelist a means of conceiving of a more authentic way of grasping the living time of a human being. Ultimately Bakhtin aims at addressing the problem of a personal individual perfection and 'becoming' of a man, of the perfection (and growth) of the human race, of earthly immortality, of the education of the human race, of rejuvenating culture through the youth of a new generation.[123]

This is the positive towards which all of Bakhtin's strategies tend. Inauthentic life-slots prevent both the individual person and their culture from developing, from becoming more perfect. The intervallic chronotope, the playing of the actor, the donning of the mask – all of these are means by which one can challenge the political and cultural conventions that prevent this creative becoming. Can one say that Bakhtin is putting forward this kind of acting as a means of showing how things can be different? Is the popular theatre a place for democratic, horizontal mingling? Could one see a connection between these ideas and those of Brecht and Meyerhold?

Carnival and theatre

'Carnivalesque' is one of the keywords – along with 'dialogic' and 'polyphony' – associated with Bakhtin. His reworkings of his *Problems of Dostoevsky's Art* (1929) into *Problems of Dostoevsky's Poetics* (1963) and his 1940 doctoral thesis on Rabelais into *Rabelais and His World* (1965) contain sustained reflections upon the meaning of carnivalesque images in literature. After his exploration of the novelistic genre in his writings of the 1930s, is he now edging towards an ever more theatrical conception of society? As in all his other writings, trying to understand Bakhtin's references to theatre takes us to the centre of his concerns about the novel as a genre. He explains the meaning of these carnivalesque images by insisting upon their connection with a way of life.

> [Carnival] belongs to the borderline between art and life. In reality, it is life itself, but shaped according to a certain pattern of play. In fact, carnival does not know footlights, in the sense that it does not acknowledge any distinction between actors and spectators. Footlights would destroy a carnival, as the absence of footlights would destroy a theatrical performance. Carnival is not a spectacle seen by the people; they live in it, and everyone participates because its very idea embraces all the people.[124]

As ever with Bakhtin, the space in which something happens is a border between two different zones, and these are the familiar zones of art and life. He explains how carnival gives shape to life by fitting it into 'a certain pattern of play'. In passing, we should note that this is a good way of explaining how genres give shape to verbal activity – it orders them into certain recognisable patterns. This patterning renders them meaningful as symbolic activities. Having established this, Bakhtin then points out that he is writing about play and not *a* play: about an activity and not a representation. In order to emphasise that he is not writing about theatre he repeats that this is 'without footlights' and repeats the image of footlights three times in this short passage and throughout his study.

In *Author and Hero* Bakhtin had argued that a child playing by herself is not theatre until another observes her: play becomes performance only when there is an audience. Here we are still dealing with the distinction between play and theatre, but now he insists upon them being separate things because only play brings audience and actor together, theatre (with its footlights) separates them. From games being considered as possible performances they are now taken as performative: 'The images of games were seen as a condensed formula of life and of the historic process; fortune, misfortune, gain and loss, crowning and uncrowning. Life was presented as a miniature play (into the language of traditional symbols), a play without footlights.'[125] It is as if the game is the dynamic element that keeps the political-cultural-historical process moving forward. The point he seeks to make is clear: carnival is about participative celebration, and has nothing to do with a set-up where there are active and passive participants. Both his early and later arguments centre upon the role of the audience, and this is clearly crucial: but why use the image of 'footlights'? Is he really serious that 'the absence of footlights would destroy a theatrical performance'?

Theatre practitioners from the 1880s onwards were arguing precisely that theatrical performance *was* being destroyed by footlights, and that their removal was essential. Emile Zola demanded 'remaking the stage until it is continuous with the auditorium, giving a shiver of life to the painted trees, letting in through the backcloth the great, free air of reality'.[126] In many ways Zola is prefiguring Stanislavsky's demand for a theatre of reality and life, as opposed to the theatricality of footlights and the 'uninterrupted, unbearable declaiming' of neo-classical drama (once again returning us to the theatre of Racine).[127] Quite different was the demand of revolutionary designers like Edward Gordon Craig and Adolphe Appia to destroy the footlights. In his biography of Appia, Richard Beacham notes that he 'demanded the abolition of the footlights which so grotesquely distorted the actor's appearance'.[128] Gordon Craig was even more forthright: in answer to the question of why footlights exist, he replies '[t]here never was an answer, there never will be an answer. The only thing is to remove all the footlights out of all the theatres as quickly as possible and say nothing about it'.[129] For Appia and Craig it was precisely the destruction of the footlights that enabled theatrical performance. Unlike Zola their aim was not a theatre of reality and life. The same was happening in Russia with Meyerhold and other directors challenging the need for the picture-frame proscenium arch. This was most emphatically a theatre without footlights.[130]

This argument is about much more than a set of lights. It is about the very future of theatre as an artistic medium. It is about rejecting the late nineteenth-century stage with its proscenium arch picture frame and painted scenery: a kind of realism that directors like Stanislavsky no longer felt was convincingly real. He pointed out that the theatre lights were focused on the painted canvas and not the actor, and there was a contradiction between the two-dimensional set and the three-dimensional actors. Appia and Craig were creating a new sense of scenic space where lighting and stage volumes provided new possibilities for the actor to move. Gone was illusionist stage-craft and in came the plastic reality of body, light and movement. Although we have seen that Bakhtin did have a direct interest in theatre, and that he continued to lecture on 'aesthetics and the history of the theatre' when in Saransk in the 1950s, it is hard to know how to place his reference to footlights. It is even more difficult when one realises that the kind of participative celebration that Bakhtin demands in the Rabelais book is precisely what was being proposed by Appia and others.

When Appia designed the performance space at Hellerau (near Dresden) the space was called a *Festspielhaus* (a place for celebration) rather than a theatre, and there was no separation between auditorium and stage – recalling Bakhtin's delight in the frank exchange on a horizontal plane. Appia envisaged that the whole community would join together in acts of celebrative movement, with no line dividing audience from performer, professional from amateur. Beacham describes Appia's passion for this 'living art' which involved both performers and audience, and which prompted him to deny and repudiate the traditional stage. He took this 'living art' and 'replanted it elsewhere than on the dusty boards of the desecrated stage'.[131] The notion of celebrative art (*Festkultur*) was also important for Rudolf Laban who created pieces for movement choirs that were to be performed by non-professionals (and like Appia he created designs for movement theatres). Rudolf Laban created lay-dances such as *Titan* (1927) and celebrative parades such as the one of Trades and Crafts that involved over a thousand performers in Vienna in June 1929.[132] It is impossible to prove that Bakhtin was aware of these cultural currents and whether they had any effect on him, but certainly there is a connection between his notions of the body and celebrative performance and those of Appia, Laban and others – a connection which deserves future research. Bakhtin's catch-phrase, 'theatre without footlights', takes us to a turning point in the history of theatre, where the stage as a place for realist images of life gave way to a more plastic conception of time, space and movement. But Bakhtin's own conception of carnival as a kind of performative cultural practice evokes the even more recent notion of performance studies. Michael Bristol's book *Carnival and Theater* demonstrates how Bakhtin's concept of carnival games and parades can be understood in the context of the work of anthropologists Van Gennep and Victor Turner.

The space that concerns Bakhtin in his Rabelais study is not the theatre but the market square that has already been discussed in his essay on the chronotope and *Discourse in the Novel*. It was here that market stalls, puppet booths and the booth and trestle stages of Commedia dell'Arte would be erected. The market square offers innumerable pitches for players, quack-doctors, hucksters and street-sellers to shout their wares. Pushkin may take it as a model of popular theatre, but for Bakhtin the market square is a place of speech: free, popular and unofficial speech. Chapter 2 of *Rabelais and His World* is devoted to study of 'The Language of the Marketplace in Rabelais'. Dating from the writings of the Bakhtin Circle the word has been considered as something actually uttered rather than an abstract lexical item, but here it becomes a material thing hurled about:

> The role of cries in the marketplace and in the streets was important. The city rang with these many voices. […] The culture of the common folk idiom was to a great extent a culture of the loud word spoken in the open, in the street and marketplace.[133]

He writes how the 'familiar language of the marketplace became a reservoir in which various speech patterns excluded from official intercourse could freely accumulate'.[134] Once again popular culture provides Bakhtin with a resource of forms that can inform the early novel. The marketplace has a symbolic value as being the place of the people whose face 'looked into the future and laughed, attending the funeral of the past and present' which belong to 'official serious culture' which was 'strictly divided from the marketplace'.[135,136] The divisions in *Rabelais and His World* are categorical: there is the feudal darkness, seriousness and unfreedom of officialdom, that which is elevated and associated with the past, and there is the laughing, familiar, unofficial and popular which looks forward to the future. The marketplace is where the people can mingle shoulder to shoulder, on the same level, and this 'carnivalesque crowd' is 'not merely a crowd', but 'the people as a whole', 'organised *in their own way*, the way of the people'.[137] It is a place of political and cultural assembly.

Just as Bakhtin's marketplace is both a real place and a symbol, so is the human body. Bakhtin delights in the shifts of scale and perspective in Rabelais' novel: the size of his giants grows or diminishes depending on the tale being told. The body is a symbol, it is a carnival image, a comically grotesque exaggeration of the original, and it is an object of scientific interest (Rabelais was a trained doctor who was interested in contemporary advances in anatomical research). This contrasts with Appia's account of the human body which moves in scenic space and is a plastic reality: 'I shall call this corporeal space, which becomes living space, once the body animates it.'[138] For Appia the human body was the *Massgebend*, the unit of measurement for the scenic space. Rabelais' body is far from perfect or single: 'the body and bodily life have here a cosmic and at the same time an all-people's character; this is not the body and its physiology in the modern sense of these words, because it is not individualised.'[139] Bakhtin's carnivalesque body is the model for a certain kind of social interaction:

> It is not a closed, completed unit; it is unfinished, outgrows itself, transgresses its own limits. The stress is laid on those parts of the body that are open to the outside world, that is, the parts through which the world enters the body or emerges from it, or through which the body itself goes out to meet the world.[140]

Where he has focused before upon border zones of contact, here he focuses on 'convexities and orifices' because 'it is within them that the confines between bodies and between the body and the world are overcome'.[141] This contrasts with the leaden muscular heroism of Soviet statuary with their sexless, classical proportion. Bakhtin's conception of the body is, to re-use a phrase from *Author and Hero*, a whole of meaning. This literary and philosophical figure transforms our understanding of the human body in its interaction with the world. The body that Appia writes about transforms the scenic environment of the stage.

Sometimes Bakhtin very deliberately situates his argument in-between the literal and metaphorical. He is, after all, writing about 'images of the body'. Consider the mouth: the orifice of eating, drinking, speaking, singing and burping. Gargantua's father was called Grandgousier, because he had a great gullet that was capable of consuming vast amounts of wine and food; his son Pantagruel was born at a time of great thirst. The mouth acquires a cosmic significance and therefore gigantic dimensions (value is gauged in size). A wonderful example of this cosmic dimension is to be found in Book II of *Gargantua and Pantagruel* where explorers enter Pantagruel's mouth to discover that it contains its own peoples. There is a delight in this sudden expansion of scale, a thrill as we experience the explosion of perspective. Bakhtin argues that such a body contains, 'like Pantagruel's mouth, new unknown spheres. It acquires cosmic dimensions, while the cosmos acquires a bodily nature. Cosmic elements are transformed into the gay form of the body that grows, procreates, and is victorious'.[142] Later he develops this connection between the cosmic scenography of popular stage and the bodily topography:

> Bodily topography of folk humour is closely interwoven with cosmic topo-graphy. The organisation of the stage of the show and the circus ring displays the same topographical structure as the stage of the mystery: the earth, the underworld, and heaven. [...] We also find the cosmic elements in these shows: the air (acrobatic feats and stunts), water (swimming), earth and fire.[143]

One cannot help be dazzled by this display of intellectual bravura that brings into play the staging of medieval theatre, popular entertainments, the human body and the cosmos.

At this point Bakhtin makes a connection between popular literature and popular theatre, comparing the Hell's Mouth that might have been seen in a play like *Mankinde* with the mouths of these amiable giants.

> As far as I know, no author of Rabelaisiana has stressed the leading role of the gaping mouth in the novel's First Book or compared it with the organisation of the mystery stage. Yet this comparison is of great importance for the correct understanding of these books, since it proves the influence of the popular theatrical forms on Rabelais' initial work as well as on the entire character of his artistic and ideological vision and thought.[144]

It is impossible to prove this connection, but it is not a casual remark. In a footnote he reveals the depth of his research into the lay-out of the medieval stage (which takes us back to an earlier discussion in his Dostoevsky study). He describes the tripartite division of the stage into Paradise (top, right), Earth (centre, middle) and Hell (bottom, left [not centre as MB states]). 'The backdrop was formed by an elevated set which represented heaven or paradise.' He notes how the word 'gods' 'is still used in French and Russian for the top gallery of the theatre', as it is for the upper circle in English theatres. But apart from this stage architecture he grasps the importance of the Hell's Mouth in performances: the 'medieval public centred its curiosity' on these 'gaping jaws', expecting the most amusing and comic protago-nists to emerge from them.[145] And Bakhtin is totally right, the devils were hugely popular figures. In *Mankinde* the collection from the audience – i.e. the money on which the players depended for their living – was taken immediately before the entry of the devil Titivillus.[146] Without some familiarity with the literature to which Bakhtin refers, a reader of his Rabelais study might think that he was creating a cosmic fantasy, an allegory pitting the imaginary world of grotesque realism against the iron realities of Stalin's Soviet state. There may be an element of allegorising in his study, but it is also an incredibly vivid reimagining of the world of *Gargantua and Pantagruel* that renders it the more accessible to the modern reader.

These observations do not exhaust Bakhtin's references to theatre. Displaying an encyclopaedic knowledge of medieval theatre he gives as another example of a play without footlights the twelfth-century play by Adam de la Halle, *The Play in the Bower*. (Whether it was meant to be performed or is even performable remains open to question.) But of great interest are his comments on Shakespeare written when making additions and changes to his Rabelais manuscript. The first comments connect Shakespeare with the carnival tradition: 'he actualised the reserve of folk icons/characters. Shakespeare is cosmic, limitless and topographical.' This explains why 'his characters are able to develop such unusual strength and vitality in the topographical and accented space of the stage'. He then goes on to compare this stage with 'our own empty box stages' where characters 'only fuss about and there is no *real* action/movement like in Shakespeare'. He concludes that 'contemporary drama can only deal with practically thought out things, which cannot be presented in any other way. Its emptiness and accentlessness is amplified by naturalistic sets and props'.[147] In these notes to himself, Bakhtin argues that the Shakespearean stage and characters owe their vitality to the medieval tradition from which they emerge. It is a point that underpinned the work of the Medieval Players, and informed our productions of both Shakespeare and Marlowe. Bakhtin's arguments about the connection between the stage and the cosmos may seem exaggerated, but it is precisely the lack of naturalistic detail, the openness of the stage, the direct contact with the audience that accounts for the raw vitality of Shakespeare's dramas. One could argue that it was precisely this popular tradition of theatre – in his case Commedia dell'Arte – which helped Meyerhold create his own revolution in theatre. An examination of the theatre references in *Rabelais and His World* highlights the difficulties of understanding Bakhtin's connection with theatre. On the one hand there is a breadth of reference and a depth of understanding of medieval theatre; on the other there is a very limiting conception of theatre, and no connection with the revolution in theatrical practice that was happening in his own time.

Last thoughts and reflections

In his last writings Bakhtin returns to Shakespeare and how the 'semantic treasures' in his works 'were created and collected through the centuries and even millennia', and lay hidden in both literary and everyday language. Among these treasures are 'carnival forms' and 'theatre-spectacle genres (mystery plays, farces and so forth), in plots whose roots go back to prehistoric antiquity'. Developing from his Rabelais study, one of Bakhtin's later preoccupations is that the interpretation of ancient works continues for a long time after their own epoch, and thus it is that 'Shakespeare took advantage of and included in his works immense treasures of potential meaning that could not be fully revealed or recognised in his epoch'.[148] Bakhtin's notion of 'great time' extends backward into the distant past where he finds the generic roots of modern works by Rabelais, Shakespeare, Goethe or Dostoevsky, and because of these ancient roots, the interpretative life of their works will extend far beyond their immediate lifetime, and the sphere of meaning intended by the authors. He explains this long generic history with reference to Pushkin's *Eugene Onegin*, which 'was created during the course of seven years. But the way was being prepared for it and it was becoming possible throughout hundreds (or perhaps thousands) of years. Such great realities as genres are completely underestimated'.[149] In one of his last writings about Shakespeare he returns to his argument that because his was a theatre of the 'entire world (*Theatrum mundi*)', '[t]his is what gives that special significance [...] to each image, each action, and each word in Shakespeare's tragedies, which has never again returned to European drama (after Shakespeare, everything in drama became trivial)'.[150] Twice we see Bakhtin side with Pushkin in arguing that in order for theatre to refind its vitality as a popular art form it needs to leave behind the courtly tradition of Racine and return to the rich vulgarity of the market square.

Bakhtin seemed to have produced little finished writing after his 1940 doctoral thesis on Rabelais. One exception was an essay on speech genres written in 1952–1953. His other writings were preparatory notes or musings, many of which worked away at questions of genre, authorship and how we understand each other through the written and spoken word. Apart from other references to Shakespeare there are a few elliptical – and sometimes fascinating – references to theatre and acting. The connection with theatre really comes from the possible application of Bakhtin's ideas about speech genres (a concept first found in *Marxism and the Philosophy of Language*) which describes how speech works in real social situations.[151]

> The fact is that when the listener perceives and understands the meaning (the language meaning) of speech, he simultaneously takes an active, responsive attitude towards it. He either agrees or disagrees with it (completely or partially), augments it, applies it, prepares for its execution, and so on. [...] Any understanding of live speech, a live utterance, is inherently responsive, although the degree of this activity varies extremely. Any understanding is imbued with response and necessarily elicits it in one form or another: the listener becomes the speaker.[152]

Here he is holding to his earlier insistence in *Act* upon ethics being a question of actually performed actions, rather than theoretical pronouncements. Where before he had written about answerability or responsibility, here the accent is on answering, on the 'responsive attitude'. Throughout his writings he has demanded this active response, without which there could not be that communicative chain reaction which keeps a subject, a relationship or a social group alive. The meaning is not some abstract content but a putting forward of a point of view which asks for a response: does the listener agree or disagree, is it something to be acted upon or not? Throughout the pages of *Speech Genres and Other Late Essays* he lists possible responses to utterances: they can elicit 'assertion and objection, assertion and agreement, suggestion and acceptance, order and execution'.[153]

Meaning is context-specific, which explains how '[u]tterances and their types, that is, speech genres, are the drive belts from the history of society to the history of language'.[154] Here in a nutshell is Bakhtin's socio-linguistics. The second feature of this kind of meaning is that it is an attitude towards that 'particular actual reality': the meaning has an expressive intonation that is to do with the speech situation and not the particular word as a lexical item. Meaning is a result of personal engagement, either as the speaker or the listener-responder: it lies in the speaking context and not in the conceptual content of the words. Furthermore the context of an utterance 'is always personalised (infinite dialogue is where there is neither a first nor a last word – natural sciences have an object system (subjectless))'.[155] In the human – as opposed to the natural sciences – meanings are the result of personalised meanings: 'Our *thought* and our *practice*, not technical but *moral* (that is, our responsible deeds), are accomplished between two limits: attitudes toward the *thing* and attitudes toward the *personality. Reification* and *personification*.'[156] He notes that while the 'interpretation of contextual meanings cannot be scientific', it is, however, 'profoundly cognitive' and can directly serve practice, practice that deals with things.[157] To underline this very personalistic approach to dialogue Bakhtin starts to write not just about *I* and *other*, but also *I* and *thou*: should we see any connection with the ideas of Martin Buber's book *I and Thou*? 'Thou' has a much greater sense of personal, indeed, intimate address than 'other'. If Bakhtin hears voices in all dialogue, it is because he can hear real people struggling to make themselves understood. The ability to hear people speaking when reading a text might be helpful to an actor.

Bakhtin has given us a vivid and detailed explanation of how all language is alive as an utterance, and that it is addressed to someone, and takes the form of agreement, disagreement and so forth. Every speaker is trying to make sense of the world or of other people's attempts to make sense of it, and it is the actor's job to find this sense of a living voice. Bakhtin almost goes so far as to give tips about delivery. In terms of intonation he observes that, to

> a certain degree, one can speak by means of intonations alone, making the verbally expressed part of speech relative and replaceable, almost indifferent. How often we use words whose meaning is unnecessary, or repeat the same word or phrase just in order to have a material bearer for some necessary intonation.[158]

Intonative utterances like 'well!' or 'really' depend on the context – or what Stanislavsky calls given circumstances – for their meaning. He very helpfully explains the communicative status of pauses between utterances which are 'not grammatical but real. Such real pauses – psychological, or prompted by some external circumstance – can also interrupt a single utterance. In secondary artistic genres such pauses are calculated by the artist, director, or actor.'[159] Bakhtin also makes a telling distinction between quietude (the absence of sound) and silence (the absence of speech). The first 'is mechanical and physiological', but the second is 'personalistic and intelligible': it is an entirely different world. In quietude nothing makes a sound (or something does not make a sound); in silence nobody *speaks* (or somebody does not speak).[160] Again, he is distinguishing between phenomena to do with things, and phenomena to do with people.

To conclude: Bakhtin states that 'only the contact between the language meaning and the concrete reality that takes place in the utterance can create the spark of expression.'[161] An actor has to deliver lines as if they are utterances which possess this spark of expression. The speech of their characters has to 'have the quality of turning to someone', which is 'a constitutive feature of the utterance; without it the utterance does not and cannot exist.'[162] The actor's task is to deliver lines as if they were spontaneous utterances, as if they were a response to an event in the world, and in such a way that they prepare the ground for responses of other characters. Bakhtin roots the meaning of life in the speech activity of actual people: this is remarkably close to Stanislavsky, who demands that acting has to seem as convincing as actual life.

Bakhtin and theatre

This aim of this survey has been two-fold. The first was to demonstrate the extent and nature of Bakhtin's reference to theatre. Precisely because theatre was a constant source of reference throughout his writings, it has been possible at the same time to offer an account of the development of his thinking by means of these references. We can draw some preliminary conclusions from this survey. Although theatre helps Bakhtin articulate what has been described as the dramaturgy of the author and character in the novel, his primary interest is always precisely the novel and not theatre. Marvin Carlson puts the matter well when he complains that Bakhtin only offers 'dramatically flavoured observations', and he shares Tzvetan Todorov's 'frustration and puzzlement' that the reader 'waits in vain for an extended comparison of the novel and drama, parallel to the frequent comparison of the novel and the epic'.[163] The frustration is not just that Bakhtin never made his comparison himself, but that very few critics – Carlson excepted – have taken up this challenge. The chapters that follow do not so much offer a comparison of the novel and theatre, as much as an examination of how Bakhtin's ideas about the novel can illuminate questions that are central to theatre. Equally, I shall deploy theories about theatre practice to test some of Bakhtin's ideas about dialogue in everyday life and dialogue in the novel.

Notes

1 Clark and Holquist (1984) 21.
2 Clark and Holquist (1984) 42.
3 Clark and Holquist (1984) 44.
4 Clark and Holquist (1984) 327.
5 Clark and Holquist (1984) 115.
6 Brandist *et al.* (2004) 15, 25, 40–42.
7 Clark and Holquist (1984) 151.
8 Todorov (1984) 89.
9 Todorov (1984) 90.

10 Carlson (1996) 59.
11 Todorov (1984) 68.
12 'Notes from 1970–71' quoted in Lodge (1990) 97. (N.B. Vern McGee in *Speech Genres* p.110 translates 'dramaturge' where Todorov (1984) 68 translates 'playwright'.)
13 Pechey in Hirschkop and Shepherd (2001) 69.
14 Pechey in Hirschkop and Shepherd (1989) 59.
15 Pechey in Hirschkop and Shepherd (1989) 59–60.
16 Pechey in Hirschkop and Shepherd (1989) 61.
17 Pechey in Hirschkop and Shepherd (1989) 61.
18 Pechey in Hirschkop and Shepherd (1989) 61–62.
19 Brandist (2002) 92.
20 *Discourse* 327.
21 Poole (2001) 112 (citing *Discourse* 327).
22 Poole (2001) 118–119.
23 Poole (2001) 111.
24 Poole (2001) 112.
25 Poole (2001) 143.
26 Poole (2001) 144.
27 Poole (2001) 113.
28 In Poole (2001) 153.
29 *Hero* 76.
30 At Caryl Emerson's suggestion the translation has been modified from 'non-participating' to 'non-intervening'.
31 *Hero* 74–75.
32 *Hero* n.9, 236–237.
33 Clark and Holquist (1984) 42.
34 Clark and Holquist (1984) 43.
35 *Freudianism* 79.
36 *Philosophy of Language* 41.
37 Discourse in Life 106.
38 Discourse in Life 109.
39 Discourse in Life 99.
40 Discourse in Life 100.
41 Discourse in Life 100.
42 *Philosophy of Language* 87.
43 *Philosophy of Language* 87.
44 *Philosophy of Language* 89.
45 Discourse in Life 102.
46 Discourse in Life 103.
47 *Philosophy of Language* 103.
48 Literary Stylistics 126.
49 Discourse in Life 101.
50 Literary Stylistics 106.
51 Literary Stylistics 118.
52 Wölfflin (1932) 18.
53 *Philosophy of Language* 120–121.
54 Lodge (1990) 126.
55 Clark and Holquist (1984) 239.
56 Poole (2001) 143.
57 Poole (2001) 140.
58 Poole (2001) 159–160.
59 Bocharov (1994) 1012.
60 Bocharov (1994) 1020.
61 Frank (1987) 15.

62 In Sekirin (1997) 164–165.
63 In Sekirin (1997) 172.
64 Avsey (1983) xii.
65 For Stanislavsky's Letters to Madam Dostoevskaya see Senelick (2014) 51–52 [25 February 1890], 55–56 [10 April 1890].
66 *Dostoevsky* 28.
67 *Dostoevsky* 45.
68 Morson and Emerson (1990) 258.
69 *Dostoevsky* 298.
70 *Dostoevsky* 111.
71 *Dostoevsky* 47.
72 *Dostoevsky* 5.
73 *Dostoevsky* 49.
74 *Dostoevsky* 51.
75 *Dostoevsky* 238–239.
76 *Dostoevsky* 32–36.
77 Morson and Emerson (1990) 232.
78 *Dostoevsky* 17.
79 *Dostoevsky* 17.
80 *Dostoevsky* 17.
81 *Dostoevsky* 17.
82 *Dostoevsky* 252.
83 *Dostoevsky* 40.
84 *Dostoevsky* 147.
85 *Dostoevsky* 217.
86 *Dostoevsky* 154.
87 *Dostoevsky* 149.
88 Holquist (1990a) 47.
89 *Dostoevsky* 221.
90 Prehistory 55, 56.
91 *Discourse* 320.
92 *Discourse* 266.
93 *Discourse* 359.
94 Epic and Novel 36.
95 Epic and Novel 36.
96 Epic and Novel 36.
97 Epic and Novel 36–37.
98 Prehistory 82.
99 *Discourse* 338.
100 *Discourse* 281.
101 *Discourse* 354.
102 *Discourse* 354–355.
103 *Discourse* 356.
104 *Discourse* 326.
105 *Discourse* 326.
106 *Discourse* 405.
107 *Discourse* n.62, 405.
108 *Chronotope* 85.
109 *Chronotope* 84.
110 *Chronotope* 250.
111 *Chronotope* 84 – Bakhtin also published a paper on Vitalism in 1926 which touched on this same question of time, space and biological development.
112 *Chronotope* 143.
113 *Chronotope* 144.

114 *Chronotope* 132.
115 *Chronotope* n.'s' 132.
116 *Chronotope* 159.
117 *Chronotope* 159.
118 *Chronotope* 160.
119 *Chronotope* 163.
120 *Chronotope* 166.
121 *Chronotope* 166.
122 *Chronotope* 166.
123 *Chronotope* 204.
124 *Rabelais* 7.
125 *Rabelais* 235.
126 In Bentley (1968) 351.
127 In Bentley (1968) 352.
128 Beacham (1994) 25.
129 Craig (1968) 162.
130 In personal correspondence Caryl Emerson observed that in Russia there were 'the so-called "*rampa* wars" or battle over the footlights' which involved figures like 'Vyacheslav Ivanov, Sologub, Voloshin, Shpet, etc.'.
131 Beacham (1994) 187.
132 For fuller discussion of *Festkultur* and Laban's productions see McCaw (2011).
133 *Rabelais* 182.
134 *Rabelais* 17.
135 *Rabelais* 81.
136 *Rabelais* 96.
137 *Rabelais* 255.
138 In Beacham (1994) 119.
139 *Rabelais* 19.
140 *Rabelais* 26.
141 *Rabelais* 317.
142 *Rabelais* 339.
143 *Rabelais* 354.
144 *Rabelais* 349.
145 *Rabelais* 348.
146 Bevington (1975) 919–920.
147 Changes and Additions 87.
148 *Speech Genres* 4–5.
149 *Speech Genres* 140.
150 *Speech Genres* n.11, 171.
151 *Philosophy of Language* 20, 97.
152 *Speech Genres* 68.
153 *Speech Genres* 72.
154 *Speech Genres* 65.
155 *Speech Genres* 167–168.
156 *Speech Genres* 168.
157 *Speech Genres* 160.
158 *Speech Genres* 166.
159 *Speech Genres* 74.
160 *Speech Genres* 133.
161 *Speech Genres* 87.
162 *Speech Genres* 99.
163 Carlson (1996) 314.

Part II
Bakhtin and Stanislavsky

Introduction to Part II

Part II consists of three chapters which address connections between the writings of Konstantin Stanislavsky and Bakhtin. The notion of character is central to the thinking of both men; from this follows a series of related problems and questions: how a character relates to a living person; the difference between a character in verbal creation and theatrical creation; and whether an actor can be considered an author of a character. Bakhtin proposed to write a philosophy of the act, but is an 'act' the same as what Stanislavsky means by action? Stanislavsky traces the word 'drama' back to the ancient Greek '*dran*', to do. Bakhtin writes about meaning instantiated by an act as an unrepeatable 'event'; does this relate to the theatrical notion of live performance? Bakhtin writes about how time and space determine the specific meaning of an event. How does this relate to the time and space of a performance, and to Stanislavsky's concept of the given circumstances? And in turn how does the concept of the given circumstances relate to Bakhtin's notion of the given and created? They share a sense of the urgency and unrepeatability of the moment which is here and now. Both operate within the assumptions of realism, and both are concerned with establishing a relation between art and life. For Bakhtin this means that it is possible to create a verbal image of a person's life; for Stanislavsky this means that it is possible to get into the mind of a character and thus bring this verbal creation to life on stage. Crucially, both share the belief that there is a relation between a living person and a character. They both agree that the meaning of a work of verbal or theatrical art is judged in terms of its emotional truth, of how it acts upon the viewer's or reader's feelings.

Bakhtin's account of authorship begins with the author encountering a living person and ends with the creation of a literary image of that life – a work of written fiction. Stanislavsky's approach to acting begins with the written text – a playscript – and ends with the actor delivering those written lines as if they were the spontaneous utterances of a living person. Throughout this book we will see variations on this central theme, which itself is related to the bigger theme of art and life. One begins with life (a living person) and ends with art (a written work), the other begins with art (a written work) and ends with life (an actor living the role). One is about an act of verbal creation, the other an interpretative realisation. This provokes the question of whether the actor is an interpretative or a creative artist. Although working in different genres – Bakhtin in a blend of literary analysis and philosophy, Stanislavsky in theatre – both men's concepts of artistic responsibility, indeed of literary creation, are anchored in the concept of the living person.

Mel Gordon describes Leopold Sulerzhitsky, a Tolstoyan activist who had a profound influence on Stanislavsky, as a 'natural teacher with a strong spiritual tendency' who 'believed more in transforming life than improving art'. According to him, the theatre revealed the unspoken, hidden language between people. The new actor, who relies on truth and experience for his expression and inspiration, could expose – and therefore change – the everyday world of lies.[1] Key words and preoccupations in this description apply equally to Bakhtin and Stanislavsky: the focus on the 'spiritual', on life as opposed to art, on the importance of experience. For both there is an unquestioned identity between a character – a literary creation – and a living person: to understand a character is to understand another person. To go further, they argue that a character is understood in the same way as the mind of another person.

Much of Bakhtin's early philosophy consists of a description and an analysis of first-person experience, what it feels like to be an *I*. Chapter 2 will examine how this might help an actor understand how to create a living character from a written script. Michael Holquist writes about Bakhtin's attempt 'to get back to the naked immediacy of experience as it is felt from within the utmost particularity of a specific life, the molten lava of events as they happen'.[2] English director Declan Donnellan – who has spent much time working in Russia with Russian actors – argues that Stanislavsky's artistic quest, as actor, director and teacher, was to find the life in acting. 'When he uses the word "art" it often reads as a code for "life". This fusion is clear even in the title of his autobiography *My Life in Art*.'[3] He continues that Stanislavsky 'saw, or had a vision of, a form of acting that brimmed with life. […] The first question must always be "*What is good acting?*" And the answer will remain the same: "*When it is alive*".'[4] This sense of the live-ness of good acting constituted his definition of what is 'real' and defines Stanislavsky's revolution in the art of acting.

Although Holquist may be able to see that Bakhtin is writing about 'the naked immediacy of experience' such a sense of immediacy may not be obvious to many readers since the language of his early writings is dense with unfamiliar philosophical terminology, and these terms are crammed, one after the other, into long sentences. Thus a secondary aim of these three chapters is to render the rather opaque argumentation of Bakhtin's early writings into a more accessible form for the student of theatre. Such a task is made possible because the central concepts in Bakhtin's early philosophy are not intrinsically difficult to understand, dealing as they do with action, value, will and the living sense of time and place: they are to do with the experience of living in the first person, being an *I*.

Texts and contexts

Part II of this book is based on close readings of two of Bakhtin's earliest works – *Toward a Philosophy of the Act* and *Author and Hero in Aesthetic Activity* – and of

Stanislavsky's *My Life in Art* and *An Actor's Work*, along with transcripts of him at work.[5] Thus while these three chapters only deal with the early part of Bakhtin's thinking (up to 1929), it follows Stanislavsky's entire career from his amateur debut in 1877 to his death in 1938. I am not proposing a comprehensive overview of the contents of these books, but rather an exploration of the themes and preoccupations outlined above. Since this book will probably be read more by students of theatre than of philosophy, I shall begin by giving a brief overview of the contents and structure of the two works by Bakhtin under consideration. This will be followed by an overview of the publishing history in Russia and America of Stanislavsky's two books (most quotations are from the comparatively recent translations by Jean Benedetti).

The dating of Bakhtin's early manuscripts is the subject of some disagreement between critics: Clark and Holquist argue that they were written 'in the years from 1918 to 1924', a date with which Morson and Emerson agree, though they add that *Philosophy of the Act* was written before *Author and Hero*; Brian Poole argues from evidence in Bakhtin's notebooks that they were written around or after 1927.[6,7,8] *Toward a Philosophy of the Act* is the shorter of the two manuscripts, the English translation running to seventy-six pages. Its subject matter is wholly philosophical, offering a context for Bakhtin's vision of a moral philosophy which, as its title suggests, is centred upon the act. On page 54 he offers an outline of the scope of his study:

> The first part of our inquiry will be devoted to an examination of these fundamental moments in the architectonic of the actual world of the performed act or deed – the world actually experienced, and not the merely thinkable world.
>
> The second part will be devoted to aesthetic activity as an actually performed act or deed, both from within its product and from the standpoint of the author as answerable participant, and [two illegible words] to the ethics of artistic creation.
>
> The third part will be devoted to the ethics of politics, and the fourth and final part to religion.[9]

From this description one can infer that the first part of his projected work corresponds to what editors have titled *Toward a Philosophy of the Act* (1993) and the second part to *Author and Hero in Aesthetic Activity* (1990). There is no record that the third and fourth parts were completed. *Author and Hero in Aesthetic Activity* is a much longer manuscript – the English translation runs to 238 pages – that takes the discussion from questions of pure philosophy into literature. Of the seven sections only the third one 'The Expressive and Impressive Functions of Aesthetics' addresses questions of philosophy. The other six sections focus upon the representation and the meaning of the hero, and how the hero relates to the author. In brief, *Philosophy of the Act* is more concerned with ethics and *Author and Hero* with aesthetics.

The political background to the period when Bakhtin was writing his early manuscripts and Stanislavsky was writing his books saw immense changes in the Soviet Union. Lenin died in 1924 and the ensuing power struggle between leading

Bolsheviks was resolved only in 1928, when Stalin was elected General Secretary. In 1929 Bakhtin was arrested, having been accused of religious activities. Following Bakhtin's trial in 1930 he was sentenced to five years' internal exile when he was aged thirty-five. In 1930 Stanislavsky was fifty-seven and two years earlier had suffered a major heart attack which prevented him from ever acting again. Stalin's increasingly repressive regime came in the middle of Bakhtin's most productive period of his life (the 1920s and 1930s) and coincided with a final creative burst in Stanislavsky's career when he formulated his Method of Physical Actions and worked furiously on writing *An Actor's Work*, whose redrafted Russian version in two volumes remained unpublished in his lifetime. Anatoly Smeliansky detects a political watershed in the writings of Stanislavsky. Referring to his later *An Actor's Work* he notes,

> The pressure of the given circumstances can be felt in his last book. There is not the same freedom with which he wrote *My Life in Art*. The first book is a book of major questions. The second is a book of answers. *My Life in Art* is confessional, *An Actor's Work on Himself* is professional.[10]

My Life in Art, Stanislavsky's autobiography, was first published in America in May 1924 capitalising on the MAT's hugely successful tour there in 1922–1923. A much-revised Russian edition appeared in September 1926. Jean Benedetti's 2008 English translation is based on this revised Russian edition. Laurence Senelick notes how the American 'publishers were interested less in theories than in a colourful biography full of anecdotes and profiles' and that Stanislavsky 'was deeply disappointed. He had hoped to launch an explanation of his "system", not a memoir.'[11] The Russian version was in part a defence against criticisms from Meyerhold and his fellow constructivists as can be seen from a note that he made while preparing the Russian edition:

> In the Chapter on the Revolution say that constructivism is a good thing, but they didn't make very good use of it and it was discarded. Predict that the actor's art is on the decline. In the chapter on the Revolution state that this is the result of all that affected stylisation.[12]

This gives a glimpse of how the Russian edition was intimately linked to the political and theatrical arguments of Stanislavsky's times. In the 1920s his first book was part of a heated and unbridled debate about the nature and role of theatre. His second book appeared at the beginning of the Stalinist purges which had begun in 1937 and reached their peak in 1939 when Meyerhold was imprisoned. Initially both books were prompted by American publishers. Following the success of the American edition of *My Life in Art* his friends Norman and Elizabeth Hapgood persuaded him to write a practical manual on acting, the first volume of which appeared in English in 1936 as *An Actor Prepares* followed by *Building a Character* in 1950. Stanislavsky conceived this manual as a single work in two parts entitled *An Actor's Work on Him- or Herself* and was still working on corrections to both parts when he died in 1938. Again, Benedetti's translation (2008) is based on the Russian edition. Stanislavsky had envisaged a companion work *An Actor's Work on a Role* which would also be in two parts, but only left fragments. *An Actor's Work* takes the form of a diary kept by a young actor *Kostya* (a diminutive form of Konstantin) of the two-year acting course given by the teacher Tortsov (the older Stanislavsky).

Bakhtin and Stanislavsky as thinkers

In the writings of Stanislavsky and Bakhtin we have two different types of thinking: one is interested in 'how' questions, the other in 'why' questions. While there is a strong sense of the urgency of the place and the moment, and an insistence upon meaning being rooted in the world as it is experienced, Bakhtin's arguments remain at the level of theory. Stanislavsky's writings are all predicated upon and constantly risk being superseded by his own practice in theatre – as director, teacher and actor. Writing for him was an opportunity to stand back from the practice and try to make sense of it, to find its underlying principles. Whereas the sense in the Bakhtin's writing is generated by his arguments, the truth of Stanislavsky's writing lies as much in the studio as on the page. The writing is contingent upon a practical process.

Although Bakhtin's references to theatre are often quite general, he does make one direct reference to Stanislavsky in his last notes made in the 1970s from which it is clear that he has read *An Actor's Work*.

> Stanislavsky on the beauty of play – the actor's depiction of a negative image. Mechanical division is unacceptable; ugliness – a negative character, beauty – a performing actor.[13]

He is probably recollecting the following passage: 'And don't forget either, that there are positive things hidden among negative phenomena, that there is an element of beauty in what is most ugly, just as the beautiful contains things which are not beautiful.'[14] There is an echo of these words in a passage from *Author and Hero* where Bakhtin's states that '[i]n aesthetic seeing you love a human being not because he is good, but rather, a human being is good because you love him. This is what constitutes the specific character of aesthetic seeing'.[15] Although both are writing about aesthetic creation, there is some distance between the two positions. Stanislavsky's concern is that the actor creates fully rounded characters rather than stereotypes. Bakhtin's point is less obvious. Either it can mean that one can see a person as 'good' once they are rendered as a character, or it can mean that the love which is a prerequisite of the aesthetic process, renders the loved person good. I shall finish this virtual dialogue with a quotation from Stanislavsky: 'You love *yourself* in the role more than the *role* in you. […] Learn to love the *role* in yourselves.'[16] Although this returns us to the theme of art and life, it also reminds us of how both men approach the relation between author and character from very different ends: for Bakhtin the author is in charge, for Stanislavsky it is the actor. The author's creative work ends with a finished character, the very point where the actor's creative work begins.

Here we have some of the key themes in Part II. The first concerns the value given to a role or character. Stanislavsky argues that the role should not be a vehicle for the actor to seek the audience's attention (in his youth he too was guilty of showing off), but rather it should be the object of the actor's aesthetic attention, such that they can find something beautiful in the ugliest or most evil character. This distinction between showing off and acting lies at the heart of Stanislavsky's life-long quest to establish theatre as an art and the actor as an artist. Bakhtin will argue that it is love which makes one person invest value in another (even if it is a character who is bad). Both men place emphasis on the aesthetic productivity of love. When Bakhtin reflects on how 'mechanical division' is 'unacceptable' he touches on one of Stanislavsky's central preoccupations – the difference between an actor's mechanical or natural response, that is, between the repetition of an external form or the felt response to an inner impulse. There are many examples of this in *An Actor's Work*, for example: 'So, not a single scene, not one single step onstage must be performed mechanically, without an inner reason, that is, without the imagination'; or, when writing about an actor's score of actions, 'you followed a well-beaten track blindly, almost mechanically'.[17,18,19]

It is never easy to pigeon-hole Bakhtin as a thinker and the interests of his first writings occupy a territory somewhere between philosophy and literary criticism. However, in these writings his preoccupations are peculiarly close to those of Stanislavsky, and the notion of character is at the heart of the ethics and aesthetics of both men. They agree that a character is defined by its actions, and that the process of authoring must involve varying degrees of empathy and aesthetic distance or, put another way, that a character, though a product of art, has to be true to life. In the process of characterisation both men write about the importance of drawing upon personal experience (again related to life) as opposed to scientific generalisations, and this experience is centred upon the body. In Bakhtin's early writings there are many more specific references to the actor and the situation of acting than there are in his later writings (where he discusses specific characters and texts) and for this reason alone they demand a close reading. Even if he is mostly negative about the aesthetic relation between the actor and their role, it enables a discussion of how his thinking can relate to theatre and indeed offers the basis of a critique of his understanding of theatre.

Both Bakhtin and Stanislavsky had a vision of their role within Russian cultural life. The Bakhtin Circle had an amazing breadth of aims and interests, and hoped 'to unite new discoveries in the sciences with the study of philosophy'.[20] Clark and Holquist add another agenda:

> Their aim in conducting their philosophical nights was an extremely ambitious one, which, as Pumpiansky characterised it, was to rethink all the categories of modern thought in terms of the Russian Orthodox tradition.[21]

Later they note that 'Bakhtin and his group not only did not separate religious issues from other philosophical concerns but also did not perceive any necessary opposition between religion and a socialist revolution'.[22] As cited above, the 'fourth and final part' of his projected *Philosophy of the Act* was to be devoted to religion. Only in his early writings is his Christianity a very evident factor in his thinking, specifically in connection with incarnation and the aesthetic completion one person can offer another.[23] He suggests that '*I* and the *other* [...] is, after all, the sense of all Christian morality, and it is the starting point for altruistic morality.'[24] Elsewhere aesthetic completion is conceived in terms of grace:

> Finally, the idea of grace as the bestowal – from outside – of lovingly merciful acceptance and justification of the given, as that which is in principle sinful and, therefore, cannot be surmounted from within itself.[25]

Although not so explicit, there is a strain of Christian spirituality that runs through Stanislavsky's thinking and Rose Whyman points to one important instance of this:

> Stanislavsky's use of church Slavonic *Ia esm'* indicates the highest apogee of the actor's art – a spiritual state. Carnicke asserts that *experiencing* and *infecting* the audience with the actor's emotion are synonymous with *I am. Experiencing* is the 'sense of self on stage as in life' and Stanislavsky wants to indicate the actor's immediacy and presence on stage, and the fact that the actor must create the role afresh each time.[26]

Grotowski will continue this theme of spirituality in his theatrical and post-theatrical work.

The challenge of Bakhtin's early philosophy is that it is, in a very literal sense, complex. It consists of sentences where the terms 'valuational', 'volitional' and 'axiological' recur, knot and interlace. Taken singly they are less daunting. 'Valuational' obviously refers to questions of value, while 'volitional' to questions of will or volition. Axiological is a less familiar term. It refers to a meaning that is rooted in personal value – in the sense of a thing that *means* a great deal to someone. Bakhtin's way of thinking is concentric. His ideas revolve around one central set of preoccupations. An argument that follows any of these individual elements of his theory will always circle back to the central complex of his ideas. Take, as an example, one of the underlying assumptions in his thinking – that he is dealing with 'the world actually experienced, and not the merely thinkable world'. From this it follows that we are embodied beings and that, like all bodies, we have extension in both time and space, that is, we have duration and position. In this way, time and space can be grasped as lived rather than theoretical categories. For Bakhtin these specifics of body, time and space are not contingent considerations that need to be bracketed off in order to arrive at pure meaning (as Kant did). They are part and parcel of what has meaning for human beings.

One reason for this concentricity is that his philosophy is more a phenomenological description of an experience than an analysis of it. Experience is multilayered and felt as an instantaneous whole, while a verbal description needs to list the constituent elements one after the other. Some of the most important elements are: Bakhtin's notion that human existence consists of a constant process of answering; his conception that there are two ways of understanding humanity, as an *I* or as an *other*; and his belief that meaning is more about an individual sense of value than of general meaning (put in more philosophical terms, it is axiological rather than epistemological). His is a contingent view of human existence that values action over theoretical reflection.

My Life in Art is an account of Stanislavsky's journey towards the goal of making acting an art. He seems to have taken Russian actor Mikhail Shchepkin's (1788–1863) advice on acting to heart: 'Watch yourself sleeplessly, for although the public may be satisfied with you, you yourself must be your severest critic.'[27] It is because he was his own severest critic that his autobiography is such a compelling read. He made his first experiments with the Alexeyev Circle (his family name was Alexeyev, 'Stanislavsky' being a stage name that he took to avoid embarrassing other family members) between 1888 and 1898. There was no concept of actor training in Russia and tricks of the trade were handed down from actor to pupil. His journey was thus made the more difficult because it was mostly in uncharted territory, and much of the guidance he did receive turned out to be misleading. What pushes the young Stanislavsky forward is his remorseless self-criticism, his 'capacity to analyse his own practice' and his inextinguishable love for acting and theatre.[28]

Stanislavsky's tortuous development is achieved through a constant process of reaction to the theatrical culture of his time and to problems of his own physique, his own ideas about acting and himself as an actor. There is no 'tool', no single method or system that he begins with and then applies throughout his life-long career. The tools changed and adapted as he progressively discovers what theatre could be. Stanislavsky explains in a letter to Elizabeth Hapgood that this notion of constant process was true even when he started to write his book about his system (*An Actor's Work*):

> What does it mean, writing a book about the system? It does not mean writing down something that is already cut and dried. The system lives in me but it has no form. It is only when you try to find a form for it that the real system is created and defined. In other words, the system is created in the very process of being written down.[29]

The system may have had no written form while it lived in him but it was an informing principle through all his practical researches.

Sharon Carnicke explains this as a tension between the more labile 'lore' that is employed by practitioners and the systematic writings of theorists. She quotes from Stephen North who distinguishes

> the activity of 'practitioners' who operate on prescriptive, pragmatic knowledge, from 'scholars', who depend upon published descriptive theory. Rather than assuming the usual relationship – that scholars 'make knowledge' while practitioners 'apply it' – North sees practice itself as generating new and legitimate knowledge.[30]

Jean Benedetti explains that the system always came after his practice:

> Even if justifiable claims can be made for the scientific nature of the System, the fact remains that its formulation depended on Stanislavski's capacity to analyse his own practice and that practice could not, except within certain general limits, be anticipated. It always produced change. There is a constant time-lag between personal practice as recorded in the *Notebooks* and the System as publicly proclaimed.[31]

Thus when writing up his system Stanislavsky 'simplifies and categorises as he writes. He turns messy practice into neat theory. He makes cogent prose from often contradictory experience'.[32] Indeed he resists publication because it 'threatened to fix his ever-changing ideas into unalterable forms'.[33] This recalls Bakhtin's insistence upon the need for a 'loophole' by means of which a self can be assured of the possibility of future change and development, and not remain stuck in the evaluative image of him- or herself created by the *other*.

When editing Stanislavsky's manuscripts for publication in English, Hapgood cuts the dialogues between Tortsov and his students. Carnicke argues that deleting such interactions 'diminishes the give and take between student and teacher. While Stanislavski's Socratic style adds little factual information, it creates an attitude toward the work that is experimental and open to argument'.[34] His approach is based on engaging the student in a dialogue:

> Socrates, in Plato's *Dialogues*, behaves with his interlocutors in exactly the same way that Torzov-Stanislavski behaves with his students. He urges them, he probes them with continual questions, until the *sought-for idea* emerges from the student, like something which was already there and which only needed the maieutic power of dialogue to come to light. […] In Stanislavski's second nature, one does not believe in something because it is true: on the contrary, something is true because one believes in it.[35]

Practice is about experience, about dialogue, and it is open-ended. The procedure is heuristic, it is about actor-students being encouraged and given the confidence to find out for themselves. In Magarshack's introduction to *System and Method* he notes how the talks weren't written down beforehand, since 'Stanislavsky did not believe in "lecturing"'. As Carnicke has described, he 'always accompanied his theoretical work with practical examples, and was never afraid of repeating himself'. But, most importantly, he 'welcomed difficulties'.[36] The dialogue here is based on the teacher posing the right questions to provoke their students into action. Thus the

> secret of 'if', as a stimulus, lies in the fact that it doesn't speak about actual facts, of what is, but of what might be […] 'if' […] This word is not a statement, it's a question to be answered. The actor must try to answer it.[37]

Once again, it is about experiencing and not cognitive thinking – an approach shared by both Stanislavsky and Bakhtin.

One problem about his books is that they do not mark a fundamental change in his practice that took place in the 1930s. When he was developing his system in the 1910s and 1920s he encouraged actors to identify with a character's life by remembering events from their own life which resemble those of their character. One name for this process is emotional recall. His later approach consists in simply performing the given actions of the character and letting this generate the emotional contours of their life. One could describe this shift more technically as moving from a process of voluntary to involuntary recall of autobiographical memory. Emotional recall requires the actor to consciously seek for a corresponding memory. The involuntary recall happens when a memory is triggered through an association between a physical action and a memory. Two very different traditions of acting have resulted from these approaches. The first, concerned with emotional recall, is now better known as 'The Method' as developed by Lee Strasberg. The second is called the Method of Physical Actions, the best account of which is to be found in a book by actor Vasily Torpokov *Stanislavsky in Rehearsal*. It is this Method which was taken up by the MAT after Stanislavsky died in 1938.

Where Bakhtin's early thinking is difficult to understand because of its unfamiliar philosophical concepts, Stanislavsky's writings pose a less obvious challenge. On the surface they are accessible and easy to read. He would refer to human nature and assume that this was an unchanging phenomenon. His notion of truthful action rests on an assumption about the constant 'nature' of human beings. And because he assumed his reader would understand what he meant by the word 'nature', there was no need to explain the term. Although Stanislavsky did study some psychologists (they are listed in Chapter 3) it was to bolster rather than challenge his outlook. He did not change his assumptions about the nature of the human mind, or acknowledge the very different account of mental life proposed by writers like Nietzsche or Freud. Stanislavsky would refer to the mystery of the creative subconscious and avoided Freud's destructive and sexually driven concept of the unconscious. Stanislavsky was not part of the revolution in thinking about philosophy, culture, society, language and the mind that so engaged members of the Bakhtin Circle. However, his student Meyerhold was a very active agent within this more critical, more explicitly revolutionary world.

Concepts in Bakhtin's early philosophy

Phenomenology

Scholars like Brian Poole and Craig Brandist and the contributors to the two editions of *Bakhtin and Cultural Theory* have demonstrated the importance of understanding the philosophers who inspired Bakhtin, not least because he rarely cited references and thus gave the impression that his vocabulary and concepts came from himself.[38] Bakhtin's ethics is based on things in the world having a value to a particular person at a particular time and place rather than a factual and value-neutral meaning; value is what prompts a person to act (once again the opposition between axiology and epistemology). This notion of value is drawn from the writings of Max Scheler

(1874–1928) and Nicolai Hartmann (1882–1950). In both *Author and Hero* and *Philosophy of the Act* Bakhtin describes his approach as phenomenological.

In *Act* he notes that the 'event of being is a phenomenological concept, for being presents itself to a living consciousness as an [ongoing] event, and a living consciousness actively orients itself and lives in it as an [ongoing] event'.[39] Later he notes that the 'phenomenological account of being is to know the irreducible uniqueness of being me (as opposed to anyone else): it is not egoism or even egocentricity, rather an acute openness to response, a total absence of theoretical mediation'.[40] Dermot Moran describes this way of doing philosophy as an attempt 'to describe *phenomena* in the broadest sense as whatever appears in the manner in which it appears, that is as it manifests itself to consciousness, to the experience'.[41] Later he notes that 'all experience is experience to someone, according to a particular manner of experiencing'.[42] Continuing his description of phenomenology Moran turns to the act: 'There is no act without an object; an empty act cannot be conscious of itself. Given the presence of the intentional content or object of the intentional act, then the act is directed primarily on the object.'[43] Stanislavsky offers an echo of this passage: 'Concentrating on an object produces a natural need to do something with it. Action concentrates the attention even more closely on the object. So, concentration plus action creates a close bond with the object.'[44] Moran develops his description of how we experience the world, arguing that phenomenology rejects the notion that there is a truth beyond experience:

> One must not think of objects as existing exactly in the manner in which they are given in the view from nowhere. All objects are encountered perspectivally; all conscious experience occurs in a temporal flow, the nature of which must be recalled in any analysis of human perception. The positing of entities outside experience is ruled out as meaningless.[45]

This supports the earlier argument about Bakhtin's value-meanings being rooted in a particular time and space. All perception is perspectival, it is experienced from somewhere, and therefore all dialogue consists of views from different perspectives.

Stanislavsky explains the difference between meaning and value in terms of science and human nature:

> As you have probably noticed, whenever science and technology have not been of help, we have turned to our own natural, biological creativity, to our subconscious, to practical experience. And I invite you to do the same now. Let us move out of science into our own lives, which we know, and which provide us with wide experience, practical knowledge and information, rich, inexhaustible emotional material, skills, habits etc. etc.[46]

Although Stanislavsky brings a non-reflective bias into the discussion (which will be continued energetically by Grotowski), his point about art and science has been picked up by a wide range of contemporary writers. Noam Chomsky admits that '[i]t is quite possible […] that we will always learn more about human life and personality from novels than from scientific psychology'.[47] Neuroscientist Gerald Edelman sees the matter more as a 'dilemma': 'that phenomenal experience is a first person matter, and this seems, at first glance, to prevent the formulation of a completely objective or causal account.'[48] Edelman goes on to argue how the categories, constraints and laws of scientific discourse, and the fact that it is written in the third and not the first person, mean that it doesn't offer a very convincing account of life: its laws 'do not and cannot exhaust experience or replace history or the events that occur in the actual courses of individual lives. Events are denser than any possible scientific description'.[49] The last sentence returns us to Bakhtin's phenomenological sense of the event, and his philosophical quest to describe first and not third person experience.

Event

A central concept in Bakhtin's phenomenology is that of the event (in Russian *sobytie*, literally 'co-being'). It is this sense of the event which marks off either an act or a literary work as being something one can experience. A footnote to *Act* makes the connection with phenomenology clear: 'The event of being is a phenomenological concept, for being presents itself to a living consciousness as an [ongoing] event, and a living consciousness actively orients itself and lives in it as an [ongoing] event.'[50] But it is also related to the sense of value: 'Any universally valid value becomes actually valid only in an individual event.'[51] The sense of event is what makes an act or the representation of an act 'real' in a phenomenological sense. A performance is an event that involves two sets of beings, the actor and the audience, and it is known through bodily experience rather than intellectual reflection.

Act and action

Central to the thinking of both men is action: Bakhtin is writing about the conditions under which one can act authentically, and to a great degree so is Stanislavsky, with the difference that they both mean something quite different by the word 'act'. Bakhtin uses the verb *postupat'* which is much more about behaviour, the way people act towards each other; Stanislavsky uses *delat'* which is more about acting as in doing things. This should not surprise us: Bakhtin is proposing an ethical philosophy which centres upon how we ought to act, particularly towards each other; and here he was returning to the ancient Greek sense of *ethos* (ήθος), meaning a person's moral character, outward bearing or disposition. Stanislavsky's Method of Physical Actions is much more about helping an actor enter into a role through truthful doing. Both men are writing about how a person can make meaning: in Bakhtin's case it was about bringing moral principles to life through action. Stanislavsky's question is about bringing the lines and actions of a play to life on stage. In both cases it is about embodied action which brings forth a meaning that is realised and experienced in the present moment.

Both Bakhtin's ethics and aesthetics could be understood as kinds of 'answering'. *Philosophy of the Act* argues that we have a responsibility to consider the world around us – that is, our natural and cultural environments – as questions or problems to be answered rather than facts or truths that can be taken as given. These answers take the form of acts which are performed in a specific place, at a specific time. Somewhat damagingly, Bakhtin never defines what he means by an 'act', and gives few examples: in his writings it can range from an act of conceptualisation, to an attitude or intention, to a physically performed act. What is clear is that Bakhtin's ethical answering is active and takes place in the lived world. He is writing about decisions or acts that affect the person who takes them, and this explains how they are not theoretical. There is something at stake for the person who takes the decision or performs the act. (This sense of sacrifice has religious overtones.) In *Author and Hero* we encounter an aesthetic answering which takes the form of 'authoring', that is, where one person provides another with a sense of themselves as a completed character (or as Bakhtin has it, a 'hero'). The interface of ethical answering is between a person and the external environment, and it is interpersonal in aesthetic answering.

Answerability

The central concept in Bakhtin's ethics is that we are called to act when we come into relation with people and ideas, and that ethical behaviour is about responding to this inner sense of obligation. We are responsible and responsive when we are answering with acts. Our life is a constant and ongoing process of act-performing that cannot result in a knowledge of ourselves as whole and finished beings, precisely because it is ongoing and not finished. For this we need the activity of another person who can offer a picture of us as taken from outside. At the heart of his ethics and aesthetics is the insistence that neither meaning nor world nor self is already constituted as a meaningful whole. They are not given but are set as tasks for us to accomplish. Our sense of being and meaning derive from us acknowledging and acting upon this feeling of obligation: towards the world in ethics and towards the other in aesthetics.

I *and* other

In order to understand Bakhtin's concept of authorship one needs to grasp his master distinction between the *I* and the *other* (*ia i drugoi* in Russian). Aspects of this distinction are part of everyday thinking. There is a rough correspondence between *I* and *other* and first and third person experience, and between internal and external experience of the world; in cinematic terms one could say the first is a 'point of view' shot where the camera 'sees' what the character sees. The second is a panning shot which allows us to see the character in action and in a broader spatial context. Bakhtin develops this dualism into a very particular conception of the human condition where because the two perspectives generate two completely different sets of information, so neither renders a complete picture of human existence. Both are locked in a symbiotic relationship of co-dependency.

The life of an *I* is ethical, motivated by what it ought to do. The actions of an *I* are directed to the world ahead and are practical. But such a forward-oriented perspective means that an *I* is in no position (literally and metaphorically) to see his or her life in a broader perspective. For this they need the aesthetic activity of an *other*, who, motivated by love, fills in the limited perspective of an *I* and provides an image of this life of action. The *I* is given to the *other* as a task to render it into a hero in the same way that an object in the world is given to the *I* as a task that is to be answered with an act. However, translating the Russian *drugoi* as *other* can be misleading, since we are not dealing with an entity that is radically 'other' to self but rather a fellow human being who recognises the contingent condition of humanity and is prepared to offer aesthetic completion. Bakhtin's conception of the *other* has much more of the friend (Russian *drug*) than it does of alterity.

Notes

1 Gordon (1987) 42.
2 Holquist (1993) x.
3 Donnellan (2008) ix.
4 Donnellan (1998) x.
5 His address to Opera students in 1918 ed. Magarshack (1950).
   His workshops at the Opera Studio 1921–1926 ed. Rumyantsev (1998).
   His work as a theatre director 1924–1934 ed. Gorchakov (1954).
   His work as a theatre director 1934–1938 ed. Torpokov (1999).
6 Clark and Holquist (1984) 63.
7 Morson and Emerson (1990) 74.
8 Poole (2001) 109–135.
9 *Act* 54.
10 Smeliansky (2008) 689.
11 Senelick (2008) xvi.
12 In Senelick (2008) xix.
13 *Speech Genres* 155.
14 *Work* 114.
15 *Act* 62.
16 *Work* 527.
17 For example: *Work*, 29, 45, 85, 365, 500, 621.
18 *Work* 84.
19 *Work* 197.
20 Holquist (1990b) 5.
21 Clark and Holquist (1984) 120.
22 Clark and Holquist (1984) 122.
23 For example: *Act* 16, *Hero* 129.
24 *Act* 75.
25 *Hero* 57.
26 Whyman (2008) 254.
27 In Cooper and Mackey (2000) 247.
28 Benedetti (1988) 201.
29 *Work* 687.
30 Carnicke (1998) 66.
31 Benedetti (1988) 201.
32 Carnicke (1998) 69.
33 Carnicke (1998) 72.
34 Carnicke (1998) 84.
35 Ruffini in Barba (1991) 66–67.

36 Magarshack (1967) 79.
37 *Work* 50–51.
38 Hirschkop and Shepherd (1989, 2001).
39 *Act* n.1, 78.
40 *Act* 41.
41 Moran (2000) 4.
42 Moran (2000) 11.
43 Moran (2000) 8.
44 *Work* 92.
45 Moran (2000) 12–13.
46 *Work* 511–512.
47 Chomsky in Lodge (2002) 10.
48 Edelman in Lodge (2002) 11.
49 Edelman in Lodge (2002) 13.
50 *Act* n.1, 78.
51 *Act* 36.

2 Time and space in the novel and in theatre

Jesus help me find my proper place.

(Graffiti on a wall in the British Library)

How to act? Why act? What is an action? What kind of meaning is generated by such actions? What is the tempo-spatial perspective of the person who takes action? These are all central questions for both Stanislavsky and Bakhtin, and although they are referring to different fields when they pose them, there are some surprising overlaps in their conceptual vocabulary. This shouldn't surprise us. Both men are offering descriptions of the same thing: the sense of being a conscious self; both share the realistic assumption that we can know and therefore can represent such a state of mind. Central to the practice and thinking of both men is the concept of the act: Bakhtin began writing a philosophy of the act and towards the end of his career Stanislavsky evolved a new approach to creating a character called the Method of Physical Actions. Action, the motivation to act, the relation between meaning and action – all of these themes are common to both Bakhtin and Stanislavsky. For these reasons I shall argue that many of the conditions that Bakhtin describes in *Toward a Philosophy of the Act* could be very useful to the actor.

The quality of a performance – both for performer and audience – derives from how live it feels, how the words seem to mean something so particular on that actor's lips, how they feel like a living person's spontaneous utterance rather than lines remembered from a script. One expects to read such reflections in writings about theatre but it is a little more surprising to read the same insistence upon truth, being and the live event from a philosopher. But this is precisely what Bakhtin demands in his two early manuscripts: both meaning and being are experienced as an event rather than recognised as an already existing content. He argues that it is not enough to accept the validity of moral propositions; they must be acted upon in order that their truth can be experienced. The same thing applies to a person's being. Being is an active verb rather than a substantive state and therefore a meaningful life must consist of actions. Being is about putting oneself in relation to the world of people and objects; it is about making active responses.

Acting from the centre

Do actions come from one's centre? If so, we have to understand 'centre' both metaphorically and literally. Clive Barker explains the situation of the actor who

> stands at the centre of a three-dimensional volume of space. In fact he stands at the centre of two three-dimensional volumes of space, the actual neutral space of the stage and the virtual characterised space of the setting of the play. Both of these concepts of space relate directly to another space area – the auditorium.[1]

Although Barker is offering us an image of the actor in the theatre space, this 'centre' does not refer to a geometrical point but rather to the actor's experience of space as being around him or her. The technical expression for this orientation in which I am at the centre of my world is 'ego-centric' space where every direction has the person as its reference, hence the expression that something is on 'my left'. Deictics like 'here' and 'there' are called 'shifters' in linguistics because their direction alters according to the speaker's perspective. The other orientation in space is allocentric, where the directions are always the same irrespective of the person's perspective, as in the 'neutral' theatre directions Stage Left and Stage Right.

Bakhtin describes egocentric space as being 'arranged around me as around that sole centre from which my deed issues or comes forth' and Stanislavsky describes it as follows:[2]

> In our vocabulary, 'I am being' refers to the fact that I have put myself in the centre of a situation I have invented, that I feel I am really inside it, that I really exist at its very heart, in a world of imaginary objects, and that I am beginning to act as me, with full responsibility for myself.[3]

The expression 'I am being' is the *ia esm'* to which Rose Whyman referred in the introduction. In Chapter 5 of *An Actor's Work* Stanislavsky develops this sense of centricity into concentricity when he describes the actor as being at the centre of a widening number of 'circles of attention'. Tortsov advises:

> As the circle, with the lights at full, grows bigger, the area on which you have to concentrate grows larger. However, this can only continue as long as you are able, mentally, to hold onto the circumference firmly. As soon as it begins to waver and dissolve, you must quickly reduce the circle to dimensions you can cope with.[4]

Negotiating this transition from actual to virtual space is made all the more difficult because of the third space beyond – the auditorium. The actor has to be creative under the incredible pressure of performance for the public, and this can result in stage fright where the actor loses all connection with the virtual world being created and can only think of the present situation where hundreds of eyes are staring at him or her. Although Bakhtin writes about the role of the spectator he makes no acknowledgement of this problem which is particular to anyone engaged in public performance. With this image of a circle of attention the actor can reduce the amplitude of their attention when they realise that the actual is starting to impinge upon their engagement in the virtual world of the stage.

The time and space of Bakhtin's actions is in the actual world. One could go so far as to say that only in the moment of taking action does one become an *I*. Bakhtin argues that it is only through taking action that I actually engage with the world, and that I experience what it feels like to exist: I know I exist when I take action. One could borrow Stanislavsky's words and say that 'I am being' happens when an *I* 'acts as me, with full responsibility for myself'; the difference being that this is a real and not an imagined world. Bakhtin describes the *I*, the act-performing self, as a 'centre of operations, the headquarters of the commander in chief directing my possibilities and my "ought" in the ongoing event of Being'.[5] Bakhtin invests much meaning in the concept of the centre, insisting that it is 'not just an abstract geometrical centre' but

> constitutes an answerable, emotional-volitional, concrete centre of the concrete manifoldness of the world, in which the spatial and temporal moment – the actual unique place and the actual, once-occurrent, historical day and hour of accomplishment – is a necessary but not exhaustive moment of my actual centrality – my centrality for myself.[6]

This is a hard sentence to understand because of the way Bakhtin has piled up so many concepts: a perfect example of the complexity mentioned in the introduction above. Put more simply, the centre is a real place in the real world from which we answer. It is the locus of our will and our emotion, which are themselves both experienced in and prompted by the time and place in which we live. Bakhtin insists that the actions about which he is writing are real, performed in real time and can only ever occur once because the conditions will never again be the same. We will see that the actor's time and place is both the here and now of performance, and the represented time and place of the play.

Experiencing not thinking

Bakhtin's early manuscripts circle around a core of problems, one of the most important being how to describe the experience of being an *I*. This is not some transcendental concept, but an active – better, an 'enactive' – state of responding to and from one's particular place and time, thereby generating a feeling of being an *I*. Bakhtin's early philosophy is not simply phenomenological – a description of first-person experience – it is also performative: to experience myself as a really existing being I need to perform actions, because only through my performance of an action can I generate the feeling of engaging in the world. Bakhtin insists that the matter is about experiencing and not thinking. To know something about the world I need to experience myself in active relation to it. The knowledge has to be the result of my having performed an action. For Bakhtin knowledge is not an epistemological content that is true in all places and at all times, but a moment of revelation that happens at a particular time and place. This recalls Moran's description of phenomenology quoted earlier in the introduction: 'all experience is experience to someone, according to a particular manner of experiencing.'[7] Bakhtin echoes Moran but emphasises the first-person experience:

> What is important for us is to relate a given lived-experience to me as the one who is actively experiencing it. This relating of it to me as the one who is active has a sensuous-valuational and volitional-performative character and at the same time it is answerably rational.[8]

This is another way of saying that the experiencing *I* is and has to be at the centre of its world; only when all lived experiences are related 'to me' can they have a felt meaning. Bakhtin stresses three related aspects of action: that it is a response to something I value ('valuational'), which is why I want ('volitional') to act, and whose performance I experience physically ('sensuous'). In this quotation he omits the emotional level, but this is very often mentioned in his account of the rich tress of experience associated with the performance of a task.

Much of *Toward a Philosophy of the Act* is taken up with a description of how and why a person should act. Bakhtin offers a detailed description of what it feels like to be an *I*, which for him means one who takes action. He describes the very state of active being that Stanislavsky wishes his actors to experience in their acting. Bakhtin's quotations above list the various mental and physical levels on which one experiences the performance of an act – it is so much richer than a disembodied, cognitive response. Bakhtin argues that the truth of a moral principle can only be felt when it becomes an 'ought'. While I might be able to recognise the general – i.e. theoretical – validity of a proposition, it will not have personal meaning for me until I grasp what I ought to do in relation to it. The world has to matter to me, and his concept of ethical responsibility lies in this sense of personal engagement. Bakhtin warns against the danger of 'fatal theoreticism' which he defines as 'the abstracting from my unique self' adding, '[t]here is nothing I can do with this theoretical proposition; it does not obligate me in any way'.[9,10] Stanislavsky and Bakhtin both agree that action is what gives life and meaning to a person or character.

The first part of *Toward a Philosophy of the Act* was planned to be an examination of 'the actual world of the performed act or deed – the world actually experienced, and not the merely thinkable world'.[11] The distinction between a world 'actually experienced' and one that is 'merely thinkable' is central to his notion of being and doing. In one statement Bakhtin sheds light on the discovery that Stanislavsky made in the early 1930s when he realised that an actor could experience their character through performing actions in the given circumstances rather than through time-consuming table work where they tried to work out their characters through analysis and discussion. Bakhtin's word 'actually' helps to convey the nature of how the self is situated in both time and space: the *OED* defines it as 'making actual or real, in a way that is characterised by doing practically […] as opposed to possibly, potentially, theoretically, ideally'.

Dermot Moran has already been quoted in the introduction: 'There is no act without an object; an empty act cannot be conscious of itself.'[12] Stanislavsky gives similar advice to young opera singers: 'An actor does not believe in the object itself but in his relationship to it. Therefore no matter what prop you are handling I shall believe in its reality on the stage if you establish the right attitude towards it and are sincere.'[13] Bakhtin describes the moment when a person comes into relationship with an object as a connection 'with that which is to-be-achieved'; the object then becomes part of a future project, part of what we want to do (our 'will' or the volitional aspect of the self).

> An object that is absolutely indifferent, totally finished, cannot be something one experiences actually. When I experience actually, I thereby carry out something in relation to it: the object enters into relation with that which is to-be-achieved, grows in it – within my relationship to that object.[14]

The difficulty for the actor is to make the character's scripted actions take on this sense of ethical and volitional weightiness that Bakhtin writes about. The thing has to be a part of the character's future project, and not something that is part of a finished narrative. Moran also stresses the fact that all objects are seen from somewhere, they are grasped perspectivally:

> One must not think of objects as existing exactly in the manner in which they are given in the view from nowhere. All objects are encountered perspectivally; all conscious experience occurs in a temporal flow, the nature of which must be recalled in any analysis of human perception. The positing of entities outside experience is ruled out as meaningless.[15]

A particularly useful phrase is 'the view from nowhere': this is precisely the theoretical position that Bakhtin rejects in favour of the lived perspective that is centred in time and space.

Another word for this particular place in time and space is 'situation'. To illuminate Bakhtin's notion of ethical responsibility further let us consider 'situation ethics' which Rowland Stout defines as when a 'concrete situation of infinite particularity is presented to us, and what constitutes our responsibility is to answer this situation in the fullness of our being'.[16] Bakhtin's difficult phrase, the 'concrete centre of the concrete manifoldness of the world', is very elegantly glossed by Stout as a 'concrete situation of infinite particularity'. In one sentence Stout has described the solidary relationship between being and answerability. We all occupy a unique physical place from which only we can answer. The argument so far can be reduced to a set of master oppositions:

Impersonal	Personal
Abstract	Embodied
General	Particular
Possible	Actual
Theoretical	Experienced

Space, then, is not a theoretical extension but an actual territory in which we are situated, a place from which we see things, and from which we issue our answers to those things. We see things perspectivally, each person seeing a different face (or facet) of an object or event: 'the compellently actual "face" of the event is determined for me myself from my own unique place.'[17] Bakhtin goes on to argue that this situatedness is an essential ingredient in our understanding of truth: 'validity is conditioned […] by its being correlated with the unique place of a participant.'[18] He puts this pithily: 'Any universally valid value becomes actually valid only in an individual context.'[19] Later he expresses this as an opposition between an embodied being, which necessarily entails time and position, and unlocated theory:

> Historically actual once-occurrent Being is greater and heavier than the unitary Being of theoretical science, but this difference in weight, which is self-evident for a living and experiencing consciousness, cannot be determined in theoretical categories.[20]

Bakhtin adds that 'everything in this world acquires significance, meaning, and value only in correlation with man – as that which is human.'[21] One reason actual time weighs more heavily is that we know that our own life-time is limited. It is this knowledge which lends an existential dimension to any reference to time:

> If man were not mortal, the emotional-volitional tone of this progression – of this 'before' and 'after', this 'not yet' and 'already,' this 'now' and 'then,' this 'always' and 'never' – the gravity and significance of its sounding rhythm – would be extinguished.[22]

Adverbs like 'now', 'already' and 'then' have no intrinsic meaning unless and until related to the situation of something that exists, and when related to the precarious existence of a human being they acquire their affective weight. It is precisely this feeling of the 'gravity and significance' of the time of a character that an actor has to convey. Possibly it was with this notion of lived time that the Russian director Genrietta Yanovskaya gave a workshop in 1991 entitled *The Urgency of Morality*. Where Sartre would later write about 'situation', here Bakhtin writes about 'situatedness':

> The situatedness of the self is a multiple phenomenon: it has been given the task of not being merely given. It must stand out in existence because it is dominated by a drive to meaning, where meaning is understood as something still in the process of creation, something still bending toward the future as opposed to that which is already completed.[23]

Meaning isn't already out there, but 'something still in the process of creation'; rather than being something finished, given and completed. It is 'given to' an individual as a task, a question, or a project. Possibly in a very complex manner, Bakhtin is precisely describing the sense of the urgency of mortality that the actor has to create in order, not so much to represent as to embody this sense of a living character. Bakhtin equates meaning (as in value) with embodiment. Only an embodied being could feel this urgency, could feel the given circumstances as a personal motive for action. This leads on to another of Bakhtin's master distinctions between the 'given' and the 'created'.

Given and created

Holquist explains this difference between 'given' and 'given to' by noting that the cluster of terms used by Bakhtin all share the same root verb *dat'* ('to give' in Russian). One's given life can only become a living event through 'the action of me fulfilling my task (*zadanie*), i.e., by making the slice of existence that is merely given (*dan*) to me something that is conceived (*zadan*)'.[24] The act of conception brings forth something new, it is inherently creative. The distinction between given and created can also be understood in terms of how we enter language as an *I*. As an example of how the word 'given' can be used, the *OED* cites the anthropologist Edmund Leach: 'The English language from the point of view of any individual speaker [...] is a "given", it is not something he creates himself.' Language is already out there and somehow we have to actualise ourselves within it. Young children start to master using the pronoun 'I' quite late in their acquisition of language. It is a difficult part of speech because everyone is an 'I' when speaking. This is why the linguist Roman Jakobson referred to it as a 'shifter'. The deictic shifters mentioned above are all part of a changing egocentric position in space. Holquist notes that while the pronoun 'I' is invisible at the level of system (one cannot describe a general 'I') it 'can be filled in any particular utterance'.[25] An utterance is a meaning event, an act that results from me putting myself in the place of 'I'. In Holquist's words, '[m]uch as Peter Pan's shadow is sewn to his body, "I" is the needle that stitches the abstraction of language to the particularity of lived experience'.[26] To be an *I*, is the result of speech activity, it is not a given. This is another example of how being is a result of doing. Is this not what Stanislavsky is trying to describe in the actor's work? Is it not about helping an actor to achieve that sense of being an *I* while working with a text that has quite probably been performed before and which she or he will have to repeat in subsequent performances?

Given circumstances

The simplicity of Stanislavsky's later approach to creating a character – the Method of Physical Actions – is that it is purely based on the exploration of actions performed in the circumstances given in the play.

> I don't start from the flowers but from the roots. My imagination springs from the given circumstances. When you work on your role, you must begin from the root of the character. My theory is to take away the text from the actor and make him work only on actions.[27]

Given circumstances is one of Stanislavsky's earliest guiding concepts and remained an essential part of his system throughout his career, especially in the Method of Physical Actions. Where Bakhtin is writing about ethical action in the real world, Stanislavsky is writing about the difficulty of faithfully representing that world, about how a dramatist can be realistic, and how the actor can bring that dramatist's lines to life. In his very early years he already had an insight that the nature of the actor's creativity is based on not living as 'ourselves but as our character within the circumstances of the play'.[28] The words he uses to describe this experiment are telling: the difficulty 'was that we not only had to be actors but the authors of one new improvisation after another'. In this double role of actors and authors they became creative artists in their own right, and thereby theatre became an art and not simply an entertainment. Although writing in a very different register to Bakhtin, Stanislavsky is also pointing to the necessity for the actor to make a creative response to the given text, which while it has a general meaning in itself, needs to be realised through the performance of acts. The actor needs to find the 'ought' which compels their character to act.

Tortsov advises his students to respond to the given circumstances 'through action, say "that's what I would do!" and do the thing you want, whatever you are drawn to do, without thinking about it'.[29] This is a more accessible version of Bakhtin's complex of terms 'performative-valuational-volitional'. It is about what the character wants to do. The given-ness of these circumstances as a task for the actor is repeated throughout Stanislavsky's writings. In his written instructions for the MAT's 1934 production of *Othello* he notes that '[a]ll these given circumstances provided by the writer, are obligatory for all and lead in the first instance to the score of your role'.[30] Again, as in Bakhtin, we see the interplay between an obligation and a creative response. Elsewhere he writes that 'the circumstances which for the dramatist are supposed for us actors are imposed, they are a given. And so we have created the term Given Circumstances and that is what we use'.[31] In this lucid distinction between the supposed and the imposed circumstances we can grasp the crucial difference between Bakhtin's act-performer and Stanislavsky's actor. The given circumstances of a play exist within an artistically designed structure in which all the elements have been chosen because they contribute to the meaning of the play. The actor's job is to make the artistically created play seem as if it were real life. Bakhtin would surely have been surprised to find his approach to philosophy being applied to the work of an actor, but the way that he describes the experience of living in the first person could, if expressed in less tortuous terminology, offer a practical guide for an actor to find – or is it 'create'? – that sense of a centre of answerability.

Value, sense, meaning

Throughout the argument so far there has been an opposition between thinking and experiencing, or put more generally between two kinds of knowing or meaning. It is here that Bakhtin articulates a kind of meaning that characterises the mental state of the character that Stanislavsky's actor aims to reproduce. In order to give the audience the sense that this character is a living being, they need display a responsiveness and connection to their environment: their movement and lines need to have the appearance of being a response to their surroundings. Whereas cognitive truth is valid irrespective of the speaker or context, Bakhtin has been describing a kind of experienced truth that involves emotion, value and context. Value has a personal and emotional dimension that abstract meaning lacks: it is experienced rather than thought. The first is embodied and for that reason not transferrable, the other is not.

While epistemology is the study of meaning, the study of values is axiology, a term that Bakhtin uses frequently in his argument. Rowland Stout explains that values are 'phenomenologically disclosed in emotional experience', and this distinction between intellect and emotion is something which informs the writings of both Stanislavsky and Bakhtin.[32]

> Everything that I have to do with is given to me in an emotional-volitional tone, for everything is given to me as a constituent moment of the event in which I am participating.[33]

The word 'participating' grasps the essence of Bakhtin's approach to meaning and being which demands personal involvement. To be alive is to be un-indifferent towards things in the world, a response which results in a person experiencing 'these individual, unique persons whom he loves, this sky and this earth and these trees': 'there-ness' and 'this-ness' are about the relation between the viewer and what is being viewed.[34] It is not simply a question of context, but of an embodied self who defines his or her relation to these things. It is this sense of personal value (this-ness) that makes us want to talk about things.

This particular, context-specific, felt kind of meaning is the stuff of the actor's work. Each production of a play offers a different reading of its meaning, each different performance of that production elicits nuances of meaning that are particular to the conditions of that particular evening. The main factors are the unique audience, the way the actors played to them and the chemistry of the cast as a whole. An actor has to transform the given, external meaning of the play into personal, idiosyncratic sense. The actor's words have to convey what Bakhtin considers are the contents of a felt response to the world: value, volition, emotion. Together these create the internal conditions for that response; they are what impel a person to act. They create a unique meaning event that lives rather than the repetition of the lines of the play. Every performance has to have the quality of eventness that Bakhtin writes about in his early philosophy. And, of course, they have to be embodied – they have to seem as if they come from someone in that particular place and time of the character's given circumstances.

Acts and tasks

Bakhtin doesn't offer a definition of what he means by an act, only that each person has a unique obligation to act from their own place: 'That which can be done by me can never be done by anyone else.'[35] Hirschkop defines an act 'as a moment of commitment or position-taking'.[36] This both captures the sense of ethical engagement and conveys the metaphorical aspect of the place or position of the act-performer. Bakhtin argues that being as a lived event 'cannot be determined in the categories of non-participant theoretical consciousness – it can be determined only in the categories of actual communion, i.e. of an actually performed act'.[37] We have already seen that the 'actually performed act' looks in two ways: firstly it affirms (but does not add to) the validity of the theoretical truth by an act of physical instantiation (that is, realising it in a particular time and place); secondly it affirms the being of person who has just performed the act.

Bakhtin insists that an act is performed once and once only. General truths are always true whereas a particular truth is experienced in the actual moment at which a person performs an act. Or, as Bakhtin puts it, 'an answerable act or deed [...] brings any extra-temporal validity into communion with once-occurrent Being-as-event'.[38] Again and again Bakhtin repeats this distinction between the possibility of general meanings and the actuality, finality and totality of an act:

> The performed act concentrates, correlates, and resolves within a unitary and unique, and, this time, final context both the sense and the fact, the universal and the individual, the real and the ideal, for everything enters into the composition of its answerable motivation.[39]

This sense of once-only-ness and unrepeatability is central to Bakhtin's phenomenological description of the experienced moment. The act creates an 'event' of meaning, a moment of realisation of a truth. Bakhtin writes about such meaning events within the context of a life. I am arguing that this kind of multi-layered meaning event – experienced at emotional, physical and cognitive levels – is precisely what can happen in the theatre: a collective and shared moment of meaning.

A key term that Stanislavsky uses in his argument is *zadacha* which means a 'task' or 'problem' which can only be solved through an action. The following discussion should be compared with the one above where Bakhtin's terms *dan, zadan, zadanie* are analysed, and which, like *zadacha*, share the same root verb *dat'*, to give. It is that which is given the person to do. Sharon Carnicke argues that when Stanislavsky's first translator, Elizabeth Hapgood, chose to translate *zadacha* as 'objective' she 'shifts the focus of Stanislavsky's concept'. An objective is very different to a problem, and implies 'not an impulse towards an action but rather the action's outcome' and thus confuses 'the path from "problem" to "action" as described by Stanislavsky'.[40] Put in Bakhtin's terms, an 'objective' is already a given: it is a line of action set out to be followed. A task or problem requires creative activity. She further argues that '[t]aken together, the concepts of "problem" (*zadacha*) and "action" (*deistvei*) comprise the heart of Stanislavski's System' which explains why this distinction is so fundamentally important: a 'problem' demands that an appropriate action be selected to resolve it while an objective already suggests a pathway towards the eventual goal.[41] The notion of the problem is a heuristic device, a means by which the actor can find out what to do. As Bakhtin has shown, the sense of a life comes through the depth of its participation; it has to be an active response. She continues,

> [b]y placing attention on actions, the actor gains focus and confidence on stage. Hearkening back to Aristotle, Stanislavsky points out that action distinguishes drama from other forms of art. In the Russian edition, he traces the origin of the word 'drama' (cognates in Russian and English) to the Greek word *dran* ('to do') in order to enforce this idea.[42]

Stanislavsky knew only too well that the successful actor needs to feel the situation as an *I*, rather than a he or she. The actor has to find that centre which the character occupies in the world of the drama and then feel the situation from that position.

> As yourself you experience a role, as someone else you imitate it. As yourself, you understand the role with your intelligence, wants, and all the elements of your mind, but as someone else, in the majority of cases, only with your intelligence. We do not need exclusively rational analysis and understanding[43]

In answer to the question What is my motivation? Bakhtin offers the concept of the character's 'ought'. What is it that your character really wants? What things or people mean a lot to your character? How does your character see the world? These are simply some of the basic ideas of Bakhtin turned into questions, and they might help an actor better inhabit the present moment. In other words, Bakhtin's description of the meaning-making activity of his *I* offers a heuristic model for the actor's work.

This focus upon the present moment helps to identify an important shift in Stanislavsky's approach to actor training. In the 1910s and 1920s he drew on the notion of emotional memory where an actor, in order to find a way into the emotional state of their character, would seek examples of that emotion from their own personal experience. In order to live the present moment in performance the actor relied on a past moment from their own life. Stanislavsky later moved towards a process that kept the actor in the present moment, warning that 'we can't put the recollections of our feelings in order the way we do the books in our library'. He goes on: 'Don't imagine you can return to yesterday's memory, be content with today's. Learn to accept memories that have come to life afresh.'[44]

> It seemed to him more and more that the actor had to be engaged, in his own person, with the problems the character had to solve, he had to experience the Given Circumstances in his own right. A great deal of time was therefore devoted to exercises on Here, Today, Now: what would I do if I were in this situation?[45]

This orientation in the present, this sense of finding the meaning from the immediate context, has many echoes of Bakhtin's sense of the moment. Very crudely put, this shift from relying on past memory to present context marks Stanislavsky's move away from an approach to acting based on emotional memory to the Method of Physical Actions. Torpokov wrote that 'through the correct execution of physical actions, through their logic and their sequence, one penetrates into the deepest, most complicated feelings and emotional experiences'.[46] The aim is still to generate an emotional response within the actor; it is simply the means that has changed. Throughout his book Torpokov emphasises this connection between action and psychological reaction. Stanislavsky states that the simplest physical actions lead 'to the awakening of intuition', later calling them 'the means to awaken one's intuition', arguing that they help the actor 'to live genuine organic life on the stage. It is inescapable and indispensable'.[47]

Torpokov's record of his time at the makeshift 'studio' in Stanislavsky's house in Leontsev Street dwells upon the fact that the actors there seemed to be engaging in living behaviour rather than acting.

> Everything was done naturally, with the utmost simplicity – as it should be. There was nothing invented, people actually live in this way, they act in this way, they suffer and are happy. Nothing was done for show, nothing was 'theatrical', but everything sank deep into the soul.[48]

We have seen that in Bakhtin's philosophy of the act the truth of a proposition and the reality of the act-performer's being are both actualised through the performance of an act. Although Stanislavsky is dealing with acting rather than act-performing, with art rather than life, he insists that the actor does rather than acts and that from this engagement in truthful doing will come believable acting. Although travelling in different directions, both men agree upon the fundamental importance of the experience of act-performing.

Stanislavsky's advice to Torpokov (who was already an established actor when he came to Leontsev Street) always centred upon action, upon how you (as a person) would behave in the given circumstances. Work on the actions within the play came before the lines of the script: 'Don't think of the lines, the intonations – they will come of themselves. Think, rather, of your behaviour.'[49] Later Stanislavsky asks, 'Why the text? Let us speak of our affairs. What is important to me is your behaviour.'[50] Torpokov sees this focus upon physical action as one of Stanislavsky's most important discoveries:

> Stanislavski long ago began to understand that the chief secret of mastering a role lies in studying the physical behaviour of the character. If the physical behaviour is correct and interesting, then the speech pattern of the role will be naturally and easily formed.[51]

Again and again he distinguishes between doing and acting or performing:

> Now try, only don't perform; be natural, be really interested in what you are doing […] Don't act anything, just play each action. Don't do anything for

us, do everything only for your partner. Check your partner's reaction, if you are acting well.[52]

Stanislavsky would insist that Torpokov played neither for the meaning (which would indicate that he was consciously thinking about the lines) nor even the emotion: 'No. I don't want your feelings, tell me how you behaved.'[53] 'Do not speak to me about feeling. We cannot set feeling; we can only set physical action.'[54] Torpokov indicates the shift that Stanislavsky had made from his earlier emphasis upon emotion to his later focus on action and the very present interaction with the other actors onstage:

> The importance of the transference of the actor's attention from the search for feelings inside himself to the fulfilment of the stage task which actively influences his partners is one of Stanislavski's greatest discoveries […].[55]

Torpokov articulates the shift elegantly: from the actor's 'search for feeling inside himself' to 'the fulfilment of the stage task'. The performance of an act, not acting.

Time and timing in performance

In these final two sections I shall explore the specific way that time and space are used in theatre performance. In Bakhtin's account of the experience of an act-performing self, there is only one time – *kairos* 'the propitious moment for the performance of an action'.[56] It is an unrepeatable moment. It is precisely this sense of lived time that theatre aims to create in a performance, but it has to be repeated again and again and at a specific time. Herein lies the artistry and discipline of the actor whose creativity has to be delivered to order. Just as Barker wrote that space is double (or even triple) in theatre, so is time: there is the duration and pacing of the performance, the represented period of the story, and the given time when the curtain rises. In the argument that follows we will see how the structures of the narrative and of the performance are woven together. In Stanislavsky's account of the actor's work he explains how a true performance can be delivered night after night.

When Stanislavsky stated above that 'we cannot set feeling' he was referring to what he calls the logical sequence of physical actions. He argues that through 'the correct execution of physical actions, through their logic and their sequence, one penetrates into the deepest, most complicated feelings and emotional experiences'.[57] This is the logic of what we (the audience, the reader) believe that we would do in the given circumstances and applies to comedy routines:

> I once saw a splendid Vaudeville actor take off his trousers and hit his mother-in-law with them. It was wonderful and did not shock anyone because the actor was able to convince the audience of the logic of his behaviour; there was nothing else to do but act in that way. He prepared us for that, step by step.[58]

There are several dimensions to this logic of behaviour. The first is an intelligible through-line, a narrative vector which carries forward the meaning or emotion of the story (what the French call *le fil rouge* – the red thread). This logic is closely linked to realist assumptions about how people act, which are underpinned by more general social codes of behaviour. At the close of *Hedda Gabler* Ibsen seems to tease his audience's sense of realism (how things are) when Judge Brack declares, 'But good God! People don't do such things!' This after Gabler had just shot herself.

The third element is the actor's job of pacing oneself when playing a role. Stanislavsky describes how his idol Tomasso Salvini (1829–1915) plotted the emotional journey of the role of Othello.

> This ladder down which Othello descended in the full sight of the spectators from the heights of bliss to the depths of destructive passion, Salvini moulded with such clearness, with such merciless logic, and such irresistible persua-siveness that the spectator saw all the detailed curves of the suffering soul of Othello and sympathised with him from the depths of his heart.[59]

Stanislavsky wonders at Salvini's technique in building 'the mathematical pro-gression in the development of the emotion of jealousy, beginning from the most restful state, passing through the almost unnoticeable birth of the passion and on to the very heights of jealousy'.[60] All this describes how an actor can negotiate between narrative logic (represented time) and the scoring of a role (performance time). One could also describe this as the diegetic aspect of acting – telling the story of the character – and the mimetic aspect – acting like that character.

There is another dimension to time which is what Stanislavsky calls tempo-rhythm. Much of Chapter 21 of *The Actor's Work* is about the relation between rhythm, tempo and mood. Quite simply: tempo-rhythm directly affects feeling.[61] Stanislavsky notes how people

> work, create, perceive, communicate and persuade in a certain Tempo-rhythm […]. Every human passion, state of mind, experience has its Tempo-rhythm. Every individual inner and outer character type […] has its Tempo-rhythm. […] In a word, there is a living Tempo-rhythm in every moment of our existence, mental or physical.[62]

He argues that an actor's 'genuine re-experiencing has to confront the use of logic and sequence of feelings. Without them there is no truth and, consequently, no belief, no "I am being"'.[63]

Stanislavsky then turns his attention to another temporal dimension – that of an actual performance. He argues that a crucial skill of the actor is to attune to the rhythm (and therefore mood) of the overall performance.

> Tradition has it that our great predecessors like Shchepkin, Sadovski, Shumski and Samarin always went to the wings long before their entrance so that could tune into the tempo of the performance. That is why they always took life, truth and the right note for the play and the character on with them.[64]

Although this sensitivity to timing might be acknowledged as essential for an actor, Stanislavsky admits that

> [n]obody is aware of the rhythm and tempo of their lives. And yet I would have thought all human being should be aware of the pace, or some other way of measuring their movements, actions, feelings, thoughts, breathing, pulse, heart rate and general state.[65]

What Stanislavsky is looking for is an actor who can understand how to shape their performance in real time through developing a sensitivity to their live interaction with the other actors on stage (though he doesn't mention the audience).

Finally, we turn to another level of organisation – the score of physical actions by means of which actors can repeat the structure of their performance, rather than trying to repeat particular moments which have worked in past performances. Torpokov remembers Stanislavsky's words on the subject:

> You will never be able to play this scene that way again. You may play worse, you may play better, but what you just did – that cannot be repeated and is for this reason priceless. Try to repeat what you played and nothing will happen. This cannot be fixed. You can only fix those paths which led you to this result. I tortured you, Vasily Osipovich, so that you would search for the sense of truth in the simplest physical actions.[66]

This notion of a formal structure by means of which there is the possibility for recreating the emotional contours of a performance is central to the actor's work. In this way the actors can square the circle: they act spontaneously, because they are working in a score. He sums up: 'All my system amounts to this: to understand the organic moments in your part and to be able to group them logically, reflecting them in a series of truthful physical actions.'[67]

It is now possible to put Bakhtin's concept of the unrepeatable moment of action into context. While this could be taken as a model for the experience of what is real, the question remains of *how* this can be realised on stage. An actor needs training to be able to recreate it over successive performances. The discussion goes well beyond theatre training when Stanislavsky explores the relation between emotion and behaviour in everyday life. While Bakhtin struggled to reconcile the phenomenological moment of the actual with the broader current of historical time, Stanislavsky offers a model.

Theatrical space

As noted in the Introduction, these chapters do not follow the chronological development of Stanislavsky as an actor, a director or as a actor-trainer. However this section on his response to the staging of plays does offer a historical perspective. Indeed, to understand the 'revolution' in theatre that he and Nemirovich-Danchenko hoped to create one needs to know what kind of theatre they were opposed to, and what models they chose to imitate. This revolution dates back to actor/director Ludwig Chronegk's (1837–1891) work with the Duke Georg II of Saxe Meiningen's troupe which toured Europe between 1874 and 1890. Above all, the Duke and Chronegk were searching for unity within the production – in the cast, props, costume and set. In his book on the Meiningen troupe John Osborne quotes a contemporary critic on the secret of their success which 'is to be explained by the harmonious and artistically beautiful overall impression of the performance': the writer continues that

> the attraction does not reside in one or other of the external aspects, in the splendid scenery, in the historically accurate costumes, in the beautiful groupings or the effective scenic arrangements, but in the fact that all the means serve the purpose of faithfully revealing the spirit of the work in a vivid and stylish manner.[68]

This points to an underlying artistic principle to which Stanislavsky would subscribe: 'namely that art must be higher than the artist, the effect of the whole […] higher than the admiration of the individual.'[69]

The Meiningen troupe was admired by other theatre revolutionaries, notably André Antoine who created the *Théâtre Libre* (The Free Theatre) in Paris in 1887 and Otto Brahm who created the *Freie Bühne* (The Free Theatre) in Berlin in 1889, both of whom were associated with the genre of naturalism. Although Antoine had some problems with the historical detail of Chronegk's productions, 'he clearly recognised in the productions a unity of style', one 'in which the figure is integrated in the ground, the actor absorbed in the action.' Antoine writes, 'Another very characteristic detail is the formal prohibition imposed on the actors and extras against stepping beyond the frame of the stage proper'. And after having seen the company twelve times, he admits that he never saw 'a single one of them advance his foot to within two metres of the prompter. It is also forbidden to look out into the auditorium, which, incidentally, is darkened'.[70] (Antoine himself used a darkened auditorium in 1888.)

The sense of artistic totality is created by the director, designer and actor all working together to sustain the illusion of a separate world being created before the audience's eyes. The actors turned their backs on the audience, completely against the older tradition of playing *en face*. Critics commented on this sense of convincing illusion: one stated that 'all the productions transported the audience into a carefully realised, alien world', another that 'I had the feeling that I was moving among people of another country and a different age, and yet also that I was not at all out of place but chatting cosily to them without any sense of strangeness'.[71,72] The English critic William Archer (1856–1924) recognised 'a further significant development of the realistic tendency in which the actor is absorbed rather than theatrical, and in which the footlights serve as a barrier between audience and stage'.[73] This is a very succinct distinction between old-fashioned theatricality and the newer psychological realism – where 'the actor is absorbed' – and one that Brahm would appreciate given his commitment to 'eliminate theatricality, in the pejorative sense it had had since the eighteenth century, from the theatre'.[74]

However, Brahm was less impressed by the scrupulously researched and reproduced detail of the decorations in Caesar's house and in the Capitol in their production of *Julius Caesar*, admitting that they 'were a wonderful sight', but as to whether 'they are historically "authentic" and whether they have, with scholarly accuracy, been brought into line with the latest research, I am, alas, not competent to decide, since I am not a professor of archaeology'.[75]

There are several significant features in these descriptions. The first is the historical detail of the properties, costume and set. The Duke acknowledged his debt to Charles Kean's historically inspired productions at the Princess Theatre between 1850 and 1859, though a criticism of his productions was that he was 'perhaps more zealous as archaeologist than actor'.[76] Kean's productions were planned 'that historical accuracy might be so blended with pictorial effect that instruction and amusement might go hand in hand'.[77] This echoes a phrase used by Osborne who describes work of the Meiningen troupe as a 'mediation between picture and dramaturgy; it is a period of convergence between the visual and the dramatic arts'.[78] The next important feature was the fact that the actors kept behind the proscenium arch so as to remain within the picture frame and thus sustain the illusion of this being a separate world, and didn't look at the audience but at each other. Osborne describes how Stanislavsky's hero Ernesto Rossi would address 'the audience, *en face* rather than in profile, and in a declamatory or elevated, rather than a natural or conversational style of speech'.[79] It is a strange contradiction that Stanislavsky, who opted for the conversational over the declamatory and famously had actors show their backs to audiences, wrote so enthusiastically about Rossi's 'truth' when acting.[80]

A concomitant of the Duke's insistence on period costume was that actors, used to playing a certain line of characters (or *emploi* – a French term taken up again by Meyerhold), could no longer wear their familiar costumes. Thus the actor Ludwig Barnay, used to playing swash-buckling heroes like Petruchio: 'expected to be able to wear his own boots (and spurs) because it was customary to express the masculinity which this role required with the aid of the military dress of the Thirty Years' War.'[81] Chronegk insisted that he wear a period costume rather than his 'uniform' and Osborne describes the effect it had:

> Only slowly did he begin to perceive that the costume issued to him required a much more subtle and intellectualised conception of male superiority than the conventional aggressiveness of his original understanding of the role: 'Thanks to this purely external element the style of my interpretation imperceptibly underwent a transformation, and came, perhaps, to correspond more closely to the dramatist's intentions.'[82]

Osborne's point is that period costume can result in a more psychologically nuanced performance – it is not simply about period detail.

Stanislavsky describes how Chronegk's 'productions gave Moscow its first view of a new kind of theatre – period authenticity, crowd scenes, visually beautiful scenery, amazing discipline, a festival of art in every respect'. He adds that he 'did

not miss a single show. I not only saw them, I studied them'.[83] But he did note
that the 'director's talent often' covered up that of the actors and it is they 'who
matter most' and therefore they 'need first to be guided'. He concludes that

> [t]he production plan was always wide-ranging and profound in its meaning
> but how was it to be realised without the actors? The centre of gravity of a
> production went over to the staging. The necessity of being creative on
> everybody's behalf turned the director into a dictator.[84]

The pictorial outweighed rather than was mediated by the dramaturgical.

When members of his family circle produced Aleksey Tolstoy's *The Death of Ivan
the Terrible*, their realist attempt 'to get away from the usual clichéd style of production used in historical plays about the boyars in old Russia' landed them in
the same creative impasse as Chronegk.[85] 'In our revolutionary zeal we went
straight for externals, the end results of the creative process, ignoring its first, most
important phase, the birth of feeling.' He offers a comic description of how the
amateur actors 'went straight for the external appearance' by using 'padding,
footwear […] false noses, beards and moustaches' in the hope of capturing the
feeling and the voice of the character's body, but it was 'at the cost of inner truth
which is the basis of all acting'.[86] Stanislavsky describes this kind of production as
his line of 'historico-realism'.[87]

It was important for Stanislavsky to distinguish himself from Meiningen, not
least because he was painfully aware of the criticism of his student Meyerhold that
he was prey to 'Meiningen-itis'.[88] He acknowledges 'I have frequently been
reproached for adopting the technique of the Meiningen Theatre in the handling
of group scenes. This is not true. The Meiningen Theatre was strong in external
organisation of mass scenes, strong and formal'. Stanislavsky then describes how
in crowd scenes each actor is given 'at least two pages of text' which they have to
memorise and then 'repeat it mechanically during the mob scenes. In this way
they created a false similarity to life'. In contrast, he wants each actor 'to create
his life on the stage on the basis of a complete knowledge of the life of the period
and his own personal observation of his contemporary life. I appeal to his conscious
independent creativity'.[89]

Antoine and Brahm may have recognised the value of the Meiningen troupe –
particularly the creation of a separate world on the stage – but their line was not
historico-realism, but naturalism, another tendency from which Stanislavsky later
wished to distance himself. The reason was the same as for the historical plays –
as a director he 'genuinely thought at the time that it was possible to tell someone
else what to live and feel. I gave directions to everyone at every moment of the
action, and they were binding'. He continues:

> I wrote everything down in my plan, how, where, in what sense the role and
> the writer's stage directions were to be understood, what kind of voice to use,
> how to move, what to do, how to do a move across and where. I made special
> little sketches for every entrance, exit, move, etc., sets, costumes, make-up,

mannerisms, way of walking, the behaviour and personal habits of the characters were all described, etc., etc.[90]

Stanislavsky's opening instructions for *The Seagull* have become famous for their exaggeratedly naturalistic detail:

> The dim light of a lantern on top of a lamp-post, distant sounds of a drunkard's song, distant howling of a dog, the croaking of frogs, the crake of a landrail, the slowing tolling of a distant church-bell – *help the audience to get the feel of the sad, monotonous life of the characters.* [my italics][91]

This is scene-setting to get the audience in the right mood for the play and it is little wonder that Chekhov disapproved of Stanislavsky's attempt to provide an emotional frame for the play before it had even started. Was this because he didn't trust or didn't understand Chekhov's text? Meyerhold, who played Treplev, argued that the production worked thanks to the actors who created the mood:

> The atmosphere was created, not by the mise-en-scene, not by the crickets, not by the thunder of the horse's hooves on the bridge, but by the sheer musicality of the actors who grasped the rhythm of Chekhov's poetry and succeeded in casting a sheen of moonlight over their creations.[92]

Meyerhold's point is that the play can work, simply by attending to the way it is written. At the beginning of his career as a director Stanislavsky seems to trust neither the playscript nor his actors, hence the elaborate settings. Later in his career he was still concerned that actors might be hiding 'behind the director, the designer and the composer', thus obscuring 'the very essence of our art – acting'.[93]

In Gorchakov's transcriptions of Stanislavsky directing there are many moments when he explicitly rejects naturalism in favour of realism; for example:

> We often have been and still are accused of falling into a naturalistic expression of detail in our pursuit of the realism of life and truth in our stage actions. Wherever we have done this we were wrong. It is definitely bad and inartistic: it misrepresents our desired attempt to create a realistic performance. Realism in art is the method which helps to select only the typical from life. If at times we are naturalistic in our stage work, it only shows that we don't yet know enough to be able to penetrate into the historical and social essence of events and character.[94]

Later in the book he returns to the selection of 'details that are typical', because the audience can then 'imagine and complete in imagination what you have suggested'. He continues,

> [t]hat is why naturalism is poisonous to the theatre. Naturalism cheats the audience of its main pleasure and its most important satisfaction, that of creating with the actor and completing in its own imagination what the actor, the director and the designer suggest with their theatre techniques.[95]

Towards the end of his career it appears that he started to trust both the audience and his actors.

As Stanislavsky moved from being the director-dictator towards an actor-trainer so at the same time he researched how to help 'the actor by his staging'.[96] He demanded a more sophisticated notion of verisimilitude: not that of a two-dimensional painted backdrop with lighting that serves the painted image, but a three-dimensional space in which the actor can move. When one thinks of the revolution in lighting and staging that took place in the early twentieth century, the names Appia, Craig and Meyerhold spring to mind. But Stanislavsky declared

> [w]e need the third dimension more than the first two. What use is it to us actors to have a backdrop by the hand of an artist of genius hanging behind us? Very often we don't see it since we have our backs to it.[97]

He argues that the truth of the stage picture comes from the actor's movement and thus they need to interact with three-dimensional objects:

> As actors we need these visible, tangible objects which excite us artistically by their beauty more than painted drops we cannot see. Three-dimensional objects live with us as we do with them, while drops behind us are quite separate from us.[98]

He describes with pride the set that he created for Hauptmann's *The Sunken Bell* in 1898 at the MAT:

> On the entire stage there were only a few rocks on which they could stand or sit. I was not mistaken. As a director, I not only helped the actors by the unusual layout but stimulated, without their knowing, new gestures, new ways of acting. How many of the performances benefited from my direction! […] In all justice I must acknowledge that on this occasion I took a step forward as a director.[99]

Stanislavsky is describing a fundamental shift in artistic emphasis: away from the stage being an artistic recreation of another world, to being a spatial environment designed to promote the creativity of the actor. But note that this staging of Hauptmann's Symbolist play was produced at the same time as *The Seagull*, so one cannot say that we have been following different stages in his development as much as tensions within his method. The approach he would carry through was realism, which relies neither on the accumulation of period detail nor on naturalistic stage setting, but suggestion and an engagement with the audience.

The quotation from Clive Barker at the top of this chapter can help us put these revolutions in acting and staging into a broader context. From the above discussion it is clear that early experiments in historical realism relied a great deal on the virtual characterised space possessing a wealth of period detail in properties, costumes and setting. The auditorium started to be darkened from the 1880s, emphasising that the stage is another 'alien' world to which the audience was 'transported'. By becoming absorbed in the virtual action rather than addressing the actual audience, this pictorial illusion was made even more convincing. Naturalism, certainly as Stanislavsky conceived it, was about creating an atmosphere and setting for the audience, another kind of virtual characterised space. But, as Stanislavsky noted, this attention to detail of staging and costumes took away from the actor's creative work. Symbolist drama offered him a chance to explore a different kind of space which was between virtual and actual: the rocks of the set weren't just to help the audience picture a scene, they were there to promote the creative work of the actor. Rather than writing elaborate plans for the actor's movements (as in *The Seagull*) here he was offering stage configurations that might prompt the actor's creativity. The realism that Stanislavsky demanded was one that came from the work of the actor and not from his technical or design team.

Conclusion

In his staging for *The Sunken Bell* Stanislavsky created an 'unusual layout' on the stage to stimulate certain gestures and movement from his actors. Movement is a concept that is conspicuously absent in Bakhtin's early writings. When he writes about the place from which we see and answer the world, if he means this metaphorically, as when we use the word 'position' to describe where we 'stand' in an argument, then there is no problem. But with Bakhtin's insistence upon the concrete, on the here and now, it does appear that he is talking about real time and space. A view of the world based on such a fixed notion of 'situatedness' would be limited and limiting. To understand one's situation one should take it from several perspectives, which involves moving. Bakhtin's account of our search for meaning is based on a single perspective and takes no account of the restless exploration and travellings of the human species.

The same goes for Bakhtin's notion of time. Is an act really performed once only? Although Stanislavsky's notions of timing and scoring are predicated upon an artistic practice rather than philosophical reflection, he does offer a very sophisticated dialectic between structure and spontaneity, between the repeatable and the unrepeatable. The actor lives in both actual and virtual time, pacing a performance in real time according to the already established emotional contours of the role. The actor's score is both about a reading of the character (showing the logic of behaviour) and a practical plan for how to perform that character in real time. Bakhtin seems to conflate eventness – the confirmation that such an event actually happened because I personally experienced it – with history. But surely history is about seeing connections that link events and thus propose meaningful patterns? If a person's life is the sum of their acts – *postuplenie* – surely these aren't considered as an unrelated number of events, each isolated from the other? One's life cannot be an unrelated series of one damn thing after another. The revelatory meaning that Bakhtin seeks needs to be balanced with one that takes account of the past and uses that to plan acts in the future.

Notes

1 Barker (2010) 135.
2 *Act* 57.
3 *Work* 70.
4 *Work* 101.
5 *Act* 60.
6 *Act* 57.
7 Moran (2000) 11.
8 *Act* 36–37.
9 *Act* 27.
10 *Act* 41.
11 *Act* 54.
12 Moran (2000) 8.
13 Stanislavsky and Rumyantsev (1998) 11.
14 *Act* 32.
15 Moran (2000) 12–13.
16 Stout (2008) 868.
17 *Act* 45.
18 *Act* 48.
19 *Act* 36.
20 *Act* 8.
21 *Act* 61.
22 *Hero* 209.
23 Holquist (1990b) 23.
24 Holquist (1990b) 24–25.
25 Holquist (1990b) 28.
26 Holquist (1990b) 28.
27 Gorchakov (1954) 375.
28 *Life* (2008) 43.
29 *Work* 54.
30 *Role* 17.
31 *Work* 52.
32 Stout (2008) 868–869.
33 *Act* 33.
34 *Act* 30, see also 58.
35 *Act* 40.
36 Hirschkop (1999) 35.
37 *Act* 13.
38 *Act* 10–11.
39 *Act* 28–29.
40 Carnicke (1998) 87–88.
41 Carnicke (1998) 88.
42 Carnicke (1998) 88.
43 *Role* 53.
44 *Work* 208.
45 Benedetti (1988) 316.
46 Torpokov (1999) 87.
47 Torpokov (1999) 138–139.
48 Torpokov (1999) 35.
49 Torpokov (1999) 48.
50 Torpokov (1999) 97.
51 Torpokov (1999) 100–101.
52 Torpokov (1999) 86.

53 Torpokov (1999) 114.
54 Torpokov (1999) 160.
55 Torpokov (1999) 58.
56 *OED*.
57 Torpokov (1999) 87.
58 Torpokov (1999) 141.
59 Stanislavsky (1967b) 257.
60 Stanislavsky (1967b) 267.
61 *Work* 503.
62 *Work* 474.
63 *Work* 474.
64 *Work* 486.
65 *Work* 486.
66 Torpokov (1999) 138–139.
67 Stanislavsky (1967a) 160.
68 Osborne (1988) 139.
69 In Osborne (1988) 68.
70 Osborne (1988) 83.
71 Osborne (1988) 69.
72 Osborne (1988) 69.
73 Osborne (1988) 110.
74 Osborne (1988) 50.
75 Osborne (1988) 89.
76 Rowell (1981) 36.
77 Rowell (1981) 36.
78 Osborne (1988) 80.
79 Osborne (1988) 48.
80 *Life* (2008) 53.
81 Osborne (1988) 163.
82 Osborne (1988) 163.
83 *Life* (2008) 113.
84 *Life* (2008) 114.
85 *Life* (2008) 184.
86 *Life* (2008) 184.
87 *Life* (2008) 183.
88 Braun (1991) 35.
89 Gorchakov (1954) 149.
90 *Life* (2008) 176.
91 Balukhaty (1952) 139.
92 Meyerhold (1991) 32.
93 *Life* (2008) 265.
94 Gorchakov (1954) 143.
95 Gorchakov (1954) 333.
96 *Life* (2008) 147.
97 *Work* 214.
98 *Life* (2008) 157.
99 *Life* (2008) 157.

3 Psychophysical acting

Introduction

This chapter deals with the mind and body in the writings of Bakhtin and Stanislavsky: the body as the agency which acts and the body that is an image for an observer. The body is a problem for both men, but for the different reasons that we have already begun to discuss. For Stanislavsky it centres upon practical questions of how the actor can get into a character. For Bakhtin it generates philosophical questions about how an *I* can understand itself as an *other*. The concerns are in an inverse relation: Stanislavsky's actor is trying to understand how he or she as an *I* can understand a character; Bakhtin's *I* is trying to understand him- or herself as a possible character, or *other*. With attention being paid to both the act-performer and the observer, we can now consider Bakhtin's foundational concept of *I* and *other*.

It should come as no surprise that Stanislavsky goes into much greater practical detail of how the actor's body can become an instrument for artistic expression, and how his own body proved particularly resistant to this process of training. As with Bakhtin's description of how time and space shape subjectivity, his analysis of the body is characteristically general. The principal point of comparison between the two men is how they both figure the relationship between the body as experienced from within (the perspective of the actor and act-performer) and as an image from outside.

At the heart of Bakhtin's conception of *I* and *other* is the fact that an *I* cannot create an image of themselves and therefore (according to his logic) can neither value nor understand their own acts or their own body. This function of imaging has to be provided by a person outside them: an *other*. When Stanislavsky refers to images they have both a positive and a negative valency. It is poor practice for an actor to try and recreate the visual features of another actor (what Stanislavsky called 'stencils') – such an external approach results in a performance which lacks any inner life. But Stanislavsky also writes a great deal about how much he learned from great actors like Rossi and Salvini. Thus while both Bakhtin and Stanislavsky write about the inner and the outer body, they attach quite different values to them. For one, inner experience offers an incomplete and contingent account of action in the world: actions can only be understood and evaluated from the outside. For the other, to act from the outside is most often superficial, and it is only when an actor draws upon their inner experience and resources that they can act truthfully. Bakhtin's conception of human life is from the outset double – an *I* needs an *other*. Stanislavsky's is centred upon an individual, the actor, and his aim is to discover and describe the actor's work. This is a good example of why they are such different thinkers with similar concerns.

Another major difference between them is the process of training the body. Stanislavsky argues that as an artistic instrument the actor's body is not a given but has to be created through training. Indeed training is not a once-only education but a dialectical negotiation with habits which build up and changes which occur within the actor's body. A creative life is thus a constant process of retraining and renegotiation, so that the actor's body remains an instrument of expression. Bakhtin has no conception of any such progressive and continuing learning with and about one's own body. Another important feature of Stanislavsky's approach is that it is psychophysical. In his pragmatic and unsystematic way, Stanislavsky works away at how inner experience can be affected or even generated by physical activity and vice-versa. Holquist notes how Bakhtin was 'intensely interested in […] current developments in physiology, particularly the study of the central nervous system, an area in which Petersburg was one of the world centres' and echoes a reference in his and Clark's biography to 'his interest in the science of physiology'.[1,2] Despite these tantalising references, Bakhtin's early writings explore neither human neurology nor physiology: his approach is phenomenological and confined to a description of how we experience the body.

The final concern of this chapter is methodological: a comparison with Bakhtin's phenomenological account of experience which generates frozen moments of understanding, a dialogical engagement based on love that results in images that are forever finished; and Stanislavsky's pragmatic notion of training which is a dialectical engagement between the outer and inner body, a movement that is recursive, a constant revaluation of the past knowledge and competences in the light of the present needs and experience.

Bakhtin's body

Bakhtin argues that we experience the body in two ways: either we see another's body from the outside or we feel our own body from the inside. A glance at many of the headings throughout *Author and Hero* indicates how his thinking about the body (of self and other) is structured around this distinction between inner and outer; for example, the section entitled 'The Spatial Form of the Hero' has such sub-headings as:

Outward Appearance;
Outward Boundaries of the Body;
The Inner and the Outer Body;
The Value of the Human Body in History; and
The Inner and Outer Body in Self-Experience.

In the four sections below I shall describe how this categorical distinction between the outer and inner body guides his thinking about the body.

Face to face

In *Author and Hero* Bakhtin describes two individuals who are situated (sitting?) opposite each other. They look at each other. Their positions do not change, that is, they do not move.

> When I contemplate a whole human being who is situated outside and over against me, our concrete, actually experienced horizons do not coincide. For at each given moment, regardless of the position and the proximity to me of this other human being whom I am contemplating, I shall always see and know something that he, from his place outside and over against me, cannot see himself: parts of his body that are inaccessible to his own gaze (his head, his face and its expression), the world behind his back and a whole series of objects and relations, which in any of our mutual relations are accessible to me but not to him.[3]

The first thing to note is that this is a static act of contemplation, and, as such, extremely limited as a foundation for a theory of action, drama or dialogue. To extend the visual metaphor further Bakhtin's body is about *sight* and *site*: neither parties change position in order to offer themselves multiple points of view and neither *actually* speaks to each other. There is no to and fro of exchanges and no challenging of views. They sit, mute and immobile, and think to themselves about what they see. It is all about visually apprehended images of 'whole humans'. The senses of movement, smell, touch, taste and hearing play very little active role in this primordial situation. Bakhtin has stated that we cannot see or grasp ourselves as a complete image. While this is true as an account of the feedback from one's visual sense, it takes no account of the body's internal feedback about position and movement that constitute the proprioceptive senses and the kinaesthetic sense. When he writes about the concrete body he is referring to the fact of a body in space: the notion of the body as an exquisitely evolved organism adapting through a constantly looping process of sense and response is alien to Bakhtin.[4]

Bakhtin's conception of the body isn't dualist in the usual sense of a division between mind and body, but a division between sensation and image (the body of *I* and *other*). He agrees that sensation can tell what a body feels, but not what this state means. And by 'means' Bakhtin is saying, 'what it looks like', blurring visual apprehension – seeing – with knowing. He gives the dramatic example of someone in pain:

> He does not see the agonising tension of his own muscles, does not see the entire, plastically consummated posture of his own body, or the expression of suffering on his own face. He does not see the clear blue sky against the background of which his suffering outward image is delineated for me.[5]

In one sense Bakhtin is unanswerably right: a person in pain cannot see themselves. But what claims is he making for this image of agony? That the onlooker understands more than the person in pain? True, a picture of pain can be shown to other people who would all agree that the person is experiencing agony. In a sense this transferable content is all that can be communicated about the situation since the pain in itself is incommunicable. But we can sympathise with this person precisely because the 'plastic-pictorial characteristics' of the person's body remind us of how we have felt such pain. Bakhtin's categorical distinction between sense and meaning, between the inner and the outer body, is driven by his reliance on the single sense of sight, as is the distinction between the roles of observer and actor; there is no question of the *other* assisting in any practical way to change the situation. Bakhtin's notion of how we understand the body revolves around it being able to be grasped immediately as a static image rather than a mobile organism. At every step of his argument he is dealing with fixity rather than movement. It is hard to reconcile the above discussion of the body as a visually apprehended and comprehended static image, in the light of his own biography. It is an index of Bakhtin's stoicism that he could write about the 'meaninglessness' of pain when he himself suffered from osteomyelitis, an inflammation of the bone marrow of the long bones, and an incredibly painful condition that sometimes prevented him from writing – he would instead dictate to his wife – and resulted in the amputation of his right leg in February 1938. Bakhtin made no acknowledgement of his own body which caused him immense pain and continual problems of mobility and function. How could he possibly join in a conversation about the training of the body to become an artistic instrument when for him it was a constant impediment?

I and *other* in space

In Chapter 2 we dealt with first-person experience of time and space and now we can compare this perspective with that of the *other*. There is a section in *Author and Hero* called 'Horizon and Environment' which describes the spatial perspective of the act-performers (*I*) and their observers (*other*), respectively. I aim my actions towards the horizon before me, while the contemplator views my actions taking place in the environment of the world.

> The world of my active fantasies about myself is disposed in front of me, just as is the horizon of my actual seeing; I enter this world as its leading actor, i.e., as the one who conquers all, hears, wins extraordinary glory, and so forth.[6]

This is the perspective of the act-performer whose eyes are focused entirely upon the goal ahead. He argues that any temptation to become aware of oneself results in the action becoming self-conscious and inauthentic:

> If, on the other hand, the plastic-pictorial characteristics of an action are present-on-hand in the action-performer's own consciousness, then his action instantly breaks away from the compelling seriousness of its purpose, breaks away from the needfulness, newness, and productiveness of what is being actualized, and turns into mere *play* or degenerates into mere *gesture*.[7]

I shall argue that, while this is in part true, it is a very reductive model of human behaviour, not least because it categorically forbids an *I* any capacity to guide their action through creating images of them.

Bakhtin's exclusive categories forbid act-performers any awareness or knowledge other than what is directly involved in the performance of the act. Their eyes are directed forward towards the horizon. Their time is always a calculation between now and the future, the interval in which the act is performed. The problem of always being thrown forward into the project of doing is that subjects are never present to themselves in the now but always 'dispersed'.

> In the dimension of time, […] I find only my own dispersed directedness, my unrealised desire and striving – the *membra disiecta* of my potential wholeness; whereas that which could assemble these *membra disiecta*, vivify them, and give them a form – namely, their soul, my authentic *I-for-myself* – that is not yet present in being, but is set as a task and is yet-to-be.[8]

This is the nub of Bakhtin's sustained description of the experience of being an *I* – the soul, the real self, cannot ever be present in being because it is always thrown forward to the next task. It is a situation of agonising contingency. Put another way, 'I am really unable to see my own pure givenness – I really never believe completely that I am only that which I actually am here and now'; do what I can 'the centre of gravity of my self-determination will continue to shift forward, into the future'.[9] 'Already-to-be is to be in a state of need: to be in need of affirmation from outside.' In its constitution in both time and space Bakhtin argues that the *I* needs the *other*. My soul is set as a task for the *other* to render into form: 'The soul is an externally perceivable category: the soul is the spirit the way it looks *from outside*, in the other.'[10] Everything hinges upon this outside perspective. He insists that '[i]t is only in the other human being, in fact, that a living, aesthetically (and ethically) convincing experience of human finitude is given to me, the experience of a human being as a delimited empirical object'.[11]

To know the body, to value the body

We encounter the same kind of limitation and partiality when it comes to knowing and giving value to one's own body. This might seem contradictory coming from a philosopher who takes a phenomenological approach to proof: why does Bakhtin argue that the direct physical experience of the activity of my body provides me with insufficient knowledge about my actions? The answer is by now familiar: knowing is linked to seeing, and I cannot grasp myself immediately as an image. Value is also dependent upon this detached perspective (of oneself as a possible image, but not of one's actions). Bakhtin describes how babies come to recognise and value their own bodies through a mother's loving activity; they are the passive recipient of her outside evaluations. 'The child receives all initial determinations of himself and of his body from his mother's lips and from the lips of those who are close to him.'[12] The words of the loving *other* help to create a bridge between the inner experience of the body and the body which is seen and thus can be valued by others.

> For what I experience from within myself is not in the least my 'darling little head' or 'darling little hand,' but precisely my 'head' and my 'hand' – I act with my 'hand', not my 'darling little hand.' It is only in relation to the other that I can speak about myself in an affectionate diminutive form, in order to express the *other*'s actual relationship toward me or the relationship I wish he would show toward me.[13]

Bakhtin focuses on the value but omits to mention that this naming of the body also allows infants to recognise these discrete body parts and thus learn how to piece together an image of themselves as articulated moving structures. Bakhtin misses out this crucial aspect of dynamic learning. Each part named and learned becomes part of a dynamic, living whole.

When reading the above we should remember Vygotsky's account of a person's interaction with both the world and other speakers which assigns an active role for the speaker/learner. With Vygotsky the person is in a constant state of revaluation, assimilating new information into models of understanding which are then deployed in future thought or speech acts. Bakhtin's focus is much more upon the recognition that one can be the object of love. The need for this love returns us to the inherent chaos of inner experience:

> Words of love and acts of genuine concern come to meet the dark chaos of my inner sensation of myself: they name, direct, satisfy, and connect it with the outside world – as with a response that is interested in me and in my need. […] it is his mother's loving embraces that 'give form' to him axiologically.[14]

Bakhtin's account emphasises the positive, evaluative role of the loving *other*, but wholly diminishes the sense-making activity of the infant. While Bakhtin is undoubtedly right that there is an important developmental need for parental love and affirmation, this account in no way acknowledges the learning achievement of the infant, both in terms of movement and language. Bakhtin's categorical insistence upon the roles of *I* and *other* in turn informs the dialectic of the given and created resulting in the self becoming almost pathologically needy: 'In this respect, the body is not something self-sufficient: it needs the other, needs his recognition and his form-giving activity.'[15] The body is created by the mother through an act of kindness which Bakhtin defines as 'a principle of comportment toward something given, because kindness constitutes a domain of that which is not yet given but imposed as a task'.[16] Bakhtin's *I* doesn't seem to develop but always presents 'itself as indigent, as weak and fragile, as a forlorn and defenceless child'.[17] But he goes further with his argument:

> While my thought can place my body wholly in the outside world as an object among other objects, my actual seeing cannot do the same thing; my seeing, that is, cannot come to the aid of thinking by providing it with an adequate outer image.[18]

Is Bakhtin actually writing about the body, or the aesthetic image of the body? To whom is the body a 'given' – the experiencing *I* or the observing *other*?

The question is not simply about whether Bakhtin is writing about the body or an image of the body, but also about the necessary connection between seeing and knowing. Is it the case that because I cannot see my own body as 'an immediately intuitable experience', I therefore can neither create an aesthetic image of it nor value myself?[19] Bakhtin argues that even when I look in the mirror it is only a partial reflection of myself and not an image, because I cannot grasp myself as another would see me; I am still, as it were, attached to the reflected image.[20] Furthermore he argues that all self-portraits lack ontological weight because they lack an 'optical purity of being' and have an 'emptiness' and 'ghostliness' because of the 'fact that we lack any emotional and volitional approach to this outward image that could vivify it and include or incorporate it axiologically within the outward unit of the plastic-pictorial world'.[21,22] Would Bakhtin's approach provide a very fruitful reading of the self-portraits that Rembrandt made during his life? Bakhtin doesn't actually argue the connection between seeing, knowing and valuing, it is just taken as a given of his categorical distinction between *I* and *other* and then repeated over and over again.

There is a broader philosophical argument to be had about the fundamentally metaphorical connection between image, seeing and understanding. In the Introduction I briefly discussed Bakhtin's connection with German thinkers (Hartmann and Scheler), and it could be that his use of the Russian word image (*obraz*) has taken on the dimensions of the German *Bild* (picture or image) and *Bildung* (education or culture). Interesting as it would be, such a discussion takes us too far from our subject. The main point for this argument is that in the context of knowledge and value the early Bakhtin is predominantly interested in the visual sense, and ignores all others. Although he briefly mentions the feeling of a body in pain, this is mainly to highlight the suffering person's inability to grasp this as an image. As concerns the sensory feedback a person gets from their physical activity and the core sense of self that this generates – Bakhtin is silent. Despite the interest Holquist claims he has in physiology and the nervous system, Bakhtin says nothing of the multi-sensory faculty of proprioception, not to mention our kinaesthetic sense which informs our every movement.

The value of the human body in history

This is the title of a section in *Author and Hero* where he proposes a history of the literary representation of the body according to whether a value is placed on '*self* experience' or on the 'experience of the *other* human being' and that 'the living experience from which the "idea of man" arises is founded either in self-experience or in the experience of the other human being':[23]

> Accordingly, either the distinctiveness of self-experience is reduced under the influence of experiencing other people, or the distinctiveness of experiencing the other is reduced under the influence of and in favour of self-experience.[24]

Thus far in his account he has presented the necessity for the two experiences in everyday life: here he explores the means whereby first one and then the other had the ascendancy. And at this point his study shifts from philosophy to literary analysis.

Bakhtin's history of the body begins with the 'antique body' which he argues was entirely external. Only with the Dionysian Cult was there the beginning of a concept of the inner man – that of sexuality. But this 'infracorporeal lived experience' involves simply the physical experience of one another's bodies, and doesn't yet allow a person to experience themselves as an *I-for-myself* which is 'an essentially different category of experiencing a human being; as yet, only the ground is being prepared for that separation'.[25] At the other end of the pole is Platonism where the experience of the internal body is valued to the exclusion of the phenomenal external body. 'The pure relationship to oneself (a relationship that has no aesthetic constituents and can only be ethical or religious) becomes the sole creative principle of experiencing and justifying man and the world axiologically.'[26] Thus these two historical moments in Classical Greek thinking define two opposite but equally incomplete accounts of how one can understand and value the human body.

The section finishes with a reflection on what might be called the 'unaesthetic' heroes in Dostoevsky's novels and stories, who invent images of themselves based on what they think others must think of them. Considered as living people many of Dostoevsky's characters – the Underground Man in *Notes from Underground* and Raskolnikov in *Crime and Punishment* spring to mind – are tragically or comically ineffective, principally because their attention is directed inwards rather than outwards towards the world. As acting subjects they both fail because they worry too much what others will think of them. Underground Man never acts, Raskolnikov acts (by killing the old lady) but never recovers from the guilt resulting from his action. They are prevented from dialogue for fear of what other people might say about them. Above all, Bakhtin rejected any imagining of oneself because it lacks the authority of the outside eye, and here he notes 'an authoritative position for such concrete axiological seeing – for perceiving myself as another – is absent'. He goes on to explain that that exterior part of myself, 'my being-for-others' rather than going out to another, loops back into one's self-consciousness 'and a return into myself occurs'. Dostoevsky's characters indulge in imagining themselves rather than imaging forth another. Although Bakhtin appears to present this returning into oneself as both aesthetically and ethically suspect, Dostoevsky was a constant source of inspiration in his writings.

The resistant body and the image of the body – Stanislavsky's resistant body

Both in his autobiography and *An Actor's Work* Stanislavsky writes about how the actor's body is not a given but has to be created through the constant practice of training. Passages in *My Life in Art* describe his struggle with his 'natural' body as he strives to become an actor. A fundamental difficulty in the art of acting is that it is before hundreds of people at a set time in the day when the actor has to be creative. Returning to Barker's distinction above, Stanislavsky experienced a contradiction between the actual and the virtual space of theatre: being on stage made him cripplingly aware of his own body and its shortcomings, which prevented him from being able to engage in the business of embodying a character. Bakhtin's act-performers, on the other hand, seem to be unconcerned by the *other* looking at them. Within the descriptions of the struggle with his body is another struggle with the terms that are available to describe the first. Stanislavsky wants to find a way to control his muscles, but conscious control only makes them more rigid with tension. He wants to learn the art of acting, but it has to be artless, closer to nature. He wants a theatre without theatricality. This explains why actors need to retrain themselves to be able to perform the most basic of tasks 'naturally' onstage. Tortsov explains '[t]hat is why we have to learn to walk, move, sit, lie down all over again' – later adding, 'you must learn to look and see, listen and hear onstage, too'.[27] Later the student Kostya reflects on how art and nature are involved in the actor's work of 'remaking' their bodies:

> We would have to remake ourselves completely, body and soul, from head to foot and adapt to the demands of our art, or rather, to the demands of nature. For art is in harmony with her. Life and bad habits that have been grafted onto her mar our nature.[28]

Again and again art and nature are in a paradoxical relationship: art must not draw attention to itself as art, but seek to harmonise with nature. Training thus must become 'second nature', something learned so well that its effects are not achieved through conscious, external control. The actor 'must make muscular control part of your physical being, make it second nature. Only in this way can the muscular monitor be of help to us when we are acting'.[29] He argues that '[a]ny system has to become so familiar that you forget about it. Only after it has become part of your flesh and blood and heart can you begin, unconsciously, to derive real benefit from it'.[30] Technique has to be developed as 'a habit to the point where it becomes an unconscious reflex'.[31] So, training becomes 'second nature', an 'unconscious reflex' or, quite simply, habit which itself can be 'a two-edged sword. It can do great harm when badly used on the stage and be of great value when proper advantage is taken of it'.[32]

Stanislavsky describes his own stage fright with painful vividness. In his early years on stage he 'only understood the word *control* in the external sense' and forcing himself not to move 'resulted in making [him] even more wooden'. Here control 'in the external sense' means conscious control of the muscles. He goes on to describe how he would concentrate all his 'bodily tension in one particular spot': 'I clenched my fist so hard my nails drew blood. I tightened my toes and pushed them hard against the floor with all the weight of my body so that I often had blood in my shoes.'[33] He accurately describes the state of panic:

> [...] uncontrolled feelings reduce the entire body to anarchy. The muscles involuntarily shorten, resulting in a countless number of movements,

meaningless poses and gestures, nervous tics, etc. Feeling runs away from this chaos and takes refuge in its secret places. Can you be creative or think in these circumstances?[34]

It is clear that the interest is in creating a bodily state that is receptive to feeling. The reason for avoiding stiffness and tension is that they are 'harmful to the process of experiencing, to the external, physical embodiment of what is being experienced and to the actor's overall mental state'.[35] The two parts of the actor's work, embodiment and experiencing (whence the two parts of *An Actor's Work*), are symbiotically linked. 'The more subtle the feelings, the more precision, clarity, flexibility they require when they are physically embodied.'[36] An actor's work is to find a means by which this chaotic body that is prone to tension, stress and stiffness can be turned into a more subtle body that is open to feelings.

The teacher Tortsov proposes an exercise to test whether his students can experience the state of ease on stage. He asks them to sit on stage and be still, which turns out to be incredibly hard: they fidget and look stiff. Kostya finds it easier to 'sit onstage in a theatrical rather than a human way – unnaturally' but when Tortsov does it, 'the simple way he sat captured our attention'.[37,38] Once again, the contrast is between conscious effort and simple doing. Kostya realises that his approach is too conscious: 'When I monitored my muscles, the more consciously I related to them, the more unwanted tensions were created, and the more difficult it became to tell them apart and locate the necessary ones.'[39] This is a similar discovery to that of the young Stanislavsky who exercised control 'in the external sense'. Towards the end of his course Kostya realises that it is all about that simplicity with which Tortsov sat on the stage and thereby held the audience's attention:

> Performing all these actions directly, sincerely, brought nature and the sub-conscious into play quite normally. They would justify what I did and release the excess tension which was preventing genuine, productive, specific action.[40]

Throughout the book Kostya watches Tortsov and realises that it is through his supreme technique that 'all the Elements, the psychological inner drives' and so forth 'become normal, human – not convention-bound and actorish – activity.'[41]

Although Stanislavsky rarely analyses how his training works or defines terms like 'nature' or 'subconscious' he does make oppositions and distinctions which offer an insight into his system. Firstly he defines what he does and doesn't want from an actor. He is against 'convention-bound and actorish' acting and the theatrical; he is for that which is human, simple, natural and sincere. And how is this achieved? Through reducing bodily tension so that actors are open to the suggestibility of their subconscious and inner psychological drives. It is this sense of opening that was not present in the young Stanislavsky's attempts to achieve results through control in an external sense, through conscious effort. An internal approach enables the actor to allow rather than force something to happen.

Internal and external images

Another way of tracing Stanislavsky's artistic development is through his approach to the image of the character. He begins with memories of his earliest acting experiments where he imitates the outward physical characteristics of some of his favourite actors. He is play-acting, showing off for others, quite often to attract the attention of young women in the audience. As a youth he enjoys playing the external image of famous Russian actors in their signature roles, and in his descriptions we can see an echo of much earlier acting practices where students follow the external features of their actor-teachers. As his eye becomes more educated so he learns through observing leading European actors, less as models for imitation but as guides to good acting technique. Finally, he writes about the actor creating a score of images of the actions of their character, an example of truly psycho-physical acting in which the actor creates a mental image of their body.

Like many children the young Konstantin Alekseyev adored getting up on stage in order to show off in front of the public and as his taste and talent for performance developed his parents built a small stage for him in the family house. He describes a style of performance that is directed to the audience (the *en face* delivery discussed in Chapter 2), the theatricality that he would later reject as superficial. He makes much of his vanity – his desire to dress up as a hero:

> all I had to do was put on Spanish boots and take up a sword and everything new I had achieved with such difficulty vanished to be replaced by the powerful, old ingrained habits I had acquired in many years of amateur acting.[42]

> I was applauded because schoolgirls cannot tell the difference between the actor and the part he is playing, and I, like a fool, forged ahead making all my old mistakes. […] Once again I imitated the operatic baritone in Parisian boots with a sword.[43]

This is a good example of Stanislavsky's struggle with 'old ingrained habits' in the section above. If training is recursive (a constant process of going back over basic aspects of technique) it is because the professional actor is recidivist (old habits keep coming back).

In his search for models of good acting he imitated the successful actors of his time. He describes how he prepared for his début in December 1877 (aged fourteen) in a vaudeville called *A Cup of Tea* and admits that '[a]ll I wanted was to be like my favourite actor', Nikolai Musil, who played simpletons. 'I wanted to have his voice and his manner.' He sums up his approach to acting at that time: 'all that remained for me was to repeat something that had already been done and blindly copy the original. I felt wonderful. Free and self-assured onstage.'[44] It wasn't an approach that always worked, and he knew that there was 'no more painful duty than to have to embody, come what may, something alien, vague, something that is always outside you'.[45] Stanislavsky's vocabulary is telling when compared to Bakhtin: the actor cannot embody that which is 'alien' and 'always outside you', there has to be something which is personal and living.

His aesthetic quest is to find the *I* in the *other*, whereas Bakhtin's is to find the *other* in the *I*.

Throughout *My Life in Art* there are vivid descriptions of Rossi and Salvini, two actors who provided him with models of professional excellence, particularly in the way they prepared and performed their roles. In his biography of Stanislavsky, Benedetti notes how Rossi had advised to avoid 'opting for the "mask" from behind which he could hide' because he would 'become nothing but the mask'. He goes on: 'Something deeper was required: the integration of the actor's personality into the role and the release of personal, creative energy so that actor and character became indistinguishable.'[46] This fuels his self-questioning when creating the role of Benedict in *Much Ado About Nothing*:

> How was I to make it my own? I thought much and laboured much over this problem, and this was useful, since in my search for characterisation I looked for it in real life and when I found it, tried to carry it on to the stage. Before this, in my quest for the methods of acting in a given role, I only buried myself in the dust-covered archives of old and lifeless traditions and stencils.[47]

While Meyerhold may have championed theatricality as the real truth of the stage, Stanislavsky wanted to 'get rid of mouldy theatricality – that was our greatest care at the time.'[48] More than once he refers to the 'destructive and revolutionary aims' with which he and Nemirovich-Danchenko planned to rejuvenate the art of acting by declaring 'war on all the conventionalities of the theatre wherever they might occur'.[49] While this might involve a rejection of the external, it most certainly did not mean a rejection of the visual, particularly of the image.

Stanislavsky argues that '[t]here are visual and aural actors' and admits to being 'the first kind'; for him 'the easiest way to create an imaginary life is through mental images' and describes this imagining as passive: 'I choose the path which is easiest for me by being an audience, through the visual.'[50] He later analyses this process of seeing: 'I observe as an outsider, passively, without taking part in someone else's life.'[51] This is an uncanny echo of Bakhtin's account of the outside perspective of the observing *other*, and it provokes a similar question as to what is meant by an image. Is a character an image created by the actor? In *My Life in Art* Stanislavsky and his fellow actors wonder, '[i]f we could only see the image, see how he walks, talks, laughs, and come to know the quality of his voice', when they approached a role. 'If we can find the image, all the rest will come of itself.' But then realise that they were simply 'using an external stimulus to provoke an internal reaction. […] We played the image.'[52] Once again, they were copying a model rather than creating their own mental image. Both Bakhtin and Stanislavsky write about work on the character in terms of the image.

In another passage from *My Life in Art* Stanislavsky explains the difference between how a painter and an actor give form to a human image:

> A painter's canvas can assume the lines and forms his imagination conceives. But what are we to do with our own physical body? […] I did not know

how to achieve onstage the shadowy feelings that were almost inexpressible in words.[53]

He describes how he studied paintings by the Russian Mikhail Vrubel (1856–1910):

> [...] as a director and actor I try mentally to get inside the frame, to slip into the picture, so as to become part of its mood and become physically accustomed to it, not from the outside but from the inside, like Vrubel himself.[54]

Vrubel was an interesting artist to choose since his images are very far from being realistic, the distorted human figure often set among abstract swirls and roils of thick paint. He goes on to describe how he would try and reproduce the image himself, recalling the sensations that passed 'right through you, your body, muscles':

> Remembering what you have discovered physically, you try to take it with you to the mirror, so as to verify with your own eyes the lines of your body and what they express but, to your amazement, all you encounter in your reflection is a caricature of Vrubel, actors' posturing, and above all, the old, familiar, hateful operatic clichés.[55]

Where Bakhtin eschews the mirror on principle, Stanislavsky describes in painful detail the difficulty of reconciling his attempts to embody a painting and the reflected image he sees before him. In his description we see the difference between imitating and embodying an image. In Chapter 2 we saw how Charles Kean and Duke Georg of Saxe Meiningen began their revolution in theatre with the pictorial, but here Stanislavsky is seeking to establish his theatre not on external images but inner experience. And yet it would still involve images.

Another way of understanding how Stanislavsky arrived at his notion of the inner image is to compare his approach to that of the actor and writer Benoît-Constant Coquelin (1841–1909), whose book *L'Art du comedien* (1894) Stanislavsky had studied. In describing the creation of a character Coquelin also turns to the art of the painter:

> The actor creates a model in his imagination, then like a painter, captures every trait and transfers it not onto canvas but onto himself. [...] He sees Tartuffe in a particular costume. He puts it on. He sees a certain way of walking and copies it. He forces his own face, and, as it were, like a tailor cuts and sews his own flesh until the critic inside his *One* is happy and says that this indeed looks like Tartuffe.[56]

The process, like that of Bakhtin's, is once-only, the creation of a static and finished image. In Tortsov/Stanislavsky's eyes this would be simply 'a superficial resemblance, the outside of a character, not the character itself – the actor needs to find the character's voice and way of moving – "the very *soul* of Tartuffe"'.[57] The opposition is still between external and internal: between the art of Coquelin which 'impresses you only at the time you are watching him' and that of Yermalova which 'enters into your heart, into your life'.[58] Both are ways of embodying a character: one focused on how it looks, the other through its principle of movement. Stanislavsky pursues this comparison with the work of a painter when describing his later Method of Physical Actions:

> The line of physical actions has precisely the same significance in the art of the actor. The actor, like the painter, must make the character sit, stand or lie down. But this is more complicated for us in that we present ourselves as both the artist *and* the model. We must find, not a static pose, but the organic actions of a person in very diverse situations. Until these are found, until the actor justifies the truth by the correctness of physical behaviour, he cannot think of anything else.[59]

The passage above touches upon a fundamental difference between Stanislavsky and Bakhtin: firstly the actor is both artist and model, whereas the hero is categorically separate from the author. Part of the actor's creative process is to create images of him- or herself in motion, much as sports training relies on visualisation. The later Stanislavsky connects images with feelings (again returning to his shift from emotional memory to physical action): 'Considering the fact that there is no difference between the art of the stage and the art of emotional experience, that is, the art of embodiment, Konstantin Sergeyevich refused to let us play *feelings*, we must always play *images*.'[60] Torpokov helps to tease out what Stanislavsky meant by the terms 'image', 'visualise' and 'imagination' in his later years. He distinguishes between playing aimlessly and playing according to a visual score: 'Don't play anything, just visualise it for yourself. You still want to *play* something, but you will not be able to really play anything until you have built up images.'[61] It isn't clear whether these are images of the actor's score of movements and gestures, or the image of the character performing them. What is clear is their importance as a means of giving form and clarity to the actor's playing.

At a more metaphorical level Stanislavsky also asks his actors to consider their scores of images as films. He advises Torpokov that '[a]n unbroken film of images like a motion picture must be created in your mind. If this doesn't exist, you cannot play the fragmented scenes convincingly'.[62] In *An Actor's Work* he repeats this advice at some length. I shall quote only a brief passage: 'Constantly watching the film of your mental images will, on the one hand, make sure you stay within the play, and, on the other, unfailingly and faithfully guide your creative work.'[63] The score of the actor's actions is now compared to a film reel through which they guide their actions. We should bear this image in mind when we turn to Meyerhold who didn't use film as a metaphor for the actor's imaginative work, but as a model for constructing his pieces: he very consciously talked of montage.

Bakhtin, Stanislavsky and psychology

The word 'psychology' can be used in two very different ways: on the one hand it refers to the scientific study of mental phenomena or the treatment of mental pathology; on the other hand it has a much broader cultural meaning to do with our inner mental life and our understanding of others and characters. When Stanislavsky writes about a psychotechnique, or the 'psychology' of a character, it is in this informal sense, though we shall see him refer to a range of psychologists from France, the United States and Russia. Thanks to these assumptions about the human psyche there can be agreement about a character being 'believable', about a course of actions being 'logical', about what is and what is not 'realistic'. And it is thanks to this cultural agreement – quite as much as his reading in faculty psychology – that Stanislavsky can write about the 'psychology' of a character. We shall see in Part III that it is precisely this assumption about how people 'are' that will be challenged by Meyerhold. The challenge is located both in the realm of medical science and of culture and politics. The early Bakhtin rejects psychology as a means of accounting for the process of authorship. He concedes that 'there can be no doubt that, phenomenologically, co-experiencing of another being's inner life does occur, whatever the unconscious technique of its actualisation might be.'[64] In other words, he is interested in the phenomenon of co-experiencing and not the psychological mechanism by means of which it happens. Like Stanislavsky, he is interested in the product and not the facultative process whereby it is produced.

Bakhtin's quarrel with psychology is the same one we have seen in respect of philosophy: that it deals with 'hypothetical individuality' and not with actual people:

> *What-is-mine* in the experience of an object is studied by psychology, but it is studied here in complete abstraction from the axiological weight of the *I* and the *other* – in abstraction from their uniqueness; psychology knows only a 'hypothetical individuality'.[65]

In the same passage he goes on to argue that in faculty psychology unity is defined in terms of a 'regularity conforming to psychological rules' rather than the living unity of a person (or character). Once again we come back to a sense of meaning that is to do with value which in turn means value to a particular person. The axiological weight of an object is that it has a particular value to me as an individual person, rather than to 'people' in general (or as he puts it 'hypothetical individuality'). Behind this pragmatic account of meaning there is another question: what is it that makes us think of a character as a whole?

We have already seen how Stanislavsky felt compelled to invent a systematic approach to acting. One could argue that he was in a constant process of research and experiment, and (as already suggested by Sharon Carnicke) the system always lagged behind the process of practical experimentation. Apart from the trial and error experiments he conducted on himself, he was constantly on the lookout for sources of information and inspiration that might help him in his quest. Benedetti writes about him being 'driven, therefore, to cobble together a "jargon" that was unknown outside the Art Theatre'.[66] So, he drew on the yoga of his friend Sulerzhitsky. Mel Gordon argues that it was only Sulerzhitsky, 'a theatre non-professional', who understood the significance of Stanislavsky's early discoveries: 'the secret of great acting involves unearthing the mind's potential; the development of affective physical and psychophysical exercises must be the first path to a consistent awakening of the Creative State of Mind.'[67] Stanislavsky was also familiar with the work of Russian psychologists like Ivan Pavlov (1849–1936), with the American William James (1842–1910) and with Théodule Ribot (1839–1916).

Psychology, along with all other aspects of scientific and cultural life, was a very hotly contested subject following the Russian Revolution. In the early years of the Revolution there was a determination to re-evaluate all questions of art and science in the light of Marxism, and this meant putting into question the pre-revolutionary image of man. This project was enthusiastically embraced in the work of Lev Vygotsky who has already been cited above. Benedetti describes how Stanislavsky 'was locked in a bitter battle with pseudo-Marxist Soviet psychology, which was Behaviourist and did not recognise the existence either of the subconscious or of the Mind. Consequently, he substantially rewrote whole passages' of *My Life in Art* in an attempt to appease the authorities.[68] Stanislavsky was aware of the dangers he was courting by using outdated terminology: 'the greatest danger of the book is "the creation of the life of the human spirit" (you are not allowed to speak about the spirit). Another danger: the subconscious, transmission and reception, the word *soul*.'[69] We shall see that throughout Stanislavsky's career he took a keen interest in psychology, but that this was driven by his spirit of pragmatic enquiry: everything he did was in aid of trying to find a more reliable means of acting. Thus his 'psychology' was a mixture of different, even contradictory elements: the yogic notion of *prana*, the religious notions of spirit and soul, the vaguer concepts of the subconscious and superconscious, the cultural notion of 'human nature'. The underlying conflict was methodological: Soviet policy was to demand an objectivity and scientific rigour while Stanislavsky took a more pragmatic and artistic approach.

We have already seen that Stanislavsky's first approach to acting was based on emotional recall and as such demanded the actor to work on their own 'psychology'. Richard Boleslavsky describes this faculty for emotional recall:

> We have a special memory for feeling, which works unconsciously by itself and for itself. It's right there. It is in every artist. It is that which makes experience an essential part of our life and craft.[70]

He gives an example of an old couple at a dinner party who are prompted when cucumber is served to remember making love many years earlier in a cucumber patch and their emotions at that moment. Boleslavsky explains that at first they were unaware of the source of their emotion. This explains how the process of recall, or association, isn't conscious: 'They just naturally yielded themselves to the feelings as they came.'[71] He goes on to explain that the same process can be applied by the actor and advises that the feelings will come of their own accord, 'involuntarily'.[72] He warns that this is not about the representation but the reliving of an emotion: 'To imitate is wrong. To create is right.'[73]

Whyman points out that 'the central idea that Stanislavsky verified from his reading of Ribot' was 'affective memory' and that it was based on a person's sensuous experience of the world.[74] Whyman quotes Ribot: 'every recollection must be a *reversion*, by virtue of which the past once more becoming a present, we live at present in the past.'[75] Ribot distinguishes this emotional memory from what he calls 'intellectual' memory, which today we would call episodic or explicit memory whereby we recall facts as a conscious act of remembering. Emotional memory is, as Whyman puts it, 'based in "nature", that is, in "real" experience', a process over which we have no conscious control, as opposed to the voluntary but purely intellectual process.[76] The key conceptual opposition at work here is that between memory which is consciously retrieved (with just the mind) and a past emotional memory that 'appears' or is suggested by association with a present sensory experience. One is the product of conscious and willed mental activity; the other is based in nature, is connected with the body, and is involuntary or non-conscious.

Creativity and the subconscious

While Stanislavsky tirelessly searched for an approach to acting that was systematic, he freely admits that *An Actor's Work* 'has no pretensions to be scientific', adding however that 'art should be on good terms with science'.[77] The word 'subconscious' is not a scientific term and has nothing to do with Freud's 'unconscious', even if both men proposed that the only way to access these zones was through the conscious mind. Stanislavsky explains that '[t]he essence of my book is access to the subconscious through the conscious methods in an actor's work to study and stimulate subconscious creativity – inspiration'.[78] On the next page he asks what must the actor do if that inspiration 'doesn't happen? Then there is nothing for it but to stimulate subconscious creation through the conscious means, by our technique'.[79] Chapter 16 of *An Actor's Work* is entitled 'The Subconscious and the Actor's Creative State' which indicates the equation between the two in Stanislavsky's system. In a few words, 'the basic task of our psychotechnique is to bring the actor to the state in which his creative subconscious can burgeon', or again, this technique 'has the capacity to create […] the favourable conditions in which the work of nature and the subconscious can take place.'[80,81] Once again, we see the association of creativity with 'the work of nature'. The actual neurophysiology of creativity is irrelevant to Stanislavsky – 'Matters of the subconscious are not my field':[82]

> So, we won't get in the way of the subconscious when it's working but rather learn how to involve our natural mental processes in our creative work, and ensure that our vocal, aural, indeed, all the mechanisms of physical embodiment by which we communicate our feelings, thoughts, mental images, etc., are sensitive and receptive.[83]

When dealing with a process which you don't fully understand but whose power is undeniable, one should just allow it to happen rather than interfere with it consciously. In essence, this is a forerunner of Grotowski's *via negativa*, which we will encounter in Chapter 6.

There is very little consistency in Stanislavsky's use of terms when describing this creative process: at one time it involves the subconscious, at another the actor's nature is 'freed from the tyranny of reason, from the power of conventions, preconceived ideas, forcing, and engages with its own superconscious initiative (intuition)'. He concludes '[s]o, the only way to the unconscious mind is the conscious mind'.[84] The superconscious 'elevates the human heart and so it should be prized and protected in our art' while the subconscious is that part of the mind which lies beneath the threshold of consciousness.[85] He quotes a statistic from Elmer Gates (an 'American experimental psychologist 1859–1923') that 'ninety per cent of our mental life is subconscious'.[86,87] For all that he quotes a number of psychologists Stanislavsky's 'constant concern is the living human spirit, the life of the human soul. You cannot create or come to know a living spirit through your brain, you do it, first and foremost, through feeling.'[88] Indeed there is creative advantage to be had in not knowing: 'Mystery is beautiful in itself and is a great stimulus to creativeness.'[89] If he has drawn on terms from psychology, these are balanced with much more traditional terms like feeling, emotion and intuition, all of which are part of nature. Consciousness should only be deployed to create the conditions under which a non-conscious process can take place. 'Nature is a better guide to a living organism than the conscious mind and well-known famous "acting" techniques.'[90]

Both Stanislavsky's psychotechnique of emotional memory and his later Method of Physical Actions are psycho-physical in that they require the actor to connect experiencing and embodying. The difference lies in the sequence and emphasis. Rather than waiting for an emotional association which will result in the actor being able to embody the character, the actor begins by embodied activity within a specific context and then waits for the emotional associations suggested by that activity. Mel Gordon recaps the difference between this action-based approach to the earlier approach based on affective memory.

> Without relying on their memories, imaginative powers, or analytical abilities, actors were compelled by the direction to decide which Physical Actions they would execute in the Given Circumstances of the play. Only that which could be physically performed and seen by an audience was allowed. […] The Method of Physical Actions was predicated on a simple discovery that Stanislavsky borrowed from Michael Chekhov and Vakhtangov's followers (who in turn, were influenced by Meyerhold): all physical action is psychophysical. This means that internal feeling and character identification could be stimulated by pure movement, action, and rhythm.[91]

Sharon Carnicke puts Stanislavsky's later approach in context with his earlier experiments.

> That actors speak through their actions becomes as important to Stanislavsky as what they say. If, as Ribot teaches, emotion cannot exist without motion however subliminal, and if, as Yoga professes, the mental and physical exist as an indissoluble whole, then, Stanislavsky reasons, neither can emotional content be torn from physical embodiment.[92]

However she goes on to argue that this is precisely what happened to the legacy of Stanislavsky's work. Following the influence of Boleslavsky, Lee Strasberg focused on the emotional aspect of his work to the exclusion of the physical. In the Soviet Union they opted for a purely materialist account of acting: 'Just as history culminates in the creation of Communism, the System culminates in the Method of Physical Actions.'[93] What united the Americans and the Soviets was that neither integrated yoga into their account of acting.

Conclusion: a body that learns

Much of the argument of this chapter has been driven by questions that come from the practice of theatre: 'how to' questions that revolve around psycho-physical acting. Both experiencing (the 'psycho') and embodying (the 'physical') are techniques that the actor needs to learn and refine through a process of life-long training. Stanislavsky's approach to actor training is illuminated by Bakhtin's formulation of the given and the created: a person's given body has to be created anew before it can become an actor's body, a creative body. Stanislavsky offers two accounts of the creation of such a body: his personal story and then the fictional account of a two-year training programme (first year 'psycho', second year 'physical'), giving the perspective of both teacher and student. Both in his early and in his later approaches Stanislavsky insisted upon the connection between experiencing and doing. Without experiencing doing is simply mechanical. One could argue that what drove him in his research was the demand that acting should involve this dimension of personal experience or feeling.

Bakhtin's is a profoundly different approach to experience and act-performing. There is experience and there is act-performing, but they are not connected functionally. Where the actor's body (Stanislavsky's) is not given but has to be created through training, the act-performer's body (Bakhtin's) is a given as concerns the performance of actions. The body is just there to perform the actions. Bakhtin is not interested in the performance of the action, the difficulty it poses or the skills it demands of the performer – it is simply performed. It requires no helpers, and there are no stages leading up to or following the performance. The questions that concern Bakhtin are both external. The act-performer's eye is trained upon the horizon and upon the object that demands action; either that, or upon a given truth that can only be experienced through the performance of an act. Once performed, the act can only be given meaning or value by an observer. In both instances the attention is outside the act-performer's body. An *I* can neither attribute meaning to an individual act nor create a narrative linking a series of acts: this is a notion of selfhood where one has no position on oneself.

Bakhtin does not write about the act-performer experiencing the performance of the action internally, and thus being able to perform it better or worse. There is no feedback either from the performance or from the effect of the deed. It is as if the body Bakhtin writes of has motor nerves which execute actions, but no sensory nerves that provide information about how it feels to execute them. (How different from Bakhtin's own body, wracked with pain and rendering him partially immobile.) In this sense Bakhtin's body never learns from its actions: as feedback only comes from outside, from the *other*, they remain a series of discrete, and from his perspective, unknowable events. The (performing) body – the self – has no memory of how any of its acts were performed and thus there is no lived sense of continuity through these acts. This memory of how movements are performed is one of the bases of Stanislavsky's account of acting, and in broader terms is what gives us as humans a continuing sense of selfhood that is generated through the sense of physical agency. For all Bakhtin's interest in physiology he takes no account of the body's outer envelope of skin and the various nerve-endings beneath its surface. Indeed he rejects a sense of proprioceptive totality:

> From within myself, I can perceive my own boundaries as an impediment, but not at all as a consummation, while on the contrary, the aesthetically experienced boundary of the other does consummate him, contracting and concentrating all of him, all of his self-activity, and closing off this self-activity.[94]

In passages like this Bakhtin seems to argue against the direct experience of our bodies in pursuit of a philosophical theory (and thereby in the context of his own life achieves a triumph of thought over lived experience).

While Stanislavsky writes about *his* body, Bakhtin writes about *the* body, a particular body from a methodological point of view, but effectively impersonal. The same is true of the act: within his theory it is a particular, once-only and therefore never to be repeated act. Bakhtin's act is not an 'action' in the sense that Stanislavsky writes about, and there is no discussion of how it is performed. It is precisely the way something is done that gives a hint about the attitude, the emotional state of the performer. To give body to or embody a character is to do things like they as that character would do. This is why an action needs to be understood in its given circumstances. Stanislavsky's famous example is catching a train; the circumstances could be that you arrive just as the carriage doors are closing, or have twenty minutes before departure, so buy a coffee and newspaper and take in the scene.[95]

When Bakhtin does write about the inner body it is described as a maelstrom of conflicting sensations. Because the *I* cannot see his or her own body, because there is no whole image, *therefore* an *I* cannot understand or intuitively grasp him- or herself as a whole. A body that is grasped in solely visual and intellectual terms is always going to be other, a thing known as a visual object rather than felt as an active agent. Bakhtin is discussing a philosophical *I*, a subject, and not a psycho-physical – or even neurophysiological – self. His theory is severely limited. Bakhtin's *I* is a thing created by the eye and for the mind and has none of the physiological resilience of an embodied self. In his account, the body generates no intelligible meaning and its inner chaos needs to be redeemed by the loving other. I cited a passage from Bakhtin in which the mother names the body parts of the child, but this is only to show the necessity for a loving other, it is not presented as an essential stage in the child's progressive knowledge and mastery of his or her own body. It is not about the development of an embodied and autonomous self.

I also cited the situation of one person seated before another, each having the advantage of seeing the other as a complete whole. Even at a literal level this is inaccurate since you can only see the frontal aspect of the other person, their back remains unseen, and their three-dimensionality is something that we learn to infer from experience – it is the result of an imaginary moving around the object. Because Bakhtin's account of meaning and value is confined to externally perceived images of action, he can therefore account for neither the agency nor character of the act-performer. There is no knowing or feeling body at work – simply an *I* whose eye is trained upon the object on the horizon. Moreover, this *I*/eye does not move in order to get a better perspective on how the action could be performed. The absence of movement in Bakhtin's account of the body is not a minor omission. According to the philosopher Maxine Sheets-Johnstone, it is movement that constitutes the *I*: 'In effect, *movement forms the I that moves before the I that moves forms movement.* Spontaneous movement is the constitutive source of agency, of subjecthood, of selfhood, the dynamic core of our sense of ourselves as agents, subjects, selves.'[96] Bakhtin's notion of body, time and space are grasped as static, frontal images.

Put in Stanislavskian terms, because he accounts for neither experiencing nor embodiment, Bakhtin's body offers little enlightenment in terms of actor training since it is deprived of all senses apart from vision and thus has no means of learning or adapting to the environment. His theory is about dialogue, but the need for the *other* is mainly created by this sensory impoverishment. For all Bakhtin's insistence upon the importance of personal experience, it doesn't constitute a dynamic or developmental process within the experiencing act-performer: the active agent in his schema is the observer/author because the only informing sense within his schema is sight. His theoretical assumptions – it must be stated that *I* and *other* is an *a priori* structure – limit the capability of an individual self to make sense of the world.

Stanislavsky's inner sensations were both positive and negative, but they were all considered as information about his bodily self that helped him develop as an actor. Thus when he offers graphic images of the tension he experienced as a result of stage fright, this set him on the path of discovering how to achieve a state of physical ease on stage. Where Bakhtin presents the body as the passive site of experiences, Stanislavsky learns from what they tell him. Although he doesn't put it in so many words, he struggles against involuntary tension which prevents ease of movement and eventually achieves plasticity within his body. In the context of acting, embodiment means changing the shape of your body and the way you move. This requires actors as people to relearn how they move, to recognise their own personal habits of movement and posture, the better to be able to take on the movement habits of their characters. He describes the process in which you first imagine your character and then give body to this image through the physical plasticity of your own body. This process of transferring the mental to the physical is guided by sensations. Stanislavsky offers both a heuristic and a creative means by which the actor discovers and solves problems the better to create characters.

Discussion of imagination takes us to the concept of image, a central term for both Bakhtin and Stanislavsky and one which highlights fundamental differences between their approaches. Stanislavsky began by copying the look or gestures of an actor as he imagined they would play or had played a role. Later he asked his actors to create mental images of their characters and actions. Put another way, he began with an image of himself as a certain kind of actor: he internalised the available *emploi* of the heroic lead, 'the operatic baritone in Parisian boots with a sword', a swaggering figure sure to impress young females in the audience. His journey from these external images to a more internal approach is echoed in the historical account of the touring actor Barnay, who was persuaded by Chronegk to leave his high boots and sword – the traditional accoutrements of a romantic hero – and try a more historically authentic costume. In this instance he and Barnay were being asked to let go of their fixed mental images of themselves as actors because this was preventing them from experiencing the characters they were playing. Stanislavsky argues that these images do not result in artistic acting because they are fixed like stencils, and prevent the physical embodiment being experienced as a felt state. In his later Method of Physical Actions he argued that the actor needed to see the unfolding of their role as a series of images of action, like the spooling forward of a film. The image is not of someone else acting the role but of themselves, and the mental process of imaging is an integral part of the actor's work on their role. These images are very different to those of Bakhtin. Through his career Stanislavsky worked towards a means by which actors can imagine themselves in their roles; in other words, an aesthetically productive kind of self-imaging. This flatly contradicts Bakhtin's claim that one cannot create an image of oneself. The actor's experiential resources – their memories of past actions – inform both present and future actions; that is how to plan the score of a role in rehearsal and how to monitor an actual performance. The actor's body is a living sculptural medium which is shaped and guided by the actor's proprioceptive sense of themselves.

Finally this chapter reflected on how both men considered psychology. Bakhtin rejects 'psychology' precisely because it studies hypothetical 'subjects' rather than actual people (not that his own theory ever examines actual people). He used a very structured phenomenological description to disclose the nature of mental life as it was actually lived. Stanislavsky was open to any means which might help him understand the processes by which he could experience and embody characters. He drew upon the literary 'psychology' of character as well as a wide range of scientific psychologists. For all that, there was an anti-cognitive bias in both men, who argue against abstract thinking and for feeling and experiencing: meaning is generated in the body in a specific situation. But we also saw how Soviet psychology was becoming increasingly politicised, and how this informed a very tendentious version of Stanislavsky's Method of Physical Actions. It is one thing to say that emotion is connected to movement, quite another to assert that such and such a movement will generate such and such an emotion through a reflex reaction. Reflex conditioning reduces human behaviour to little more than a programmed, mechanical response to the outside environment – a very far cry from the mysterious process of which Stanislavsky wrote. From the beginning to the end of his career Stanislavsky realised that there are no easy recipes for creating a convincing emotion – what worked yesterday may not work today. His desire to have an objective psychology based upon observable material processes explains why Stanislavsky's references to the subconscious, the soul or to yoga would all be unacceptable to the Soviet authorities. The reciprocal functions of the psychical and physical that he had proposed throughout his teaching were sundered by two opposing ideologies: emotional memory being enshrined in Lee Strasberg's Method in the United States, and physical action being the basis of acting in the Soviet Union, both rejecting the psycho-physical approach of yoga.

Notes

1 Holquist (1990a) xv.
2 Clark and Holquist (1984) 304.
3 *Hero* 22–23.
4 *Hero* 18, 23, 38.
5 *Hero* 25.
6 *Hero* 28.
7 *Hero* 46.
8 *Hero* 123.
9 *Hero* 127.
10 *Hero* 100.
11 *Hero* 36.
12 *Hero* 49.
13 *Hero* 50.
14 *Hero* 50.
15 *Hero* 51.
16 *Hero* 54.
17 *Hero* 136.
18 *Hero* 28.
19 *Hero* 49.
20 *Hero* 32–34.
21 *Hero* 32.
22 *Hero* 30.
23 *Hero* 52.
24 *Hero* 52.
25 *Hero* 53.
26 *Hero* 54.
27 *Work* 93.
28 *Work* 132.
29 *Work* 123.
30 Benedetti (2008) xxv.
31 *Work* 123.
32 *Work* 292.
33 *Life* (2008) 101.
34 *Life* (2008) 100.
35 *Work* 120.
36 *Work* 131.
37 *Work* 38.

38 *Work* 39.
39 *Work* 129–130.
40 *Work* 599.
41 *Work* 330.
42 *Life* (2008) 103.
43 *Life* (2008) 104.
44 *Life* (2008) 35–36.
45 *Life* (2008) 36.
46 Benedetti (1988) 53.
47 *Life* (1967) 276.
48 *Life* (1967) 292.
49 *Life* (1967) 301.
50 *Role* 115.
51 *Role* 116.
52 *Life* (1967) 313–314.
53 *Life* (2008) 248.
54 *Life* (2008) 243.
55 *Life* (2008) 243.
56 *Work* 25.
57 *Work* 26.
58 Torpokov (1999) 156.
59 Torpokov (1999) 161.
60 Torpokov (1999) 202.
61 Torpokov (1999) 129.
62 Torpokov (1999) 143.
63 *Work* 74.
64 *Hero* 62.
65 *Hero* 114.
66 Benedetti (2008) xvii.
67 Gordon (1987) 31.
68 Benedetti (2008) xvii.
69 In Smeliansky (2008) 689.
70 Boleslavsky (2003) 29.
71 Boleslavsky (2003) 31.
72 Boleslavsky (2003) 34.
73 Boleslavsky (2003) 35.
74 Whyman (2008) 53.
75 In Whyman (2008) 56.
76 Whyman (2008) 53.
77 *Work* xxiv.
78 *Work* xxv–xxvi.
79 *Work* xxvi.
80 *Work* 329.
81 *Work* 337.
82 Stanislavsky (1980) 174.
83 *Work* 404.
84 *Role* 165.
85 *Role* 164.
86 *Role* 259.
87 *Role* 164.
88 Benedetti (2008) xxiv.
89 Stanislavsky (1980) 175.
90 *Work* 128.
91 Gordon (1987) 208.

92 Carnicke (1998) 148.
93 Carnicke (1998) 150.
94 *Hero* 91.
95 *Work* 472–473.
96 Sheets-Johnstone (2011) 119.

4   Authoring a character

This chapter is about how Bakhtin and Stanislavsky describe the creation of a character, and how they define this phenomenon. We return to the figures of *I* and *other* and see how they transform into author and hero. The central argument will be about how Bakhtin and Stanislavsky figure the roles of empathy and identification in their accounts of authorship. Although they might seem at opposite poles, a close reading of Stanislavsky reveals that their positions are not so far apart. In the course of my argument other questions will be answered: firstly, who authors the character in theatre – the writer, the director, the actor or the audience? We will return to the theme of the image (*obraz*) and ask in the context of character what does an image consist of? Related to this is the question, what is a character?

I and *other* become author and hero

We have already discussed the absolute need of *I* for the *other*, but how does this relate to the process of authorship? Can the solidary relationship of *I* and *other* be considered independently from that of author and hero? Another way of framing this problem is to ask whether the *other* is in fact the form in which we see the rest of humanity – as possible heroes – and by means of which we can understand ourselves as members of a speaking community. Bakhtin explains that 'it is about the other that all the stories have been composed, all the books have been written, all the tears have been shed', and concludes 'it is only others who are known, remembered, and recreated by productive memory, so that my own memory, of objects, of the world, and of life could also become an artistic memory.'[1] It seems Bakhtin is arguing that the *other* is the form in which a living person's life can 'become an artistic memory'. He argues that it is only 'the other's seeing' which is capable of producing an *I*'s 'outwardly finished personality. This outward personality could not exist, if the other did not create it: aesthetic memory is *productive* – it gives birth, for the first time, to the *outward* human being on a new plane of being'.[2] Echoing Hannah Arendt's comment that a hero is 'someone about whom a story can be told', Bakhtin argues that stories can 'exist only around a given human being as a hero'.[3,4]

Whether Bakhtin is writing about an interpersonal dialogue or the literary creation of a hero is complicated by the fact that he uses the words 'seeing' and 'image' for both. This would seem to conflate the visual image that is *given* to the *other* and the verbal image of the hero *created* by the author in response to seeing the *I*. The hero is already a complete image – a given – simply because an author (the authorial eye) can see him or her from the outside. But surely this is only a point of departure for the creative work ahead in which the author will give artistic form to the literary image of the hero? At one point Bakhtin writes that '[t]he excess of my seeing is the bud in which slumbers form, and whence form unfolds like a blossom'.[5] At another it is the author 'seeing the hero that engenders the hero as a determinate whole'.[6] What (or who) is the author seeing? Is it the person who will be transformed into a hero or the person *as* that hero? Bakhtin argues that

> [t]he author-*artist finds* the hero as already given *prior* to and apart from his own purely artistic act: he cannot engender the hero out of himself – such a hero would be unconvincing.
>
> Of course, the hero we mean is the *possible* hero, that is, the one that has not yet become a hero, has not yet been shaped aesthetically, for the hero of a *work* is already invested in an artistically valid form, that is, we mean the givenness of a human being as *another*. It is this givenness of the *other* that the author-artist finds prior to his own artistic act and it is only in relation to this givenness that his act of aesthetic consummation acquires axiological weight.[7]

To summarise the above: the hero who is 'given' to the author is and has to be *there already* since the author cannot create 'the hero out of himself' because the result would be 'unconvincing'. It is as if 'given' means 'given to the other's sight'. This categorical assertion reminds us of Bakhtin's earlier claim that self-portraits are unpersuasive because they do not involve another person's evaluative and aesthetic seeing. Bakhtin's insistence upon this seeing of a necessarily present person who then becomes transformed into a hero suggests that we are dealing more with an interpersonal dialogue that contains an aesthetic dimension than a theory of literary creation. As will be noticed in his later writings, Bakhtin's interest covers a zone that is between literary analysis, interpersonal dialogue and philosophy. Having made that caveat we now turn to Bakhtin's theory of authorship.

Bakhtin describes the creation of a character as a three-stage process: it begins with the recognition of someone with whom one sympathises. This point of connection impels one to engage further with that person by empathetically putting oneself in their place. In order to create a character based on this person, Bakhtin argues that one has to return to one's own place where the process of selection and the ordering of relevant features of that character can begin. After this brief overview, let us examine each of the steps in a little more detail. The first is recognising a person to whom the author wants to reach out. One could call this the sympathetic stage:

> In order that we should start co-experiencing with someone, he must first become sympathetic for us, for we do not co-experience with an unsympathetic object, we do not enter into it, but, on the contrary, we push it away, we draw away from it.[8]

It is this sense of fellow-feeling with the hero that motivates the author to enter into the risk-fraught process of aesthetic creation:

> The author sees and wants in the hero and for the hero only that which the hero saw and wanted in himself and for himself in his own life. [...] What the hero believes in, the author believes in as well; what the hero regards as good, the author also regards as good.[9]

There are two motivations for creating a hero: this particular agreement with the person-to-become-hero's beliefs and secondly a more general sympathy for the unfinished nature of a human being, that 'same insanity of not coinciding (in principle) with himself, the same unconsummatedness of life'.[10]

The second stage in the process is the moment of empathy:

> I must empathise or project myself into this other human being, see his world axiologically from within it as *he* sees this world, I must put myself in his place, and then 'fill in' his horizon through that excess of seeing which opens out from this, my own, place outside him.[11]

Bakhtin's description of the second stage of aesthetic creation, empathetic projection into the other person, is telling. It is about seeing the world through the *other*'s eyes, grasping what that person values. Bakhtin is categorical that such a transposition can take place even if he cannot explain *how*, '[b]ut there can be no doubt that phenomenologically, co-experiencing of another being's inner life does occur, whatever the unconscious technique of its actualisation might be'.[12] Both he and Stanislavsky take empathy or co-experiencing as such a self-evident faculty that neither man questions how it comes about. In the extract above Bakhtin has described the entire process of authorship in terms of seeing; firstly the author sees the world through the hero's eyes, and then having returned to his or her 'place outside him' it is possible to offer a wider view of the hero thanks to this perspectival 'excess of seeing'. Only once an author has returned to his or her own place can they attribute meaning to what has been experienced: 'only from this place can the material derived from my projecting myself into the other be rendered meaningful ethically, cognitively, or aesthetically [...].'[13] This is the third stage of the process.

Brian Poole explains that Bakhtin's three-part aesthetic theory was adapted from the philosopher Nicolai Hartmann (1882–1950) who argued that while it was possible to put ourselves in someone else's place, to co-experience with them, it was only possible to *understand* the other person's experiences once we have returned to the circle of our own thought. Poole explains:

> [In Hartmann's language] The subject thus cannot 'grip' the object without leaving itself (transcending itself); but it cannot be conscious of what has been grasped without being back again in its own sphere. Thus the cognitive function may be represented in a tripartite act: as a *going outside*, a *being outside the self* and *a return* of the subject to itself.[14]

The question is a balancing between feeling and cognition, a balance to which Bakhtin was most sensitive. Poole points out the critical importance of this 'return' to the subject's own place, adding that 'distance is an integral part of the author's design, for it alone guarantees genuine objectivity in the representation of a character'.[15] Returning to the visual theme, one could call this a perspectival distance. Bakhtin expresses the author's *return* thus:

> Aesthetic activity proper actually begins at the point when we *return* into ourselves, when we *return* to our own place outside the suffering person, and start to form and consummate the material we derived from projecting ourselves into the other and experiencing him from within himself.[16]

Bakhtin is emphatic (the italics are his) that it is neither possible – at least for genuine and convincing aesthetic creation – nor desirable to create a character while still being in a state of empathetic projection. This is a reformulation of Diderot's paradox: whether true acting consists of merging with or maintaining a distance from the character. The rest of this chapter will explore the consequences of Bakhtin's insistence on the 'return' to our own place.

First we will consider the quite similar terms that Bakhtin and Stanislavsky use to describe the process of empathising. The difference occurs when we explore what happens when one does not make this return to one's own place and continues to be in a state of empathetic engagement – what Bakhtin calls 'playing' at being the other person. Stanislavsky also uses the word 'playing' and it has similarly negative associations. For Bakhtin the opposite of playing is aesthetic seeing, for Stanislavsky it is being. Does Stanislavsky's insistence on 'being' the character bring him into direct opposition with Bakhtin? Next we turn to what the author does having returned to his or her place – the aesthetic activity of creating a character, which Bakhtin describes as a process of creating an image. This in turn opens the question of how Stanislavsky describes the creation of a character.

Being, playing and imaging

Empathy is central to both Bakhtin's and Stanislavsky's conception of authorship, and yet neither question how it is achieved. When thinking of Bakhtin's conception of empathy we should recall the situation of two people sitting opposite looking at each other – the exchange is purely visual. It is as if he argues that just by looking at another person I can thereby know what they are feeling. He doesn't explain how it is that information can be picked up from someone who is not moving. Bakhtin uses the Russian word *vzhivanie* (literally, 'living into') to describe how one person 'enters into' the life of the other in order to experience it from the inside. *Vzhivanie* is most probably a literal translation of the German term *einfülung* (literally 'feeling into') coined by philosopher Theodor Lipps (1851–1914) and translated into English as 'empathy'.[17] Lipps states that '[o]ne empathises when one puts oneself in the place of – and even to some extent imitates – someone or something else.'[18]

Vzhivanie shares the same root verb – *zhit'* ('to live') – as *perezhivanie* (literally, 'to live through'), the term that Stanislavsky uses to describe how the actor can experience the life of the character. Where Bakhtin (and Lipps) describe a moment in which one consciousness 'enters' (or more accurately, imagines what it is like to be) another's, Stanislavsky seems to suggest a more sustained 'living through' of the character. This opens the question as to the duration and the function of empathy in the creation of a character.

Bakhtin argues that an author who continues to identify with the hero runs the risk of *playing at* being that hero, joining in the hero's life, rather than standing back and *authoring* a hero. Bakhtin has already noted that the author believes in what the person-to-become-hero believes in, thus this 'playing at' is not an aping of that person, but a taking on, even a taking over of their ethical mission in the world. It is a case of over-identification rather than mimicry. But in the use of the word 'play' his argument starts to sound like Stanislavsky's, especially since he explicitly uses the figure of the actor to make his point when he describes someone playing at being the hero.

> All I can do in it [the other's life] is play a role, i.e., assume, like a mask, the flesh of another – of someone deceased. But the aesthetic answerability of the actor and the whole human being for the appropriateness of the role played remains in actual life, for the playing of a role as a whole is an answerable deed performed by *the one playing*, and not the one represented, i.e., the hero.[19]

Elsewhere he poses the rhetorical question: 'And what would I myself gain by the other's merging with me?' His answer is that the author 'would merely repeat in himself' what he had experienced in the other.[20] It is a duplication of the other person's actions rather than an aesthetic image of them. The aesthetic process has to be lifted out of the purpose-driven ethical negotiations between these two people, otherwise their exchange will begin 'to degenerate into self-interested disputations in which the centre of value is located in the problems debated'.[21] Again we come back to the question of meaning: Bakhtin's interest is not in the ethical content, the sociological or psychological facts of the hero's activities, but in the aesthetic image that the author creates of them. He argues that sociological and psychological analyses 'lack a sufficiently deepened form-aesthetic understanding of the fundamental creative principle in the author-hero relationship'.[22] His aim is to offer up an aesthetic image of a loved and valued human being. Only an *other* 'is capable of constituting the axiological center of artistic vision and, consequently, the hero of a work of art'.[23]

Bakhtin offers a critique of the actor based on his theory of authorship. An actor is an author depending on the degree to which

> he produces and shapes *from outside* the image of the hero into whom he will later "reincarnate" himself, that is, when he creates the hero as a distinct whole and creates this whole not in isolation, but as a constituent in the

> whole of a drama. In other words, the actor is aesthetically creative only
> when he is an author – or to be exact: a co-author, a stage director, and an
> active spectator of the portrayed hero and of the whole play […].[24]

The critical part of this argument is in the last two lines where he admits 'to be
exact' that the actor is a 'co-author, a stage director and an active spectator of the
portrayed hero'. Later in this chapter we will examine who exactly it is that
authors the character in theatre.

Not only the actor but also the spectator has to refrain from sustained empathy
with the character. For a response to be aesthetic the spectator must maintain 'his
place *outside* and *over against* the imaged life event of the dramatic personae',
otherwise he 'experiences the life of one of the characters inside and from inside
that character – seeing the stage through his eyes, hearing other *dramatis personae*
through his ears, co-experiencing all his actors from within him'.[25] Bakhtin
here conflates and thus confuses the actor's experience with that of the character, for
it is the *actor* who sees the staging and hears the other actors, and the *character* who
lives in the world and the time being represented: he has conflated the actual and
the virtual stage which were described in Chapter 2. In any case, the spectator
would be more likely to identify with the world being represented rather than the
theatrical means of representation. Nonetheless his argument does look forward
to Brecht's concept of *Verfremdung* which also warns both the actor and the spectator
against losing themselves in the stage action.

The argument as so often centres upon the creation of images: early and late
Bakhtin insists that aesthetic work results in an image of something.

> Play *images* nothing – it merely imagines. […] it is only in art that life is
> *imaged forth*, whereas in play it is imagined […] this *imagined* life becomes an
> image of life only in the active and creative contemplation of a spectator.
> [Play] is not an active aesthetic relationship to life.[26]

Note 8 in *Author and Hero* explains that '"Image" should be understood here and
throughout in the sense of a plastic (sculptural) as well as pictorial configuration or
figure'. Although the meaning of the word 'image' will change throughout Bakhtin's
career (in *Discourse*, he writes about 'images' of other languages) the concept of
image is central in his aesthetic thinking as being the form in which we present
the *other* both to ourselves and to others (in literature, painting and sculpture). The
Russian word *obraz* means, variously, 'shape, appearance, image (literary), type,
figure (literary), mode, manner' with a secondary meaning of 'icon'.[27] 'Imaging-
forth' is a translation of *obrazovanie* which has the meanings of 'representation' and
'education'. An image (like a hero) is the result of aesthetic action and is positive
whereas imagining or day-dreaming is negative, the equivalent of playing the
fool. Bakhtin argues that it is because an image is presented to *others* that image-
making becomes *aesthetic*: 'what radically distinguishes play from art is the absence
in principle of spectator and author.'[28]

Bakhtin takes the example of a child playing which was discussed in Chapter 1:

Playing begins really to approach art – namely, dramatic action – only when a new, non-participating participant makes his appearance, namely a spectator who begins to admire the children's playing from the standpoint of the whole event of a life represented by their playing, a spectator who contemplates this life event in an aesthetically active manner and, in part, *creates* it (as an aesthetically valid whole, by transposing it to a new plane – the aesthetic plane).[29]

In this passage Bakhtin confuses two fundamentally different types of 'playing'. In an actor's playing there is an aesthetic intention; it is a performance that has been rehearsed with an audience in mind. A person watching a child playing sees in the beauty and carefreeness of that play an image. Stanislavsky makes another point again when he criticises an actor for playing: by this he means they are deploying aesthetic effects rather than acting truthfully. In the use of this one word 'play' there are three very distinct meanings. Bakhtin distinguishes between playing and imaging, Stanislavsky between playing and truthful acting, or living the part.

Now to turn to Stanislavsky's term *perezhivanie*, which in Chapter 5 of Sharon Carnicke's *Stanislavsky in Focus* is called 'Stanislavsky's Lost Term' and 'invokes the experiential nature of acting' and results in actors being 'fully present on stage'.[30]

This elusive, subjective concept serves a highly practical function within the System. It gives actors a way to evaluate their work in an art form which precludes the artist from seeing objectively his or her own creation. Actors, after all, literally cannot watch themselves while they perform; even film denies the actor this experience during the process of working.[31]

The first thing to note about the above passage is that, while Stanislavsky may be drawing on theory, it is in the service of a practical endeavour: to find the best means by which an actor can act truthfully. Secondly, where Bakhtin's theory is very much about seeing, Stanislavsky acknowledges that the actor cannot see him- or herself, and therefore needs to rely on feeling and experiencing (and the outside eye of the director).

Perezhivanie is the actor's means of being aware of what they are doing. Stanislavsky argues repeatedly that in the field of acting, knowing is feeling: 'It is no accident that in our terminology "to know" means "to feel". The desired result is not achieved by cold, intellectual analysis but by the workings of creative nature.'[32] Later he develops this argument by adding: 'Artistic analysis is, above all, the analysis of feelings conducted by feeling.'[33] Ivan Lapshin (1870–1952), a philosopher-friend of Stanislavsky's, develops the theme:

Stanislavsky demonstrated it is possible to train oneself in the 'art of *experiencing*' and to 'get accustomed to a role' so that it is possible to perform it in a 'much more lifelike way thanks to the actor's constant experimentation on him/herself, and getting into the feelings of (*vchuvstvovanie*) the role'.[34]

Vchuvstvovanie – literally, 'to feel into' – is such a useful word to describe how an actor can get into the feeling-state of a character. But how does an actor truthfully embody a character over successive performances? Stanislavsky argues that experiencing is a means of repeatedly realising a character and keeping it alive in each performance: Carnicke quotes an unpublished manuscript where she notes that 'it is necessary to experience the role, that is, to have the sensation (*obschushchat*) of its feelings, every time and on every repetition of creativity'.[35] While Bakhtin wrote of finished moments of artistic creation, Stanislavsky was describing a continuing process. All these terms (living, feeling, sensing) very literally give flesh to this concrete engagement in the life of the character. 'In a word, you must make sure you do not approach a new role in the abstract, as to a third person, but concretely, as to yourself, your own life.'[36] Stanislavsky advises that it is essential to 'define, that is, feel what you, as a human being, would do in real life if you found yourself in the character's situation, given circumstances. You will be guided by your own human feelings, your own life-experience.'[37] When describing his portrayal of Old Uncle in his adaptation of Dostoevsky's *The Village of Stepanchikovo* he uses the word 'become':

> In a word, I became him for the duration of the play. To try to understand the magic of that word for the actor, *become*, Gogol said that any second-rate actor can 'play at and capture the walk, the movements' and give 'flesh and clothing' to a character, but only someone of genuine talent can 'capture the very heart of a role, *become* the character. If that is so, it means I have talent, because in that role I *became* Old Uncle whereas I more or less "played at" other roles, copied, mimicked other people's or my own versions'.[38]

It is the familiar opposition between creating a character through external imitation (drawn from outside observation) and a more internal process of becoming or being the character.

Although it appears that there is some considerable distance between Bakhtin and Stanislavsky, both men are opposed to the idea of the actor playing at being another person. Stanislavsky demands a much closer level of identification. The actor is being asked not to imitate a role in the third person, but to experience it in the first person.

> As yourself you experience a role, as someone else you imitate it. As yourself, you understand the role with your intelligence, wants, and all the elements of your mind, but as someone else, in the majority of cases, only with your intelligence. We do not need exclusively rational analysis and understanding.[39]

Does this mean that there is a complete identification with the character? In several passages Stanislavsky argued that the actor had to merge with the character.

When playing Stockman in Ibsen's *An Enemy of the People*, 'Stockman's mind and body and Stanislavski's mind and body came together as one being'.[40] Stanislavsky used the Russian word *sliianie* (meaning fusion or merging) and his literary amanuensis Lybova Gurevich added that 'the main attraction and quality of art is in such *fusion* with others', adding that this too was 'a Tolstoyan concept'.[41] Benedetti's translation of *An Actor's Work* also uses the word 'merging': 'Understand that you must behave like the character in the given circumstances and according to his social standing. We call this merging with the role *the sense of oneself in the role and the role in oneself*.'[42] Clearly, this merging or co-experiencing distinguishes truthful acting from external imitation. Towards the end of this chapter I shall argue that Stanislavsky does have a notion about aesthetic distance between the actor and the role, but in the meantime we return to the aesthetic activity that Bakhtin describes when the author has returned to his or her place.

Creating the image of the character

Whyman comments on how Stanislavsky's successors considered character as an image, which was 'a central concept in Chekhov's method'. She notes that

> Michael Chekhov's ideas on archetype and the mask of the character no doubt emerged from the same theatrical experimentation as those of Meyerhold; like Vakhtangov and Chekhov, Meyerhold uses the term image (*obraz*) rather than character, and in Russian particularly image has wider connotations.[43]

This is obviously a theme that will be pursued more fully when we address Meyerhold, but it does open out the debate as to the nature of the image that Bakhtin and these post-Stanislavskian producers are writing about.

Bakhtin argues that the establishment of the author's own attitude towards the hero is essential to the creation of an aesthetically effective image – but it is hard-won and involves an internal struggle within the author. Bakhtin warns that at first 'the hero is going to exhibit a great many grimaces, random masks, wrong gestures, and unexpected actions' and this is because of the shifts in the author's attitudes towards the hero. He continues,

> [i]n order to see the true and integral countenance of someone close to us, someone we apparently know very well – think how many masking layers must first be removed from his face, layers that were sedimented upon his face by our own fortuitous reactions and attitudes and by fortuitous life situations. The artist's struggle to achieve a determinate and stable image of the hero is to a considerable extent a struggle with himself.[44]

In this passage we see a subtlety of interpersonal engagement that is rare in Bakhtin. He observes that very often our relations with another are overlaid ('masked') by 'fortuitous reactions and attitudes' that come from our everyday, purpose-driven reactions. Aesthetic imaging demands a finer level of seeing.

The work of the author can be detected in the selection of 'meaning-bearing features'.[45] As ever, authorship is about selection – finding the features that will most effectively convey an image of the *other*. This is an axiologically driven choice: 'What the other rightfully negates in himself, I rightfully affirm and preserve in him, and, in so doing, I give birth to his soul on a new axiological plane of being.'[46] Another way of putting this is that there will be some ingredients of the hero's image that the real person would not recognise as being important, or of which he or she might not even be aware. Bakhtin invents the term 'transgredient' to describe such elements that are evident to the outside, creating consciousness but not to the person being observed. Translator Vadim Liapunov explains that while *ingredients* are immanent constituents of consciousness, *transgredient* elements 'are external to it but nonetheless absolutely necessary for its completion, for its achievement of totalisation'.[47] Bakhtin explains the term as follows: one can detect the work of the author through singling 'out all those moments or constituent features which bring about the consummation of the hero and the event of his life and which are in principle transgredient to his consciousness'.[48] He goes on to explain that notions of value, of 'determinations that possess aesthetic validity are transgredient to lived life itself' and have to be supplied by the author.[49] The actor is not creative when he 'experiences the hero's life as his own life', that is, 'when his consciousness includes nothing that would be transgredient to the consciousness of the hero he is playing. […] the actor is aesthetically creative only when he is an author'.[50]

Although Bakhtin writes of the necessity for the 'outsideness' of the author, this in no way indicates an emotional distance from the hero. He insists that as authors

> we must vividly feel the presence of that possible human consciousness to which these moments are transgredient and which they cherish and bring to consummation […] we must vividly feel *another* consciousness – the consciousness upon which our creative self-activity is directed as upon an *other* consciousness.[51]

In other words, all the work of aesthetic activity is to render this other consciousness alive (that very liveness that Stanislavsky uses as the measure of truthful acting). The author achieves something that 'is impossible for me in myself, namely: the axiological affirmation and acceptance of another's interior being'.[52] Once again there is a connection with Stanislavsky, who is also interested in the interior life of the character. The author declares of his hero: 'Yet for me that is not his last word […] the last, consummating word belongs to me.'[53] This explains why he describes aesthetic consciousness as 'a consciousness of a consciousness: the author's (the *I*'s) of the hero's (the *other*'s) consciousness.'[54]

The question of finishedness, of having the last word, is about the aesthetic form of time given to the hero, or what Bakhtin calls rhythm. He points to the 'essential difference in the significance of time' in the real-time experience of living, and in the representation of a life.[55] The meaning of a particular event within a person's life is contingent upon future events; not so in a finished story where it forms part of a meaningful whole. When one thing happens after another in a written story, it is the result of an artistic choice: this is entirely different to the open-endedness of real-life action where the outcome is fraught with risk and uncertainty. Just as the author's is 'a consciousness of a consciousness', so 'rhythm' is 'not an emotional-volitional reaction to an object and to meaning, but a reaction to that reaction'.[56] In other words, it isn't the hero's present-day ethical activity but the author's aesthetic response to that activity. Bakhtin describes the time of the author as being 'always later, and not just temporally later, but later in meaning'.[57] As far as the hero is concerned all the events are predetermined in a story, and thus from his perspective there is 'a certain hopelessness with respect to meaning'.[58] Bakhtin delights in these paradoxical distinctions which emphasise the difference between the created and the creator, the aesthetically passive and active, thus the hero is 'not someone who expresses, but someone who is expressed', the 'creator is free and active, the created is unfree and active'.[59,60]

None of the above discussion answers the question of whether Bakhtin's theory of authorship is about interpersonal dialogue or the process of creating a literary character. For all Bakhtin's insistence that he is describing a theory of literary creation, he admits that his interest is 'more oriented to general philosophical aesthetics' than to practical questions of fictional portrayal.[61] This could be said of many of his later writings which are a blend of literary analysis and philosophical reflection.

Who authors the character – writer, director or actor?

Stanislavsky, the playwright and the play

Stanislavsky describes the different roles of the writer, director (a relatively new figure in the history of theatre) and the actor in creating a character. The process begins with the author, with the director as a creative intermediary, and the play is finally delivered to an audience by the actors. Stanislavsky's interpretation – both as an actor and a director – of a writer's *oeuvre* and of individual works is driven by his understanding of the creative process.

> Just as a seed grows into a flower, so a writer's work grows out of an individual thought and feeling. These individual thoughts, feelings, living dreams run through the writer's life like a golden thread and guide him when he is creating. He makes them the basis of his play and from this seed he develops a work of literature.[62]

Bakhtin's use of the image of the bud describes a dialectical relation between literary form and seeing: the author's 'excess of seeing' is 'the bud in which slumbers form, and whence form unfolds like a blossom'.[63] For Stanislavsky '[t]he theatre's task is to create the inner life of the play and the role and give theatrical form to the seed, or thought that gave rise to the writer's or composer's work'.[64] Only in this way can the actor 'live the inner life of the character, behave in the way the author, the director and his own living feelings prescribe'.[65] Unlike Bakhtin, he considers form as an external shell within, behind, or beneath which lies the transcendental human meaning. Meanings are intuited through a spiritual communion rather than by reading words on a page. Stanislavsky's ability to understand the author's intentions and the nature of a character is explained by laws which 'already exist' and 'have been laid down once and for all by nature itself' and 'are obligatory for all those people, without exception, who do creative work in the theatre'.[66] The seed is more of an analogue than a metaphor: the inference being that human nature operates in the same way as processes in the natural world. Such a blurring of categories results in a prescriptive rather than descriptive account of the actor's work on the play text. At every turn we will see Stanislavsky reject the verbal form of the written script – it will be variously described as cold, lifeless, incomplete and fragmentary – in his attempts to access the meaning of the play through 'experiencing' it.

The first step in the actor's work on the play is to identify the 'creative seed' of a work, the big idea it contains, or its 'supertask'. The term comes from Gogol's notes on how to act in *The Government Inspector*. He advises that the actor should:

> observe the main, chief concern of the character, on which his life is supported, which is the constant subject of his thoughts, the eternal nail sitting in his head. Having grasped this main concern of the character, the actor must perform such that the thoughts and aspirations of the character have been assimilated by him and remain in his head continuously during the performance of the play.[67]

It is the actor's job to create a supertask 'which is analogous to the writer's thoughts but which unfailingly evokes a response in the actor's personality. That is what can evoke not formalistic, not cerebral but genuine, living, human, direct experiencing'.[68] (Note once again, his opposition between experiencing and form.)

When producing *The Lower Depths* Stanislavsky describes how '[w]e had to plumb the secret depths of Gorki's mind, as we had done with Chekhov, to find the hidden key to his psyche'. His aim was to bring the words of the play to life 'with the spirit of the author'.[69] To find answers to questions about the script he examines the writer's mind – a transcendental process. At best this has to be an intuitive process based on hints gleaned from a wide reading of Chekhov's plays and stories. However David Magarshack notes how the dialogue between Chekhov and Stanislavsky was made difficult because of his 'amazing ignorance of literature' and his 'primitive literary conceptions'.[70] According to Magarshack, Stanislavsky produced *The Seagull* in 1898 while remaining 'completely in the dark as to the meaning of the play' and utterly failing to 'understand the character of Trigorin', the role he played.[71]

Could one of these 'primitive literary conceptions' be that reading isn't a transaction with verbal material but a process of revealing a transcendent (i.e. nonverbal) content that somehow lies beneath the literary form? (According to this idea, form is a superficial layer and the truth lies beneath.) Reading is thus a kind of 'creative experiencing'.[72] In *An Actor's Work on a Role* Stanislavsky describes the importance of the first reading because it is 'the first acquaintance with the role, which is the first phase in creative work'.[73] The term 'acquaintance' is literal not metaphorical since the role is considered as a person who is to be 'met', and not a set of instructions that the actor has to interpret. Far from describing this first reading as an interpretation of verbal material, it is a meeting between two people that is frustrated by the printed word: an actor is 'given someone else's thoughts and feelings in a role which has been created by a writer and appears in cold print on the page. It is difficult to *experience* that kind of *material*.[74] Kostya complains that the literary form is not an aid but a hindrance: 'rather than helping me, the actual lines got in my way. […] Not only the words but also the author's thoughts, which were not mine, as well as the actions he indicated.'[75] This lends weight to Magarshack's argument that Stanislavsky was a poor reader of plays and could not 'distinguish between a great dramatic work and a play that merely gave him an opportunity of dazzling an audience by a pyrotechnic display of his original methods of production'.[76] In Stanislavsky's first production of *Othello* '[w]hat he wanted was not the text of the play so much as various hints in the text he could improvise on'.[77] A colleague remembers that 'Shakespeare's text was pushed into the background […] and what we heard was just Stanislavsky's version of the action of the play'.[78] An example of this is his rejection of a line in *Othello*: 'I do not in fact like the words "*Ha! false to me? To me?*" [III iii 337] because they contain a threat and there is no element of threat in his state of mind.'[79] The actor can intuit the mind of the character, and thus contradict the word of the author.

To be able to understand and then live a character as a person one has to imagine them having a mind: 'a well-written part will be as human as we are, just as we sense another human being.'[80] Getting into the mind of the character is at the heart of Stanislavsky's 'psychology'. Another feature of this psychology was his belief that there were universals of human nature. Thus, for example, Moliere's 'Tartuffe was not just Monsieur Tartuffe himself but all human Tartuffes rolled into one. He described life, events, individuals, and the result is a picture of universal human vice or passion.'[81] A theatre must look for 'the grain of eternally pure human feelings and thoughts […] and is understood by everybody in every age and in every language […] only that which can never under any circumstances lose its sense of beauty.'[82] This knowledge of the unchanging nature of human 'feelings and thoughts' constitutes an informal psychology.

Stanislavsky argues that the written script is incomplete. Tortsov asks,

> [f]or example, does the author always tell us in enough detail what happened before the play begins? Do we get an exhaustive account of what will happen after it is over, or what goes on in the wings from which the characters come and go? The dramatist is sparing with that kind of commentary.[83]

He encourages his young students to 'fill out' and 'give depth' to the characters they find on the page. Benedetti describes how Stanislavsky prepared for the role of Salieri in Pushkin's *Mozart and Salieri*.

> The result was a full biography, with every circumstance of the character's off-stage life vividly experienced. The subtext became so dense that it over-powered the text itself, which runs at most to a dozen printed pages, and it was the sub-text which Stanislavski tried to play rather than Pushkin's actual words.[84]

Benedetti's description is telling: Stanislavsky plays his own text rather than 'Pushkin's actual words'. Stanislavsky was turning the play-text into a novel in order to generate the descriptive detail that constitutes a 'fully-rounded' character, one that is psychologically convincing.

Stanislavsky's detailed *mise-en-scènes* for *The Seagull* and *Othello* have been published, and the latter reads very much like a novel in its vivid imagining of what was going on in the characters' heads at crucial moments in the play. Repeated throughout his text are phrases like 'from that he concludes' and 'from that follows', all of which seek to create a continuous line of thought, the 'psychological' through-line of a character. It is as if the realist novel provides Stanislavsky with the model for constructing a character. (As if Bakhtin and Materic were right about a character being a novelistic conception.)

The director

Stanislavsky admitted that at the beginning of his career he was a dictatorial director. He had a revolutionary vision of theatre as an art and although he believed that actors could and should be artists, at this early stage they were too inexperienced to make this vision a reality – thus they had to be told what to do. Being both a director and a teacher from the outset, it was clear that once his teaching started to have an effect then so his directing could become less dictatorial. Stanislavsky describes his approach to producing *The Seagull* (1898):

> I genuinely thought at the time that it was possible to tell someone else what to live and feel. I gave directions to everyone at every moment of the action, and they were binding. I wrote everything down in my plan, how, where, in what sense the role and the writer's stage directions were to be understood, what kind of voice to use, how to move, what to do, how to do a move across and where. I made special little sketches for every entrance, exit, move, etc., sets, costumes, make-up, mannerisms, way of walking, the behaviour and personal habits of the characters were all described, etc., etc.[85]

This is borne out by his detailed production notes. Rather than letting the actors find their characters through given actions or tasks, he wrote down the actions they had to perform in order to convey the emotion of the character. Note 17 on a scene from Act I between Sorin and Konstantin reads: 'In disgust, slaps his leg nervously, gets up and bends over Sorin, trying to convince him. Even beats his breast in his agitation.' Other actions include smoking and 'tearing off blades of grass – nervously'.[86] Their positions and moves on stage are indicated in small drawings. The actor is simply being told what to do and where to move – they are left with no creative autonomy at all.

Stanislavsky's early attitude towards direction was characterised by mistrust of his inexperienced actors and of playscripts which he regarded as 'incomplete'. And yet he is supremely confident in his ability to divine the spirit of an author or of a character in their works. However we have also seen a number of figures (from Chekhov and Meyerhold to Magarshack and Benedetti) voice their reservations about Stanislavsky's competence to interpret a play. Stanislavsky's confidence rests in his belief that the meaning of a text lies beneath the verbal surface; he can feel the characters in a play or novel because they are real presences within the text. There is no textual exegesis: his interpretation is based on his belief in being able to experience the character behind (in spite of) the words.

The 'double life' in Bakhtin and Stanislavsky's theory

Carnicke stated above that experiencing allows the actor to 'evaluate' their performance, and Whyman makes the same point that actors can '*experience* and observe themselves at the same time'.[87] Although this capacity for reflection isn't explained – in some way it must be to do with proprioceptive feedback from one's actions – it is critical to an argument about how an actor can be both emotionally involved in a performance and at the same time aware of its features. Stanislavsky quotes his hero, the Italian actor Tomasso Salvini, on an actor's faculty for observing their own performance: 'The actor loves, weeps, laughs onstage but weeping or laughing he observes his laughter and tears. And it is in that double life, that balance between life and the role that art lies.'[88] Stanislavsky himself noted how an actor when in the correct creative state 'has no difficulty in splitting himself in two, i.e. on the one hand he corrects something which is wrong and, on the other, continues to live his role'.[89] So while there was a discussion of the actor merging with the character, Carnicke also points out that this can also be interpreted as a doubling: 'He uses hyphens to yoke the "human being" with the "actor" (*chelovek-akter*) and the "actor" with the character (*artist-rol*) typographically connecting the experience of the performing actor with that of the person and role.'[90] Two quotations make quite clear that Stanislavsky demands that the actor maintain some distance from the role:

> This does not mean that while he is on stage the actor must be subject to some kind of hallucination, that he must lose, while he is acting, the consciousness of surrounding reality, accept the canvas as real trees, etc. On the contrary, a part of his consciousness must remain free from the trammels of the play in order that it exercise some supervision over whatever he is feeling and doing as he plays out the part of his character.[91]

The crucial part of the argument is that a part of the actor's 'consciousness must remain free' to 'exercise some supervision over whatever he is feeling and doing'. Another example of this double consciousness is when Stanislavsky was acting Stockman and had to draw on 'my double, the actor and stage director that resided in me', because

> I wanted all the more to say my speech as sincerely as it was given me so that the spectator might be more excited than he was, that he might be all the angrier at Stockman and love Stockman all the more for his childlike truthfulness.[92]

A degree of outside-ness is necessary since a total identification would be aesthetically (and psychologically) catastrophic for both actor and audience. Stanislavsky points out that the actor must not break down physically when conveying powerful emotions – this should be left to the audience such that 'the spectator is more upset than the artist and the artist preserves his powers to direct them where he most needs them to convey *the life of the human spirit*'.[93]

This returns us to the double time and space that was discussed in Chapter 2. While the actor-as-character must live in the virtual time of the story, the actor-as-performer must live in the actual time of the performance. Stanislavsky analyses this interplay between these two timeframes in Chapter 20 of *An Actor's Work*, 'Perspective of the Actor and the Role'.

> The character knows nothing about perspective, or his future, while the artist must always have it in view, that he must bear in mind the perspective. [...] Hamlet must not know his fate and the end of his life, but the artist must see the whole perspective the whole time, otherwise he will not be able to order, colour, shade and shape the different parts.[94]

To express this in Bakhtinian terms the actor maintains a double perspective, both *I-as-character* and *other-as-author*. He relates rhythm to this 'doubleness' of the artistic image; rhythm is 'not an emotional-volitional reaction to an object and to meaning, but a reaction to that reaction'.[95] It is not an ethical purpose-driven primary reaction to the world, but a secondary aesthetic reaction to that reaction. To develop Stanislavsky's thought above: an actor playing Hamlet must decide how he will play Hamlet's 'emotional-volitional reaction' to his father's death and his mother's over-swift re-marriage. Stanislavsky gives another example of an actor's performance plan for playing the role of Othello:

> the artist must remember that he has to play many similar, ever mounting moments of passion right through to the end of the play. It is dangerous to play the first scene too intensively, and not hold back for his growing jealousy. Wasting mental energy ruins the entire plan for the role. We need to be economical and sparing and never forget the climax of the play. Artistic emotion is measured in ounces not in pounds.[96]

The actor's decisions about how to pitch the emotional arc of Hamlet or Othello is what Bakhtin means by a 'reaction to a reaction'. It is the actor/author's aesthetic reaction to the character's reaction to an event in the world of the play. Bakhtin explains that 'the author-contemplator always encompasses the whole temporally, that is, he is always later, and not just temporally later, but later in meaning'.[97] Once again, the distance is necessary for the author-contemplator to understand what they have experienced. The time of the author and actor is a time in which they make sense of the life of the character. However there is a substantial difference between the time schemas of Bakhtin and Stanislavsky: the first is structured in order to create a final, finalised meaning for the hero's actions; the second is about the organisation or patterning of an event that unfolds in real time and will be repeated in many subsequent performances. It is the difference between creating a finished image of a hero, and a means by which an actor can embody a character through movement and speech. While Bakhtin is writing about embodiment in a figurative sense, Stanislavsky is writing about the work of a living body.

In his early philosophy Bakhtin's 'double' time consists of the contingent time of the living person-who-will-be-hero and the finished time of the image of the hero's life. He has not yet included the reader as that interpretative and therefore dynamic figure who will carry on the meaning of a work into areas unthought of by the author. This will come in his writings about the novel in the 1930s. Bakhtin's seemingly poor grasp of stage production means that he would not recognise that an actor has to be doubly creative: firstly in bringing a character to life in rehearsal, then in sustaining that life throughout each successive performance.

Conclusion: image and human being

Although Bakhtin and Stanislavsky might disagree as to why and how one creates a character, both agree on the importance of the notion of character itself. And there are other points of agreement: that the process is about a dialogue between the actor/author and the character, and that it is 'a struggle with himself'; that truth of the characterisation lies in its being rooted in reality rather than fiction (and therefore there is little role for the imagination); and, as a corollary to this last point, that empathy has a central role in creating a character. Meaning and value are experienced through the vehicle of a character, are focused on particular (images of) human beings, and this embodied truth has an immediacy that is lacking in general meanings arrived at through thinking.

One difference in their approaches lies in their points of departure. Bakhtin's is a theory of authoring rather than authorship. Authoring is about the relationship between *I* and *other* where one person authors another as a hero and thus redeems them from the contingency of everyday life. Bakhtin is concerned to create an image which in its totality renders a person's life intelligible. He insists that '[o]nce you annihilate the moment constituted by the life of a mortal human being, the axiological light of all rhythmic and formal moments will be extinguished'.[98] This living moment is probably to do with the ethical quest of the hero – that which motivates him or her. Stanislavsky described the actor's work as the 'creation of the life of the human spirit in a role and the communication of that life onstage in an artistic form'.[99] The end of the actor's work is the creation of what Bakhtin calls 'the life of a mortal being'. There is a cross-wise movement in both men's approach to character: Bakhtin begins with a living being and ends with a verbal image of a hero; Stanislavsky begins with a verbal image of a role and ends with a human being. Both theories include a living moment: for Bakhtin it is that past 'life of a mortal being', for Stanislavsky it is in the present moment of embodying 'that life onstage'. Stanislavsky's character is a construct that unfolds over time, while Bakhtin's is protected from any temporal contingency. There are other differences, the first of which lies in why they wrote their books. Bakhtin's was an attempt at creating a phenomenological philosophy focused upon ways of accounting for the meaning of living experience. Stanislavsky was trying to understand how acting could be considered a legitimate art form. For Bakhtin the actor – and theatre more generally – was a source of metaphor for understanding relations between author and role.

For all that Bakhtin's primary interest was not theatre, his early writings could make a valuable contribution to our understanding of characterisation. He makes us re-examine the question of empathy in the creation of a character: to what degree is the moment of empathy separate or separable from the moment of aesthetic creation? Is (as Stanislavsky seems to suggest) empathy already a form of understanding? Both men understand the necessary difference between the time and space of the actor and the time and space of the role. Bakhtin's comments about character make us return again to the ever-productive actor's paradox.

Notes

1   *Hero* 111–112.
2   *Hero* 35–36.
3   Moran (2000) 314.
4   *Hero* 209.
5   *Hero* 24.
6   *Hero* 8.
7   *Hero* 199.
8   *Hero* 82.
9   *Hero* 163.
10   *Hero* 128.
11   *Hero* 25.
12   *Hero* 62.
13   *Hero* 26.
14   Poole in Hirschkop and Shepherd (2001) 119.
15   Poole (ibid.) 119.
16   *Hero* 26.
17   For a discussion of this term see Emerson and Morson (1990) 53, 99.
18   Bochert (2006) 363.
19   *Act* 18.
20   *Hero* 87.
21   *Hero* 74–75.
22   *Hero* 9.
23   *Hero* 188.
24   *Hero* 76.
25   *Hero* 73.
26   *Hero* 74–75.
27   Smirnitsky Russian–English Dictionary (1961).
28   *Hero* 74.
29   *Hero* 74–75.
30   Carnicke (1998) 65.
31   Carnicke (1998) 108–109.
32   *Role* 70.
33   *Role* 103.
34   In Whyman (2008) 51.

35 Carnicke (1998) 49.
36 *Role* 61.
37 *Role* 62.
38 *Life in Art* (2008) 121.
39 *Role* 53.
40 *Life in Art* (2008) 216.
41 Whyman (2008) 28.
42 *Work* 60.
43 Whyman (2008) 215.
44 *Hero* 6.
45 *Hero* 8.
46 *Hero* 129.
47 Todorov (1984) 100–101.
48 *Hero* 13.
49 *Hero* 134–135.
50 *Hero* 76.
51 *Hero* 200.
52 *Hero* 128.
53 *Hero* 128.
54 *Hero* 89.
55 *Hero* 108–109.
56 *Hero* 117.
57 *Hero* 118.
58 *Hero* 117.
59 *Hero* 84.
60 *Hero* 119.
61 *Hero* 76.
62 *Work* 306.
63 *Hero* 24.
64 *Work* 570.
65 *Work* 62.
66 *Work* 345.
67 Whyman (2008) 100.
68 *Work* 308.
69 *Life* (2008) 223.
70 Magarshack (1950) 169, 170.
71 Magarshack (1950) 181.
72 *Role* 9.
73 *Role* 6.
74 *Work* 240.
75 *Work* 8.
76 Magarshack (1950) 149.
77 Magarshack (1950) 92.
78 Magarshack (1950) 92.
79 *Role* 35.
80 *Role* 63.
81 *Life* (2008) 96–97.
82 *Life* (2008) 105–106.
83 *Work* 62.
84 Benedetti (1988) 211.
85 *Life* (2008) 176.
86 Balukhaty (1952) 147.
87 Whyman (2008) 98.
88 *Work* 302.

89 *Work* 302.
90 Carnicke (1998) 119.
91 Stanislavsky (1999) 188.
92 *Life* (1967) 406.
93 Whyman (2008) 56.
94 *Work* 459.
95 *Hero* 117.
96 *Work* 461.
97 *Hero* 118.
98 *Hero* 209.
99 *Work* 19.

Part III

Meyerhold and Grotowski

5 Meyerhold, a revolution in the stage

Introduction

The relationship between Stanislavsky and Meyerhold was based on their mutual, monomaniacal passion for theatre. The dynamic of that relationship was fuelled by their often diametrically opposed notions of theatre. In the first decade of the 1900s both directors were fascinated by Symbolism, particularly the plays of Maurice Maeterlinck, but Meyerhold's 1906 production of Alexander Blok's *Balaganchik* (*The Fairground Booth*) broke with this serious, otherworldly style. Commedia dell'Arte and clowning took the place of ethereal and static meditation. Meyerhold's fascination with Commedia dell'Arte and popular traditions of theatre lead to his post-Revolutionary productions, some of which were designed by the constructivists Liubov Popova and Varvara Stepanova. An invitation to work in the Opera Studio in 1938 meant that Meyerhold began and ended his career working with Stanislavsky. Their intense dialogue may have been driven by a passion for theatre, but it was equally fuelled by fundamental differences of philosophy, aesthetics and pedagogy. Although Stanislavsky might have embraced the 'modern' movement of Symbolism, Futurism and constructivism were beyond the pale, and while he remained apolitical after the Russian Revolution and subsequent Civil War, Meyerhold embraced leftist politics and aesthetics. Stanislavsky's ideas and project can be understood in terms of Bakhtin's early philosophy; Meyerhold's ideas resonate with the writings of Voloshinov and Medvedev in the 1920s, and Bakhtin's later writings.

Like Stanislavsky, Meyerhold was trying to elevate theatre as an art in its own right, and for him that meant distinguishing it from literature. But where Stanislavsky sought for the truth in theatre by denying its theatricality, Meyerhold embraced theatricality as the truth of theatre:

> The theatrical theatre is such that the audience does not for one moment forget that the actor it sees is acting, and the actor does not for one moment forget that he has before him a theatre, beneath his feet a stage and at his back a set.[1]

As Hoover puts it, he saw theatre as not 'merely illustrative of literature or imitative of reality'.[2] Meyerhold explores and exploits all the possibilities of theatrical signification. This in turn led to his rejection of the 'literary' tendency of MAT (an egregious example of which was Nemirovich-Danchenko's 1910 adaptation of Dostoevsky's *The Brothers Karamazov*). Indeed Meyerhold reverses Bakhtin's claim that theatre had been 'novelised' and argues that Dostoevsky should be considered a dramatist. In terms of theatre design, Meyerhold was among the first directors to open the stage to the public, extending the stage into the auditorium. In the way his performances were structured, staged and lit he left them open to the interpretation of the audience, challenging Bakhtin's assertion that theatre as a genre is closed. Although Meyerhold's practice seemed to contradict Bakhtin's theory, both drew on the images of popular theatre, and from Pushkin's affirmation of this tradition. Meyerhold's revolution in theatre involved him rejecting the realist assumptions that provided a common ground between Stanislavsky and Bakhtin. Although it might seem that all three men shared a common preoccupation with rhythm, for Meyerhold this had everything to do with a musical conception of performance time, rather than the double structure of narrative time that Bakhtin and Stanislavsky were discussing. When it came to questions of actor training, Meyerhold turned to the behaviourist theory of Ivan Pavlov and the management science of F.W. Taylor – gone were any references to nature, the spirit and the subconscious so often mentioned by Stanislavsky.

Meyerhold and Stanislavsky

Of the three theatre practitioners in this book Vsevelod Meyerhold is probably the least known and his concepts of actor training are much less known than Stanislavsky's system. I shall argue that his answers to those questions of theatre posed in the preceding chapters have fundamentally shaped theatre practice throughout Europe and for this reason were taken extremely seriously by his mentor Konstantin Stanislavsky. There are various narratives that one can read into their relationship: the first is of the headstrong and wayward Meyerhold who like the prodigal son finally returns to the MAT and its realist aesthetic in 1938. Another narrative is of the two men arriving at the same conclusion towards the end of their careers. Meyerhold has already described himself and Stanislavsky 'approaching the solution of the same problem like builders of a tunnel under the Alps. He is moving from one side, and I from the other. And inevitably, somewhere in the middle we must meet'.[3] In 1938 he was reported mentioning 'more than once' that 'Stanislavsky's "system" in its latest stage of teaching about "physical action" was close to his own objectives in directing and teaching. With great pride, he would repeat that now nothing divided Stanislavsky and him'.[4] For his part Stanislavsky noted that his opera singers didn't know 'how to handle their bodies', adding 'I'm counting a great deal on Meyerhold. He's a master of that. If emotions influence the physical actions of a person, then physical actions must to an equal degree influence the emotions'.[5] Even before this in 1935 or 1936 when asked whom he considered to be the best Soviet director, Stanislavsky answered: 'The only director I know is Meyerhold.'[6] If we have learned anything from Bakhtin it is not to foreclose dialogue by reducing two voices into one: this would be the case by adopting either the 'prodigal son' narrative or arguing for a final dialectical synthesis of their highly contrasted approaches. It is to be expected that with such an intense relationship moments of agreement would have great significance for both men, and that indeed they may have shared a vision of coming to a final agreement. But this should have nothing to do with a study of that relationship. Let us rather follow Bakhtin's injunction to keep the two voices in play rather than merging them.

Bakhtin insisted upon the aesthetic productivity of love: the act of authoring being motivated by the love of the other person. I would argue that the same is true of any committed dialogue. One would only be moved to disagree or agree if the other person's opinion carried some weight. Certainly there was a great affection between them: Gladkov reports that throughout his life Meyerhold 'retained an almost childlike admiration for Stanislavsky. It was more than respect; it was love'. This extended to him refusing to allow anyone to 'speak badly of Stanislavsky in his presence' and sharply cutting off 'anyone who did not in his opinion regard Stanislavsky with sufficient respect'.[7] When Stanislavsky's seventy-fifth birthday was celebrated, Meyerhold wrote to him:

> How can I tell you how much I love you? How can I tell you the magnitude of my gratitude to you for what you taught me about such a difficult business as the art of directing turns out to be?![8]

Their relationship can be understood as a dialogue in Bakhtin's sense of the word: although they didn't often directly address each other, their writings are permeated by a constant awareness of each other. In the index to Senelick's *Stanislavsky: A Life in Letters* there are forty-seven references to Meyerhold but only one letter directly addressed to him (and a particularly bad-tempered exchange at that). This dialogical shadowing was not always positive – there were many moments where one would quite explicitly disapprove of the other – but it could also have been a means of figuring their own image of theatre, acting and teaching. For this kind of dialogue to work the other person must matter (must have value) to you, otherwise their absent presence would have no shaping force on your own actions. For either man to have influenced the writings of the other, their presence needed to have a sufficient gravity.

For all this talk of distant dialogue, Meyerhold and Stanislavsky did work closely between 1898 and 1905. In 1898 students and actors from Nemirovich-Danchenko's Philharmonic School and Stanislavsky's Society for Art and Literature were selected to create the Moscow Art Theatre (MAT). Having won first prize for acting at the Philharmonic School, Meyerhold was chosen to join the troupe and remained at MAT until 1902 where he took on a number of important roles, including Treplev in Chekhov's *The Seagull*, and Tusenbach in *Three Sisters*. In 1905 Meyerhold was invited to be director of a Theatre-Studio that Stanislavsky created with his own money (and in the face of opposition from Nemirovich-Danchenko). One of the aims was to explore acting methods appropriate to Symbolist dramas which were of interest to both men. However the results were not what Stanislavsky had hoped for and he closed the Theatre-Studio in October of that year. Robert Leach writes that Meyerhold's 'work, for whatever reason, horrified Stanislavsky when he attended a dress rehearsal and not one of the plays worked on so assiduously [...] was ever presented to the public.'[9] There are possible reasons for this horror: both men took very different approaches to Symbolist drama, approaches that were informed by their conceptions of theatre, of the roles and relations between director and actor, and between actor and audience.

Even after this close association there were still moments of direct reference or even communication. In notes for a planned article from 1910 or 1911 Meyerhold argues that Stanislavsky needs to find a 'third path' in between naturalism and modernism – 'that of the realist'. Later he notes that

> [i]t is quite correct that Craig be invited. To each his own. If Stanislavsky gives over the fantastic and mystical element to Craig and leaves for himself the realistic theatre, this would be to Stanislavsky's benefit. He can be *masterful* in realistic theatre and will not allow himself to be ordered about as it seems to me he was by Egorov in *The Blue Bird*. There, with a well-chosen director, he can be most productive creatively. His erudition. His growth in the sense of characters.[10]

From these notes it appears Meyerhold feels that Stanislavsky should avoid either the modernism of Craig or the Symbolism of Maeterlinck: his strength is in realism and a theatre based in character. A letter of 1912 from Meyerhold and his painter/designer Golovin repeats this impression that Stanislavsky's artistic vision is being thwarted by conservative elements in the MAT.

> Here in Petersburg [...] there is a rumour that you alone are carrying the full brunt of the awful crisis of the conflict between two currents in the Moscow Art Theatre: the old one whose adherents are grouped on the side of naturalistic theatre, and the new, which you represent together with the youth, seeking new routes for stage art. With all our souls we wish you victory in your battle![11]

Alexander Blok recorded a conversation in December 1912 where Meyerhold had complained that 'his world view' was being confused with 'his technical methods as a director', arguing that 'he was closer to Pushkin, i.e. to the humane' than Blok and many others think.[12] It is telling that Meyerhold should seek to distinguish his 'technical methods' from his 'world view' which he aligns with Pushkin and the humane and therefore comes close to Stanislavsky (and to Bakhtin). He makes this connection with Pushkin very explicit in an article of April 1921 entitled 'Stanislavsky's Solitude'. Here he and a colleague repeat the argument that Stanislavsky is being betrayed by his colleagues at MAT.

> He and only he in his solitude is capable of restoring the lost rights of theatrical traditionalism with its *'relativistic improbability'*, *'diverting action'*, *'masks of exaggeration'*, *'truth of passions'*, *'verisimilitude of feelings under the proposed circumstances'*, *'freedom of judgment by the street'*, and *'blunt openness of popular passions'*.[13]

The phrases in italics are all from Pushkin. In an address to his theatre in the 1930s Meyerhold insists that '[i]t is necessary [...] to finish with this nonsense, with this foolishness that Konstantin [Sergeyevich] and I are antipodes. This is not true. We are two systems, each of which completes the other'. He continues that 'the system is not only what he thought through himself, but includes a lot of what was done by other comrades in art – Vladimir Ivanovich Nemirovich-Danchenko, and Vakhtangov, and me, sinner that I am'.[14]

And so to the other side of the dialogue. In 1925 Stanislavsky returned from a performance of Erdman's *The Mandate* 'completely satisfied', in particular with his staging of the difficult final act: 'Meyerhold has achieved in this act what I have dreamed of.'[15] In an unpublished record that 'probably dates from the 1920s or early 1930s' Stanislavsky notes that '[t]ruest of all is Meyerhold's path. He starts with general possibilities and principles of stage and direction. He resolves them boldly and simply (the same cannot be said of his work with actors; he is weak in that respect)'. His boldness includes dispensing with the proscenium arch and the stage curtain: 'He reveals the entire behind-the-scenes part of the stage. It is well whitewashed and clean. This is the building itself, an extension of the auditorium.'[16] In both passages Stanislavsky admires the decisions of Meyerhold the director – be it a complicated staging device for a new play, or his revelation of the stage itself as a device. Other less flattering references show how Stanislavsky defined his own project in distinction to that of Meyerhold: he describes the MAT as a theatre in which 'we could create the life we had dreamed of for so long, purify our art, and build a temple, not a fairground slum.'[17] Robbins translates this as 'I can create a temple instead of a market place'.[18] Torpokov records Stanislavsky reflecting on those 'not so distant times', when

> many of our theatres were still in the grip of a reactionary formalism. In search of the greatest expressiveness and in an attempt to present 'ideological trends', they got lost in paths of vulgar society, presenting the author's concepts in sharp form of exaggeration which were called by the then-fashionable name 'grotesque'.[19]

A dialogue about Symbolism

Although Stanislavsky's name might seem synonymous with realism, he was very curious about plays by Symbolist authors, particularly those of Maurice Maeterlinck whose work was also admired by Anton Chekhov (who had suggested his work to Stanislavsky).[20] The closure of the Theatre-Studio in 1906 didn't deter Stanislavsky from pursuing his interest in Symbolist drama. Even at the planning stage of his production of Knut Hamsun's *The Drama of Life* he knew this production would be a costly experiment (this after the closure of the Theatre-Studio had cost him 18,000 roubles). In a letter of July 1905 to Maxim Gorky he notes: 'The play will not be a success, but there will be plenty of discussions and arguments about it. That is the best way to shake up the public.'[21] Just as Meyerhold would later advocate creating a division in the spectators' reaction, Stanislavsky split the MAT audience between the left and right, progressives and conservatives:

One half of the audience, the Left with their customary assertiveness, applauded and shouted: 'Death to realism! No more crickets and mosquitoes' (a reference to the sound effects in Chekhov's plays). 'Long live the avant-garde! Long live the left!' At the same time the other half, the conservative Right, booed us and shouted angrily: 'Shame on the Art Theatre! Down with the decadents! Long live the old kind of theatre!'[22]

Stanislavsky's aim was to educate the public as well as his own actors. To a certain degree he succeeded: his production of Maeterlinck's *The Blue Bird* opened in September 1908 and had 1,788 performances.[23]

Stanislavsky recalls the inspiration behind the Theatre-Studio as an attempt to engage with contemporary non-realistic movements in the arts:

> The *credo* of the new studio amounted to the fact that realism and the mundane had had their day. Now was the time for the unreal onstage. We needed to depict life not as it is in the real world but as we are vaguely aware of it in our dreams and visions, our moments of exaltation. That was the state of mind we had to convey onstage, just as it was being shown by new modern painters on their canvases and new composers in their scores and new poets in their verses. Their works have no clear outlines, no complete melodies, no precisely expressed ideas. The strength of the new art lies in its combinations, the blending of colours, the lines, the musical notes, the sounds of the words. They create a general mood that unconsciously takes hold of the audience.[24]

Although Stanislavsky might seem to be breaking with realism, there is a continuity of vocabulary since his writings contain countless references to the subconscious or unconscious as the source site of an artist's creative impulses. Ever the practical man of theatre he realises that while a

> painter's canvas can assume the lines and forms his imagination conceives [...] what are we to do with our own physical body? I could not see any way of giving living embodiment to what my imagination conceived or to what I saw in paintings, heard in music or read in poetry.[25]

The challenge, as ever, is one of embodying a certain kind of experience, but this time the experience is not rooted in everyday conscious life. This tussle between form and content is at the heart of the broader argument about the nature of the theatrical sign.

Maeterlinck's *The Death of Tintagiles* (1894) was one of the four productions rehearsed in the Theatre-Studio under the direction of Meyerhold. Valentina Verigina, a member of the company, wrote of the 'statuesque plasticity' of the production: 'the hands with the fingers together, certain turns and inclinations of the head, were typical of primitive painting. [...] In this way an almost unbearable dynamism was created beneath an outward calm.'[26] Edward Braun notes that Meyerhold undertook various attempts to break away from the realism of the contemporary state and to embrace stylisation wholeheartedly as a principle of dramatic art. In movement there was plasticity rather than an impersonation of reality; groups would often look like Pompeian frescoes reproduced in living form.[27]

Looking at photographs of his Symbolist productions one can see how the groupings are meticulously arranged, not realistically à la Meiningen, but stylistically, that is, for their expressive potential.[28]

Stanislavsky conceded that there were some 'beautiful-looking groups and mise-en-scène', but the 'director had tried to use his own talent to conceal actors who were no more than putty in his hands', and 'in the absence of any technique on the part of the actors all he could do was demonstrate his own ideas, principles, research'.[29] At the heart of his critique is a very different conception of the role of the director. Stanislavsky (and Grotowski after him) considered that the role of the director was to release the actor's creative potential in their work on a character. Judged from this perspective Meyerhold's approach would appear to be wholly external and more about the creative ideas of the director than the actors. His directing style was more about demonstration than discussion, the important dialogue being that between the actor and the audience. This discussion returns us to the question of authorship: Bakhtin and Stanislavsky write about authoring a character whereas Meyerhold is auteur of the production, and the audience the judge of its affect or meaning.

The challenge of Symbolism for Stanislavsky was the expression of spiritual content through the material form of the actor's body; for Meyerhold it was the creation of a stylised form of theatre. Another word for Symbolist theatre was *uslovnyi*, or conditional theatre, which Hoover explains is a theatre which operates on 'an agreed upon condition or assumption: in particular the assumption that the theatre is an art in its own right, not dependent upon reality as its point of reference'.[30] In his 1929 study Volkov argues that Meyerhold 'firmly and consistently carried out in his productions the principle of *uslovnyi* theatre'.[31] This was a theatre that not only acknowledged its own theatrical nature, but was dedicated to exploring (to repeat Medvedev's expression) the 'definite semiotic material of' theatre. Whyman explains how *uslovnost'* helps differentiate the aesthetics of Meyerhold and Stanislavsky.

> Meyerhold's revolution, of theatricality versus psychological verisimilitude (a theatre no longer dominated by the text), asserted conventionality (*uslovnost'*). Like Japanese theatre it relied on the audience reading and interpreting a set of signs particular to the form. As such, it posited a completely different aesthetic from that of Stanislavsky's Tolstoyan aesthetic, where the actors *infect* the audience because of their truthful *experiencing*. Before the revolution Meyerhold found in the theatricality of Commedia dell'Arte a vehicle for his sign-system; after the revolution he attempted to develop a sign-system for post-revolutionary audiences by means of biomechanics.[32]

The challenge for Meyerhold was to find an outward means of expression, a form of movement (what will later be described as *risunok*):

> The *truth* of human relationships is established by gestures, poses, glances, and silences. Words alone cannot say everything. Hence there must be a *pattern of movement* to transform the spectator into a new vigilant observer […] The difference between the old theatre and the new is that in the new theatre speech and plasticity are each subordinated to their own particular rhythms and the two do not necessarily coincide.[33]

Each sentence of this passage announces a significant aspect of Meyerhold's approach to theatre: it is a theatre of physical action where movement and gesture are recognised as having equal value to the written text, a principle at the heart of his critique of what he calls literary theatre. The old theatre is the literary, illusionist theatre where image and word coincide in the recreation of scenes from real life. In the 'new theatre' word, image and their shift through movement were subject to their own rhythms, both compositional and in performance.

Leach analyses Maeterlinck's drama in the context of time and space: 'If place and time are at the heart of all performance' then they are 'at the heart of hearts' in his work. Leach's argument is particularly interesting in the way that he focuses his argument on the figure of the actor where 'place and time are united on the stage'. There is a fascinating echo of *Author and Hero* in the way that Bakhtin centres the action and values of verbal art in the body of the hero. As ever, where Bakhtin is writing about an image in a symbolic or literary sense, Leach is writing about the physical reality of the actor.

> Place and time are united on the stage in the figure of the actor. The actor on stage moves in space through time. Since it is, therefore, through the person – the physical being – of the actor, that these dimensions meet, it is in the figure of the actor that the deepest truths, the theatrical truths, the truths which are only and uniquely expressible in theatrical terms, are to be found.[34]

Leach might be slightly overstating his case, but isn't this an answer to the most fundamental of the questions of this book? He may well have had the ideas of Adolphe Appia when he made his point. Appia writes about how the actor's body becomes the yardstick by which the audience measures space (and time) in the theatre:

> To Appia the actor was *massgebend* – the unit of measurement. Unity could be created only by relating every part of a setting to him. He was three-dimensional, therefore the entire would have to be consistently three-dimensional.[35]

This prompts a question about Bakhtin's concept of the chronotope: can one talk of a chronotope as a particular type of rhythmical form of time and space that is experienced by a present viewer, or is it confined to modes of deploying time and space in the representation of a previous reality?

Meyerhold states that '[f]orm and content are a union which demands the firmest cementing, which can be achieved only through the pressure of a living force – and that living force is the will of man (the artist)'.[36] Just as he had insisted upon the artificiality of the stage sign, here he argues that what brings together form and content is the creative activity of the artist. The totality of the art work lies in its *formal construction* of the work of art, a subjective vision of the world as seen through the artist's eyes. This explains why a major study of Meyerhold would be called 'The conscious art of theatre'.[37] Where Stanislavsky locates the creative process in the inaccessible depths of the unconscious/subconscious, Meyerhold's way is entirely conscious and willed. This conception of the director as a conscious artist elaborates a little further the notion of Meyerhold as an auteur.

While Stanislavsky seemed to look back to a nineteenth-century aesthetic, Meyerhold was part of the broader cultural debate about what is theatre art, how it is made, by whom and for whom. Meyerhold engaged in the questions that were being debated by the formalists, and by members of the Bakhtin Circle. He considered creativity, composition and acting in terms of gesture, sound and movement and it is here that one can see a useful connection with the writings of Medvedev and Voloshinov. Medvedev offers a *tour d'horizon*:

> All the products of ideological creation – works of art, scientific works, religious symbols and rites, etc. – are material things, part of the practical reality that surrounds man. […] Nor do philosophical views, beliefs, or even shifting ideological moods exist within man, in his head or in his 'soul'. They become ideological reality only by being realised in words, actions, clothing, manners and organisations of people and things – in a word: in some definite semiotic material. Through this material they become a practical part of the reality surrounding man.[38]

Medvedev could have added to this list the 'gestures, poses, glances, and silences' mentioned by Meyerhold above. This materialist account of 'ideological creation' is totally at odds with Stanislavsky's ideas of the artist's soul or subconscious. Reality is not a moment before but after the act of speaking or writing and this act of signification happens in the external realm of social life. Voloshinov explains further that '[m]eaning does not reside in the word or in the soul of the listener', but is 'the effect of interaction between speaker and listener produced via the material of a particular sound complex'.[39] In other words meaning is brought forth through acts of dialogue. Elsewhere Voloshinov takes on the notion of creativity being an inner process:

> We are most inclined to imagine ideological creation as some inner process of understanding, comprehension, and perception, and do not notice that it in fact unfolds externally, for the eye, the ear, the hand. It is not within us but between us.[40]

'Not within us but between us' underlines the fundamental importance that the audience held in Meyerhold's conception of theatre. The ultimate meaning of a play was not something laid down by the director-auteur but something arrived at through the dialogue between the actors and the audience. This very important distinction helps articulate the fundamental difference between Meyerhold and

Stanislavsky. When Medvedev states that 'ideological reality' can be realised only 'in some definite semiotic material' he strikes at an underlying assumption of realism: the notion that content is transcendent and therefore independent of form. This form-content split echoes Descartes' argument that one's mind is independent of the material substance of the brain. In some respects this brief period in Soviet Russia was the high-water mark for a materialist conception of communication and theatre production.

Robert Leach makes a very useful connection between Meyerhold and Shklovsky and the formalists in the way that he explains their 'quite new and challenging way of approaching art'.

> The function of art, they proclaimed, was to 'make strange' the subject matter, thereby forcing us to 'see it anew', and a frequent method by which art achieved this was by drawing attention to its own artistic devices – the painting did not attempt to conceal its paint, the poem its conscious use of words, and the theatrical presentation its theatricality.[41]

Although Bakhtin, Medvedev and Voloshinov all criticised the formalists for focusing on sensation and ignoring the cognitive aspect of language, Leach explains how it was that they tuned in to a fundamental shift in artistic practice. To grasp the shift away from representational art one has to grasp this feeling for the material reality of the means by which art is created. It is an engagement with, an attention to, the stuff itself. Philosophically, Bakhtin *et al.* have a valid point, but we will understand the art of Meyerhold and Mayakovsky (and Brecht) by attending to Shklovsky. In this feeling for the multiple nature of theatrical signification – involving volumes and shapes of space, light, movement, music, image, song, voice, text – Meyerhold points to the fundamental difference between literature (which operates with one signifying language) and theatre.

Where Meyerhold is talking about the materiality of the sign some Symbolist writers were straining against this very materiality. Nikolai Efros argued that Maeterlinck's plays should be performed on the puppet theatre because the theatre 'which by its very nature is material and real, with its ponderous mechanism of living people and stage settings, does not enhance but actually harms drama of this kind'.[42] Braun emphasises this point:

> hard as he [Meyerhold] tried to discern a relevance to contemporary events in Maeterlinck's dramas, there was in the Symbolists' rejection of the material world and their striving for the ideal of a disengagement from everyday reality that amounted to escapism and elitism.[43]

In Braun's eyes this points to a 'fatal contradiction' within the very project of Symbolism:

> The subject of art lies always in the conceptual world, but all the means of art lie in the material world. It is not possible to overcome this fatal

contradiction; one can only make it as painless as possible by sharpening, refining, spiritualising art.[44]

Braun's phrase 'all the means of art lie in the material world' echoes Medvedev's insistence on 'definite semiotic material'. Meyerhold puts the contradiction between theatre and Symbolism succinctly: 'The way of the Mystery and the way of the Theatre do not merge.'[45]

In both Symbolism and realism the theatrical sign refers to and is guaranteed by a reality and a truth beyond the stage. In their metaphysical aspiration both realism and Symbolism deny the *material existence* and the formal validity of the theatrical sign, one referring to a material reality that is not present; the other to a reality which transcends materiality. The *form* of the theatrical sign is a necessary evil which must under no circumstances draw attention to itself. Theatrical illusion relies on a double denial: the audience's willingness to accept that the means of representation *on stage* are artificial, and that as active participants they are also physically absent in the auditorium. Pushkin underlines this fundamental division by pointing out that the architectural space of the theatre is split into two halves: stage and auditorium. His rejection of verisimilitude, of the illusion of the real, is based on this fundamental division.

> What verisimilitude can there be, damn it, in a room divided in two, in one part of which there are two thousand people who are mostly invisible to those who are on the stage? Verisimilitude is always considered as the essential condition and the basis for the art of theatre. And what if we showed that the very essence of the art of theatre precisely *excludes* verisimilitude?[46]

Pushkin's earthy tones prepare us for Meyerhold's flamboyant break with the ethereal mysteries of Symbolism in his 1906 production of Alexander Blok's *Balaganchik*.

A dialogue about physical action

What did Meyerhold mean by the notions of action and movement and how were these developed both in his productions and in his actor training? How close were his ideas to Stanislavsky's Method of Physical Actions? In true dialogical fashion, Meyerhold's position is articulated through the careful distinctions that he makes between his and the MAT's (not necessarily always Stanislavsky's) approach to movement and gesture. One important distinction he makes is between the nature of literary and theatrical signification.

> The *truth* of human relationships is established by gestures, poses, glances, and silences. Words alone cannot say everything. Hence there must be a *pattern of movement* to transform the spectator into a new vigilant observer […] The difference between the old theatre and the new is that in the new theatre speech and plasticity are each subordinated to their own particular rhythms and the two do not necessarily coincide.[47]

It is not just that 'words cannot say everything' but that speech and movement 'do not necessarily coincide'. Meyerhold's words again echo Medvedev's argument that 'ideological reality' can only be realised through 'some definite semiotic material', that is, 'words, actions, clothing, manners and organisations of people and things'. Meyerhold develops that sense of definiteness by arguing that each of these semiotic systems has its own rhythm. Medvedev's words in the section on Symbolism were being cited to explain that meaning (the 'content' of a statement or artistic work) is not transcendent but the result of a negotiation with form. Meyerhold's post-Symbolist work continues this deepening of his awareness of the different types of theatrical expression. He admits that 'the old theatre' 'regarded plasticity as an essential means of expression; one has only to consider Salvini in *Othello* or *Hamlet*'. But although this movement capability of the actor is common to both directors, Meyerhold points out that 'the form which I have in mind is new. Before, it corresponded closely to the spoken dialogue, but I am speaking of a *plasticity which does not correspond to the words*.'[48]

'A plasticity which does not correspond to the words'

While the awareness of different signifying systems has echoes of the Bakhtin Circle, the non-coincidence of word and movement is more akin to the aesthetic experiments of artists close to the formalists, and marks a definite move away from realism. The passage above also proposes that movement is more important than the spoken word in conveying the truth of human relationships. Erast Garin, one of Meyerhold's actors, explains how 'even stationary figures can change their "character" by moving' and gives as an example how toy figures 'can be made to seem happy, sad, etc., even though the facial features never change. The secret of their expressivity is in *the change of pose*' [my italics].[49] Elsewhere, Meyerhold explains how, if we observe two people in conversation we can judge the attitude of two speakers to each other simply through their gesture, 'from the way they gesticulate, stand, move their eyes. This is because they move in a way unrelated to their words, a way which reveals their relationship'. Meyerhold argued that '[s]uperfluous words and lines should be thrown out […] the action alone will reveal the essence'.[50]

Meyerhold's polemic against literary theatre might be more appropriately directed towards Nemirovich-Danchenko, a published playwright and the literary manager of MAT who in 1910 adapted *The Brothers Karamazov* for the stage. Apart from being precisely the kind of literary theatre that Meyerhold was arguing against, it also returns us to Bakhtin's ideas about the relationship between the theatre and the novel. Where Bakhtin argues that in Dostoevsky we see the novelisation of theatre, Nemirovich-Danchenko writes about the collapse of any 'conventional' distinction between novel and theatre.

> If, with Chekhov, the theatre extended the limits of the conventions, then with 'Karamazov' these conventions have been destroyed. All the conventions of the theatre as a collective art have collapsed and now nothing is impossible

for theatre. [...] I think that this revolution will last not five, not 10 years but a hundred, for ever! This is not a 'new form'; but the total destruction of all the theatrical conventions which stand in the way of literary talents.[51]

He asks why 'novelists had not written their great works for the theatre?' and then answers 'because in the theatre what was demanded above all was *action*, movement. Chekhov put an end to that'. He finishes with a solution to the problem of reported narrative in novels: 'We have the reader. And people listen to him with bated breath [...] He blends into the darkness of the theatre, with the power the theatre has over the crowd.'[52]

Although Nemirovich-Danchenko's words were in a private letter to Stanislavsky, Meyerhold was prompted to join the debate by a favourable review by critic and stage designer Alexandre Benois, whom Rudnitsky describes as 'Meyerhold's constant and irreconcilable opponent'.[53] Meyerhold answers Nemirovich-Danchenko point for point. Firstly, the place of theatre is neither the study nor the library but *the stage*:

No time has been lost in finding a name for the reader turned actor, for now we have the term 'the intellectual actor'. The same deathly hush prevails in the auditorium as in the reading-room of a library and it sends the public to sleep. The reading-room of a library is the only proper place for such gravity and immobility. [...] How long will it be before they inscribe in theatrical tables the following law: *words in the theatre are only embellishment on the design of movement?*[54]

As to Nemirovich-Danchenko's point about action no longer being essential to theatre, Meyerhold's replies 'I read somewhere: "Drama in reading is primarily dialogue, argument and taut dialectic. Drama on the stage is primarily action, a taut struggle. The words, so to speak, the mere overtones of the action"'.[55] 'Literature' in Meyerhold's eyes is the unnecessary verbiage that needs to be trimmed from a stage production: 'If we examine what we have cut out of the text, weigh up that flabby material, we shall find that it is literature – sometimes good, sometimes poor – but still literature.'[56]

Benois' review described this adaptation as a 'mystery-play' – a very loaded expression in the context of my argument where Bakhtin has called Dostoevsky's novel 'a peculiar sort of mystery play'.[57] Meyerhold regards the use of the term 'nothing less than blasphemous':

Such an adaptation of a novel into a play seems to us nothing less than blasphemous, not only with regard to Dostoevsky, but, if the adapters were aiming to write a mystery-play, with regard to the idea of the true mystery-play as well.[58]

The true mystery play, he argues, was performed by 'Les Clercs de la Basoche' who 'resorted to the principles of mummery and went out into the streets. It was there, in the intimate relationship between the histrion and his public that the true theatre was created.[59] And if by 'mystery-play' Benois was referring to Symbolist pieties, Meyerhold repeats the warning given by the Symbolist Andrei Bely that he would be wise to '[l]et the theatre remain the theatre, and the mystery – the mystery'.[60] Although I will be dealing with the popular tradition of street theatre in depth in the next section I shall briefly mention one more point where Benois compares Meyerhold's theatre to cabotinage.

> [W]hat is this cabotinage that is so detested by Benois? The cabotin is a strolling player; the cabotin is a kinsman to the mime, the histrion, and the juggler; the cabotin can work miracles with his technical mastery; the cabotin keeps alive the tradition of the true art of acting.[61]

Compare Meyerhold's list to one Stanislavsky wrote when revising *My Life in Art* for a Russian readership. He notes with distaste that with constructivist theatre, '[a]crobats, cascade singers, pantomimists, clowns, trained animals, and others had left everywhere the vestiges of their bad taste and ill manners'.[62] It is hard not to hear echoes of Bakhtin in this roll-call of figures from popular medieval theatre. It is an irony that for Bakhtin they are part of an argument about the dynamism of the novel, whereas for Meyerhold cabotinage is what will 'rescue the Russian theatre from its own desire to become the servant of literature', and 'will help the modern actor rediscover the basic laws of theatricality'.[63]

The actor's work on a role

In the light of Meyerhold's arguments about the plasticity of the actor one might imagine that he would propose a very 'external' approach to creating a role; the opposite, in fact, of the MAT. He admits that

> [i]t's difficult to say what work on a role should begin with. A lot depends on the actor's personality. Some are helped by physical factors, others by psychological ones. Our system is often juxtaposed to the Moscow Art Theatre's, but that's not correct. […] One can start with the psychological that will prompt the correct physical position. Or one can begin with the physical factors that will allow one to find the correct inner life.[64]

Meyerhold is simply underlining what Stanislavsky has already observed: that acting is a psycho-physical process. Although I have followed Bakhtin in using the terms outer (or external) and inner (or internal), I shall argue how these terms will ultimately prevent a more nuanced account of the relationship between movement, posture and affective experience. A corollary to this is that although there is some truth in associating the 'psychological' with the 'internal' and the 'physiological' with the 'external', it is also a reductive account.

Meyerhold gives an example of how a physical action helps to generate an affective state. He recalls a problem that he was having when playing Baron Tusenbach in the MAT's 1900 production of Chekhov's *Three Sisters*. Tusenbach comes in, goes over to the piano, sits down at it and starts talking. Stanislavsky insisted he repeat this movement 'ten times' and

> [t]hen he came up from the auditorium onto the stage, tossed me a little piece of paper; and said: 'You cross to the piano, say your first three words, then suddenly catch sight of this piece of paper, pick it up, and while you're crossing to where you're supposed to sit, tear it up into little pieces as you continue your speech.' And it helped a lot. I got what I needed for the scene. […] After all, we all live by means of our experience, we all bring our experiences on to the stage, and that gesture, when I picked up the little piece of paper came from a conditioned reflex somewhere in my memory. (Someone should tell Pavlov this story.) And I got a living intonation.[55]

This long passage serves to show a very deep connection between a physical action, picking up and reading the piece of paper, and the ability to deliver a speech with 'a living intonation'. Stanislavsky created a bit of 'stage business', a simple action from which an actor got what he 'needed for the scene'. Somehow the older director knew that this action would elicit the required emotional state for the actor to deliver his lines. Meyerhold calls this relation between action and emotional state 'a conditioned reflex', a term used by Ivan Pavlov.

Training the actor's body

All three directors in this study share a belief in the importance of training. Stanislavsky was arguably the first to create a Theatre-Studio, a place for exploring the art of the actor. The studio is a place for practical thinking, for engaging in a dialectical negotiation between discovering the kind of actor training that is appropriate to a certain kind of theatre, and of changing that notion of theatre through the process of this training. Do Bakhtin's ideas have any place in such a detailed discussion of theatre practice and research? I will argue that two of his concepts can help us better grasp Meyerhold's notion of the actor and actor-training: firstly, his notion of the outer and inner body and, secondly, his insistence that a person cannot develop an image of themselves.

Chapter 3 offered detailed accounts of Bakhtin's and Stanislavsky's notions of the body and the present chapter should be read with those notions in mind: a kind of dialogical reading. It is not that Bakhtin is wrong and Meyerhold is right, but that both consider the actor's body as an image and come to almost diametrically opposite conclusions. Bakhtin argued that in terms of aesthetic creation it is a category error for a person to imagine themselves in action; in a similar vein, Stanislavsky argued how it was impossible for him to embody the details of a figure in a painting by Vrubel. In both cases there is an aesthetic (and ethical) proscription against imagining how it is that you look from the outside. Meyerhold not only argues against this proscription. He creates a training by means of which the actor must know what they look like, and indeed should take pleasure in this imagined view. Although actors cannot physically see themselves, they have to act with a consciousness of how they might appear as visual images. In this way Meyerhold adds quite new meanings to the word 'image', and a new dimension to the visual world of the stage. Stanislavsky writes about 'pictures' whereas Meyerhold writes about sculpture: in the first the framed stage creates two-dimensional pictures, whereas the unframed open stage is a three-dimensional reality.

How would Meyerhold describe 'the actor's work' (to use Stanislavsky's phrase)? Rudnitsky offers an answer:

> The actor's art is the creation of plastic forms in space. Therefore, the actor's art is the ability to utilise the expressive potential of his body correctly. This means that the route to image and feeling must begin not with experience, not with seeking to plumb the meaning of the role, not with an attempt to assimilate the psychological essence of the phenomenon, in sum, not 'from within' but from without; it must begin with motion. This means the motion of an actor excellently trained, possessing musical rhythm and easy, reflectory excitability; an actor whose natural abilities have been developed by systematic training.[66]

There are several important points here: first that the actor's art is 'the creation of plastic forms in space'. Secondly that the route to 'image and feeling' begins not from within but without. Thirdly is the list of required outcomes of this training: 'musical rhythm and easy, reflectory excitablity' (a term which brings us back to Pavlov).

'The actor's art is the creation of plastic forms in space'

Meyerhold's Symbolist productions were his first experiments in actors creating 'plastic forms in space'. Since plasticity is such an important term in both Meyerhold's and Grotowski's training (the first part of which was called 'The Plastiques'), it would be wise to offer some definition. The French use the term '*les arts plastiques*' for sculpture or any art form that deals with the creation or manipulation of three-dimensional forms. When Meyerhold writes about plasticity it is with this idea of the sculptural form of the human body. The actor is both sculptor and sculpture, and has to consider his or her body as a plastic material which can be shaped through carefully chosen movements. We have already seen how in his Symbolist phase he moved from the bas relief of the tableaux in Maeterlinck's *Sister Béatrice* to the fully three-dimensional shapes in later productions. Meyerhold's conception of the actor's movement and shaping was itself shaped by his conception of theatre space. An actor will move differently when behind the pictorial frame of the proscenium arch and when on a bare thrust stage. On a realistic set with period furniture and painted backdrops an actor in period costume is part of the image. I shall argue that the less there is on stage, the more work there is for the actor to create stage pictures.

Meyerhold's first experiment with a thrust configuration was in 1906 in Petersburg where a temporary stage was placed over the orchestra pit: 'The result was a spacious, wide proscenium, projecting to the first row of the seats. The front curtain was dispensed with, so that the audience could see the scenery before the performance began.'[67] Although Meyerhold had not yet begun a formal actor training, Leach points out how this stage configuration 'inevitably helped the process':

> The actor on the thrust stage found himself almost bound to use his body as well as his face for expressive purposes, because he was no longer supported by a surrounding clutter of furniture. Now he was, as it were, on his own, and if he succeeded it was because he employed all his potential.[68]

The more open space invited the actor to act with more than 'his face'. Hoover extends this point into a reflection on genre: 'Obviously the naturalistic theatre regards the face as the actor's major means of expression and, in consequence, disregards all other means. The naturalistic theatre does not know the beauty of sculpture, does not make its actors train their bodies.'[69] This point needs to be underlined since it makes the connection between kinds of scenic space, actor's movement and thus the emphasis on movement training. With a progressively architectural and less illusionist stage, the actor needs to express emotion through more than simply their faces – their entire body must come into play. Rudnitsky describes the effect of the actor's presence – unaided by costume, makeup or scenery – on Liubov Popova's constructivist stage in Meyerhold's 1922 production of *The Magnificent Cuckold*.

> Each motion of the actor, regardless of his desires, obtained sculptural relief and significance. Now he was compelled to strive for the most exact expression of the plastic picture, he was obliged to move with the lightness of a dancer and with the grace of an acrobat. Acting became coloured by the agility of sportsmen. The grace of the plastic picture inevitably caused a lightness of delivery of each line, with ringing and precise intonations.[70]

The above description makes a functional interconnection between scenic space and the acting style.

Now that the actor's body has become an image for the audience the student of acting needs exercises to develop this sense of him- or herself in space. Erast Garin describes how the étude 'Shooting the Bow'

> develops in the student the habit of sensing his body in space, the ability to align himself, to work on elasticity and balance, and the understanding that even the smallest gesture – of the hand, for example – resonates throughout the entire body.[71]

Picon-Vallin describes another of Meyerhold's actors: 'Broken up into different levels of biomechanical work, Ilinksi's acting concentrates its power into a look, a shrug of the shoulders which alone sets the audience off laughing. The back or even the little finger become eloquent.'[72]

Meyerhold's actor, although subject to the overall control of a directorial concept, can also be described as a 'director' in the way that he or she guides their own movements. The actor must always be 'conscious of the shape of his body' (the signifying material), and should at every moment be able to 'see himself' and during 'his pauses to focus his attention even more closely on the graphic quality of his movements'.[73] The skill of the actor lies in understanding the effect a certain move of a part of the body will have on the audience. The actor knows that each particular move that he or she makes has specific affective properties.

We need to keep these comments in mind when we read of Meyerhold's concept of the actor's 'self-admiration', the 'mirroring of the self'. Leach defines this as meaning 'a sharp awareness of the actor's own physical presence, and with each movement a knowledge of "how I look"'. It is 'the actor's ability to see himself from the side, as it were, and thus his playing more simple and natural'.[74] Although it must be drawn from a proprioceptive sense of one's shape, Meyerhold argues that the actor can grasp themselves as a visual image for the audience. Hoover lists the terms Meyerhold uses:

> The actor himself was adjured to cultivate consciousness of his silhouette in the audience's eyes, variously called *risunok* (outline), *zerkalinie* (mirroring) or even *samozerkalinie* (self-mirroring), and *rakkursi* (*raccourci*, or pose from a side view).[75]

Raccourci is a term borrowed from classical ballet which refers to the dancer's ability to imagine their bodily outline in any particular posture. Meyerhold adds yet another dimension to this discussion of the actor as a conscious creator of forms: 'It's essential that the actor find pleasure for himself in executing a given movement or action pattern [*risunok*]. If you find that pleasure, then everything will work out. Victory awaits you.'[76] The actor is an artist who takes pleasure in the process of creation, which here involves imagining how he or she looks 'in the audience's eyes'. What was the job of the spectator-who-will-be-author in the early Bakhtin's aesthetics now becomes that of the actor. Meyerhold would agree with Bakhtin that a spectator is necessary in the aesthetic process – the performance is for the public – but the work of authoring the character rests entirely with the actor.

The acting styles of Stanislavsky and Meyerhold could not have been more different as concerns their attitude towards the audience. In *My Life in Art* Stanislavsky remembers with embarrassment when he used to swagger about imitating 'the operatic baritone in Parisian boots with a sword' trying to impress the girls in the audience.[77] Either he was flirting with or was terrified by the audience. He describes the auditorium beyond the proscenium arch as a 'boundless, deep, dark void' that is a constant source of distraction: 'But the more I tried to ignore it, the more I thought about it, the greater the draw from the ominous blackness beyond the picture-frame became.'[78,79] Later, he describes how he felt he 'was being sucked into it', it 'gaped wide before me, I feel completely under its power'.[80] His struggle with stage fright prompted him to create the training concept of circles of attention (or concentration), which help to divert the actor's attention from the stage and on to the created world of the play. For Stanislavsky the actor's body dilates or contracts according to their fear of the audience.

The operatic baritone is an example of an external image he used to take on when seeking how to play a role. Acting from the inside was truthful, from outside it was false because it involved no living through the character's life. The actor's body is a medium for embodying, for taking and communicating the emotional world of the character. Remember how Stanislavsky explains the difference between how a painter – here Vrubel – and an actor give forms to a human image:

> A painter's canvas can assume the lines and forms his imagination conceives. But what are we to do with our own physical body? […] I did not know how to achieve onstage the shadowy feelings that were almost inexpressible in words.[81]

Stanislavsky argues that feelings 'are inexpressible in words'. But this is precisely the moment at which Meyerhold would ask the actor to move, because plasticity transcends words. Stanislavsky does not seem to think of embodiment as a way of moving. For him it is the outer manifestation of an inner feeling that was created by the author. Unlike Meyerhold, his actor training does not involve 'seeing' or taking pleasure in the image of oneself as a character.

> Remembering what you have discovered physically, you try to take it with you to the mirror, so as to verify with your own eyes the lines of your body and what they express but, to your amazement, all you encounter in your reflection is a caricature of Vrubel, actors' posturing, and above all, the old, familiar, hateful operatic clichés.[82]

Where Bakhtin eschews the mirror on principle, Stanislavsky describes in painful detail the difficulty of reconciling his attempts to embody a painting and the reflected image he sees before him. In *An Actor's Work* Kostya watches Tortsov and realises that it is through his supreme technique that 'all the Elements, the psychological inner drives' and so forth 'become normal, human – not convention-bound and actorish – activity'.[83] This technique is diametrically the opposite in the case of Meyerhold, who trains actors to develop an acute awareness of themselves as kinetic, plastic forms in space.

'the route to image and feeling must begin with motion'

The second point raised by Rudnitsky in the long quotation on p. 164 concerned the relation between feeling and movement, and this is also informed by the external/internal debate. Meyerhold argues that

> [i]f I sit you in the posture of a sad person, and sad phrases come out […] this is the external conception, the 'idea' part of the acting link. The idea forces the actor to sit in a sad posture, but the posture itself helps to make him sad.[84]

Rudnitsky explains how Meyerhold operated on the 'certainty that a precisely determined, polished and fixed external form "suggests" the required feeling, causes experience'.[85] The notion that an external form can suggest an emotion is at the heart of Meyerhold's later approach to actor training. This connection between external form and internal experience harks back to William James's contention

> that emotional consciousness and its transitory states were directly linked to the physical body; in fact, the body's automatic response to stimuli itself was the emotion, preceding the mental perception of the emotion. Using the dictum, 'I saw the bear, I ran, I became frightened' James attempted to demonstrate the physiological basis of his theory.[86]

The phrase 'the body's automatic response to stimuli' connects with Pavlov's theory of reflex reactions which will be discussed below. But just as Stanislavsky drew on Ribot to support his own ideas about acting, Hoover suggests that these scientists 'merely corroborated the principles of theatre art which Meyerhold had already enunciated'.[87]

'an actor whose natural abilities have been developed by systematic training'

Meyerhold did seem to be searching for an objective, scientific approach to acting. He drew on the ideas of the American F.W. Taylor, who was one of the first to analyse the movement of his workers in an attempt to find the most efficient way of performing a task, what would later be known as time and motion. In a lecture on biomechanics in 1922, Meyerhold declared '[w]e are on the eve of a new Taylorised man whose psycho-physical organisation will be radically transformed by the factory', adding that his 'constant concern' in art was 'the organisation of raw material'. The actor's material consists 'of plastic forms in space' – bodily movements which are 'subject to constant laws of mechanics'. In describing the actor as a *conscious* operator of his acting machinery he is drawing on the theory of Coquelin which he reduces to a 'formula for acting': $N = A^1 + A^2$ 'where N = the actor; A^1 = the artist who conceives the idea and issues the instructions necessary for its execution; A^2 = the executant who executes the conception of A^1'.[88,89] In his post-Revolutionary enthusiasm Meyerhold seems to want to follow his fellow constructivists in their rejection of fine art and the production of art objects, and embrace decorative art and the production of functional objects. But while in the truly plastic arts (i.e. the construction of three-dimensional objects) Popova could design fabrics, theatre, however real, is always a performance, thus movement in the theatre and movement in the factory will always be different. Yes they are both repeated, but only one is for an audience. Of course part of his aesthetic, from his Symbolist productions forward, was to pare down stage pictures and movements to their essentials. This has little to do with Taylor's motivation, which was to make financial economies, and everything to do with Meyerhold's poetic economy of stage movement.

Meyerhold's quasi-algebraic formulation can be understood better by referring back to Coquelin's:

The arts differ according to the nature of medium; well, the actor's medium is – himself. His own face, his body, his life is the material of his art; the thing he works and moulds to draw out from it his creation. From this it follows the existence of the comedian [*comédien* in French means 'actor'] must be dual. One part of him is the performer, the instrumentalist; another, the instrument to be played on.[90]

Behind Coquelin and Meyerhold lies the fundamental question about the degree to which movement is controlled consciously: where Stanislavsky opts for the 'subconscious', Meyerhold argues for conscious control. And this question of control brings us back to Diderot's paradox of the actor.

Robert Leach analyses Meyerhold's approach to stage movement with great sensitivity. Leach argues that Meyerhold's equation of the actor $- N = A^1 + A^2 -$ is the first stage in his attempt to create a science of acting which he calls bio-mechanics (a term which will be explained below) and is based on Taylor's concept of efficient performance. Later Meyerhold takes on Pavlov's notion of an animal's reflex reaction to a stimulus, and describes the phrase of a working movement as consisting of stimulus, realisation and reaction.

> Now, the stimulus (A^1 in the previous equation) triggers a reflex action, which is the realisation. When the realisation is done, it comes to rest pre-pared for a new intention, and this comprises the reaction. The aim of training is now to prepare the actor by creating in him a state of 'excitability' which can provoke the correct reflex action: the 'point of excitability' is the period of receptivity and rest.[91]

There is a connection between action (motor output) and reaction (sensory feed-back from the action), but Meyerhold's model superimposes animal reflexes (which are automatic and thus non-conscious) onto humans who are capable of consciousness, by which I mean a highly complex reflection upon the sensory feedback from action. It is precisely in this reflective moment when the moving person finds a connection with an emotional state or a past memory.

Meyerhold's attempt to express his theory of acting in terms of contemporary theories of scientific management and psychology runs the risk of reducing the actor's organism to that of a robot or a dog. It may be an unfortunate translation but a sentence in Rudnitsky's study reads: 'We must be able to show the modern actor on stage as a complete automaton.'[92] In fact, Meyerhold was just demanding preci-sion and concision of movement: for him biomechanics 'establishes the principles of precise analytic execution of each motion, establishes the differentiation of each motion for purposes of maximum precision' which is achieved through identifying 'the start and end points of motion, a pause after each accomplished motion, the geometrisation of movement in planes'.[93] Hoover argues that his teaching 'derived from the long tradition of the theatre and cannot be subsumed under the pseudoscience of biomechanics'.[94]

Igor Ilinsky, one of the stalwarts of Meyerhold's troupe, points out that bio-mechanics 'was never fully explained or codified' by him.[95] In a statement from 1935 Ilinsky also points out the emotional and experiential dimension to biomechanical training. Echoing Meyerhold he states that it begins 'with a number of techniques consisting of the ability to direct one's body on the stage in the most successful and correct way'. This is the economy and discipline of Taylorised movement (and also stylised movement). But he continues that it

> also extends to the most complex problems of acting technique, problems of coordination, of movements and speech, of the ability to direct one's emotions and one's acting excitability. The emotional saturation of an actor, tempera-ment, excitability, the emotional sympathy of the artist-actor with the creative emotional experiences of his hero – this too, is a fundamental element in the complex biomechanical system.[96]

Ilinsky's comments provide a counterweight to the notion that Meyerhold was preoccupied solely with the outer image, and had no concern for either emotion or experiencing.

Training, training, training

What are we to conclude from this argument about movement and physical action? Was this the common ground which brought Stanislavsky and Meyerhold together? Certainly both men believed that acting was a psycho-physical activity which required constant training.

Meyerhold declared:

> Training! Training! Training! But if it's the kind of training which exercises only the body and not the mind, then No, thank you! I have no use for the actors who know how to move but cannot think.[97]

A sentiment seemingly echoed by Stanislavsky:

> Remember: every exacting actor, however great, at certain intervals, say every four or five years, must go back and study anew. It is also necessary for him periodically to place his voice – it changes with time. He must also rid himself of those habits which have adhered to him like dirt, as for example, coquetry, self-admiration, etc. As an artist, it is necessary for him constantly to widen his culture. Now, do you understand the task which confronts you? I repeat once more: Do not think of performance – think only of training, training, training.'[98]

This focus on training rather than performance brings into play the importance of the studio, and although it was apparently Meyerhold who came up with the term 'Theatre-Studio', both men were committed to this place of experiment and research:

For Meyerhold, the alternation between performing or producing and teaching or learning was crucial to his development as an artist: the two kinds of activity, publication and research, existed in a dialectical and inter-dependent relationship; and paradoxically he often found that through the public production he was learning and the training exercises were becoming self-contained entities of achievement.[99]

In his own words Meyerhold was both a director and a pedagogue: 'I am not only a director but also a pedagogue, in the basis of my work on every play there is a pedagogical side too.'[100]

The studio, like the rehearsal room, is not a place of retreat but of public testing and experiment. Stanislavsky presents his training studio as a place where the actor enters a process of detoxification from all the theatricality that might have accrued over a period of performance. To say that they have all these shared values in common is to repeat my earlier claim that both men shared a monomaniacal passion for theatre. But look closely at the detail and both men meant quite different things by the words 'theatre', 'acting' and 'training'. Meyerhold delighted in the very same theatricality that Stanislavsky regarded as a 'lie': 'I know that scenery, make-up, costumes, and the fact that I have to perform my work in public is nothing but a bare-faced lie.'[101] Meyerhold has written above of the pleasure that the actor must get from performing a certain pattern or shaping of movement (*risunok*), and it is to that sense of joyous physicality and public dialogue that we turn next.

A dialogue about the traditions of popular theatre

This dialogue is even less of a direct exchange than the earlier ones. There is almost no common ground between Stanislavsky and Meyerhold in this exploration of the grotesque in theatre. I have already quoted (on p. 67) a note made by Stanislavsky when redrafting his *My Life in Art* for a Russian readership:

> In the Chapter on the Revolution say that constructivism is a good thing, but they didn't make very good use of it and it was discarded. Predict that the actor's art is on the decline. In the chapter on the Revolution state that this is the result of all that affected stylisation.[102]

By 'all that affected stylisation' we can imagine that Stanislavsky is thinking about Meyerhold. Although Stanislavsky did entertain the notion of studying Commedia dell'Arte and improvisation, the aesthetic of constructivism and the grotesque marked a limit beyond which he could not go. Although there was no overt dialogue between Meyerhold and Bakhtin, both men share the same passion for medieval and popular theatre, and use the same images and figures. They use them to discuss quite different things: theatre and cultural philosophy, respectively.

Meyerhold's *Balaganchik, Farce (The Fairground Booth)* was provocatively theatrical with the set being a replica of the theatre in which the performance took place. Meyerhold describes it thus:

> This booth has its own stage, curtain, prompter's box, and proscenium opening. Instead of being masked with the conventional border, the flies, together with the ropes and the wires, are visible to the audience. When the entire set in the booth is hauled aloft, the audience in the actual theatre sees the whole process.[103]

Everything about this theatre insisted on the present moment of the performance. Some years later Mayakovsky would tease the audience from the stage about their attachment to the outdated stage realism where

> The stage
> Is a keyhole
> You sit down calmly facing ahead or sideways
> And watch a slice of other people's lives.[104,105]

Meyerhold adds:

> A theatrical performance knows neither 'yesterday' nor 'tomorrow'. The theatre is an art of today, of just this hour, just this minute, this second. 'Yesterday' in theatre is traditions, legends, texts of plays; 'tomorrow', the dreams of the artist. But the reality of the theatre is only today.[106]

This is a very different notion to Stanislavsky's 'Here, Today, Now', where the actor imagines himself in the situation of the character, rather than the actor vis-à-vis the audience.[107] At one level all acting takes place in the present, but this present moment is significantly different for both men. The 'here and now' Meyerhold talks of is shared with the audience.

Once again we have to wonder whether Bakhtin's notion of chronotope (which is predicated on the representation of time and space) has any possible application to the theatrical use of time and space in performance. Leach seems to hint at a connection when he uses 'chronotope' in a discussion of 'the interplay between space and time' in Chekhov's dramas.[108] But the notion is not developed. Not for the first time, the argument has been encapsulated by Pushkin when he asks '[w]hat verisimilitude can there be, damn it, in a room divided in two, in one part of which there are two thousand people who are mostly invisible to those who are on the stage?' Pushkin followed this with a second question: 'And what if we showed that the very essence of the art of theatre precisely *excludes* verisimilitude?'[109] This is precisely what Meyerhold *did* show in *Balaganchik.*

Most commentators on Meyerhold underline the importance of this production in terms of his artistic development as a director/auteur. Rudnitsky argues that it was a watershed moment in theatrical history:

Up until his production of *The Puppet Show* nobody anywhere at any time had dared to reveal to the audience the secrets of stage effects. Theatre had not even dreamed of such frankness. In the old folk theatre such effects could have been noticeable, but never had been *specially* demonstrated to the public. Until this moment the idea of boldly exposing illusion and revealing the secrets of the 'theatrical kitchen' has been utterly foreign to early twentieth-century Russian theatre. This theatre had aspired to render a picture of life, the atmosphere of its life, its mood and spirit. Meyerhold rejected these aspirations.[110]

Hoover also highlights the significant break with MAT's realism, citing an anecdote where Stanislavsky 'once had a house, real to the last detail, built on stage and was downcast to hear from the lips of a child that it nevertheless remained "theatre" because no real house would ever be built inside a house'.[111] This goes back to Stanislavsky as a child who was asked to hold a log and pretend that it was a real fire: he set light to it over the naked flame because he found the injunction that '[i]t's pretend, not real' was 'stupid'.[112] This failure to accept the convention of theatrical signs marks an enduring difference between the two men. Meyerhold puts a replica of a theatre on the stage of the theatre 'with the express purpose of showing up the machinery of illusion'.[113]

Edward Braun's description of *Balaganchik* introduces most of the themes that will be discussed in this section:

> The abrupt changes of mood, the sudden switches of personality, the deliberate disruption of illusion, the asides to the audience, all demanded a mental and physical dexterity, an ability to improvise, a capacity for acting not only the part but also one's attitude to it. These devices were all waiting to be redis-covered in the *Commedia dell'Arte* and beyond. It was this theatre, the theatre of masks and improvisation, that the experience of the *Fairground Booth* led Meyerhold to explore.[114]

The four themes that I will elaborate on, all of which find a connection with Bakhtin's writings of the 1930s, are: 'abrupt changes of mood' which is how Meyerhold defines the grotesque; 'asides to the audience', which returns us to the polemic about footlights; and Commedia dell'Arte and a 'theatre of masks and improvisation'. Without making too much of what is a rather obvious point, Meyerhold seems to have reinvented a tradition of popular theatre with the very means by which Bakhtin denied the possibility of theatrical representation. Bakhtin thought that by definition a theatre without footlights could no longer be theatre. Meyerhold, following Pushkin, demonstrated that it most emphatically was possible and was desirable.

The grotesque

Balaganchik is an example of grotesque as Meyerhold defines it: 'a genre of low comedy in literature, music and the plastic arts.' He continues by noting how it will borrow 'from every source anything which satisfies its joie de vivre and its capricious, mocking attitude to life'.[115] This echoes Bakhtin's focus on how low comedy defies false seriousness. Picon-Vallin picks up on the fact that many commentators – Bakhtin included – 'devote the greater part of their energies to creating a corpus of literary and sometimes pictorial references' but take no 'account of the specifics of the stage'.[116] But it is precisely Bakhtin's vision (especially in his study of Rabelais) of grotesque licence to forge new relationships between objects in the world that underpins Meyerhold's revolutionary concept of compositional unity. The following quotations are from Meyerhold's essay 'The Fairground Booth':

> The grotesque, advancing beyond stylisation, is a method of synthesising rather than analysing. In turning away details, the grotesque recreates the fullness of life (in a perspective of 'improbable suitability', according to Pushkin's expression). In reducing the richness of the empirical world to a typical unity, stylisation impoverishes life whereas the grotesque refuses to recognise only one aspect – *only* the vulgar or *only* the elevated. It mixes the opposites and by design accents the contradictions. *The only effect which counts is the improvised, the original.*[117]

Once again Pushkin is invoked in both Bakhtin's and Meyerhold's popular aesthetics. Both agree that the grotesque doesn't operate on exclusive binary oppositions, nor is it a form of stylisation, both of which reduce the many to the one. In pursuing his account of this comic and liberating combination, Meyerhold goes so far as to argue that theatre is an '*example of the grotesque*' because it 'being a combination of natural, temporal, spatial and numerical phenomena, is itself outside of nature. It finds that these phenomena invariably contradict our everyday experience and that *the theatre is essentially an example of the grotesque*'.[118] Elsewhere in his essay Meyerhold notes that 'the artist attempts to cause the spectator to suddenly pass from a plane with which he is familiar, to another plane which is unfamiliar'.[119] A constant throughout his career is this insistence that the aim of art is not to represent the real: 'Art dismantles reality, depicting it now spatially, now temporally. For this reason, art consists either in images or in the alternation of images: the first yields the spatial form of art, the second – the temporal forms.'[120]

We have already seen Bakhtin's analysis of how things can become improbably huge in Rabelais' novel (where a mouth can become an entire country).

> Indeed, one of the oldest forms of hyperbolic grotesque was the exaggerated size of foodstuffs. In this exaggerated form of valuable matter we see for the first time the positive and absolute meaning of size and quantity in an aesthetic image, hyperboles of food parallel the most ancient hyperboles of belly, mouth, and phallus.[121]

This aesthetic of improbable exaggeration is picked up by Meyerhold. Braun describes how in *The Magnificent Cuckold*, '[m]any of the objects – for example, the inkstand and pen of Estrugo or the dustbin and shoe-brush of the Nurse — were intentionally exaggerated in size'.[122] In *The Government Inspector* Meyerhold demands that '[t]he objects ought to be bulky, terribly bulky. If there is a sideboard, then it has to be elephant size'.[123] Bakhtin connects the exaggerated size of the mouth with the Hell's Mouth, but only once links it to the theatre of his own time — a fascinating and very apt mention of Brecht as an artist who along with Pablo Neruda is in the line of the 'realist grotesque'.[124] But when Meyerhold and Mayakovsky collaborate on a play which is based on medieval drama in *Mystery-Bouffe*, their stage set is designed by suprematist Malevich and has no Hell's Mouth. The setting is abstract and while the time is in a mythical future the subject matter is very much about present-day concerns. Where Meyerhold translates the grotesque into a plastic onstage reality, Bakhtin remains in the realm of the symbol (closer to Cassirer's immense study, *The Philosophy of Symbolic Forms*). Thus the significance of the grotesque body is that it 'is not separated from the rest of the world. It is not a closed, completed unit; it is unfinished, outgrows itself, transgresses its own limits'.[125] Throughout his study of Rabelais, Bakhtin opposes the historical and semantic openness of the grotesque with 'the closed and finished world, with its distinct fixed boundaries dividing all phenomena and values'.[126] Like Meyerhold he stresses the importance of avoiding a forced unity, but where one is creating images on stage, the other is using images of theatre to address questions of philosophy.

Commedia dell'Arte, the mask and the *emploi*

Meyerhold was aware that people considered him 'a lost cause; he's obsessed with *Commedia dell'Arte*'.

> Yes they're right. But if I need to play some part, I always have to look for Brighella or Pantalone in him. Because these theatrical masks are to be found in every character. They represent a common theatrical tradition.[127]

For Meyerhold a character's past lies not in a biographical history (the novelistic) but in its stage or generic history — the role is a *repertoire* of gesture, posture and movement. Anna Muza points out how the '[m]asks of Commedia dell'Arte, conventional stage types, and circus clowns represented, for Meyerhold, the overt artifice of role-playing, the necessary estrangement from "reality" as opposed to its naturalistic imitation'.[128] Her use of the word 'estrangement' evokes again the formalist notion of *priam ostranenji* — making things unfamiliar.

Even if Bakhtin and Meyerhold might make very different uses of the carnival tradition, they do agree on its importance as a genre. Meyerhold cites the struggle between Goldoni and Gozzi to illustrate the historical roots of the struggle between bourgeois realism and grotesque realism, and both agree the grotesque can only be kept alive through active engagement. Traditions, he writes, 'need watering just like a bulb under cultivation. It is ridiculous to expect a tradition to flourish by itself; culture doesn't function like that'.

In his battles with Goldoni Gozzi placed his faith in the masses, in popular taste, and in the needs of the contemporary Italian audience; furthermore, he assembled a troupe of actors ready to fight with him to preserve the lusty traditions of the theatre.[129]

At the heart of this very public debate was the use of the mask: Goldoni wanted to explore 'realistic' characters without them, whereas Gozzi wanted to keep the 'lusty tradition' alive. The debate brings us to back to two related questions: what is a character, and is a character an image? While the mask is a certainly an image, it is much more than a pictorial likeness of a person. A mask is a three-dimensional structure which takes on expressive significance through movement in the same way that Garin talks about bringing a wooden doll to life. By taking the actor's face out of play the mask demands a rich vocabulary of movement. Meyerhold explains how naturalistic theatre 'regards the face as the actor's major means of expression and, in consequence, disregards all other means. The naturalist theatre does not know the beauty of sculpture, does not make its actors train their bodies'.[130]

Again and again the argument comes back to the plastic reality of the actor's body which can only become an image through the shaping movement of that actor. Thus even 'while the actor is gripped in the dramatic struggle' Meyerhold maintains that:

> he remains in full control of his actions by virtue of the physical dexterity and self-control that he has inherited from the *cabotin*; at the tensest moments of the drama he continues to 'manipulate his masks', thereby conveying without ambiguity the most subtle shades of irony and the most complex patterns of emotions.[131]

Meyerhold argued that one should play a role with the same calculated detachment that one plays a mask and quotes his favourite actor, Mamont Dalsky (1865–1918),

> who said that there must never be any correspondence between the personal mood of the actor and the mood of the character being portrayed. That kills art. He always played Hamlet in complex opposition to the mood in which he arrived for the performance.

He concluded that the disjunction between the actor's and the character's emotion 'is indeed the basis of artistic reincarnation'.[132] We are returned once again to the actor's paradox.

A *commedia* player would often perform their mask-character for their entire career, which raises the question of how actors find the kind of character they can play. Meyerhold used the French concept of the *emploi* to help him with casting: it was 'a serious matter' and he would begin his analysis of the role by checking 'him out against these formulas'.[133] Meyerhold listed seventeen different *emplois* in the theatre, the first one being the 'Hero':

1. Greater-than-average height. Long legs. Two types of face: broad (Mochalov, Karatygin, Salvini) & narrow (Irving). Average size of head is desirable. [...] Voice of great strength, range and richness of timbre. Medium baritone, tending to bass.[134]

In the first instance, Meyerhold is describing the plastic and vocal possibilities of the person of the actor which are then matched with corresponding roles. In order to 'make the *emploi* an effective means of character analysis' Meyerhold would 'use rehearsal time to talk about theatre tradition, from the conventions of Greek tragedy to provincial Russian actors of the last century whose work he had personally observed and admired'.[135] When working on the character Pimen in *Boris Godunov* he informed the actors: 'So now we have to decide to what type Pimen belongs. Without that one cannot even begin.'[136] An *emploi* is a type, like a mask in whose features the character's gestural repertoire is inscribed.

Following the argument of the earlier chapters we could guess that both Bakhtin and Stanislavsky would reject this notion of convention (which brings us back to *uslovnyi* theatre, a theatre of convention). In his essay on the chronotope Bakhtin explains how the figures of the fool and the clown continue the novel's 'struggle against conventionality, but along lines that have a deeper significance and are more complexly organised'.

> The primary level, the level where the author makes his transformation, utilises the images of the clown and the fool (that is, a naiveté expressed as the inability to understand stupid conventions). In the struggle against the inadequacy of all available life-slots to fit an authentic human being, these masks take on an extraordinary significance.[137]

Bakhtin describes a strategy whereby the convention of the mask is used to out-play 'stupid conventions'. There is a degree to which Bakhtin and Meyerhold agree: both are challenging the given, the familiar, and demand a fresh creative response from the reader or spectator; more broadly, both use the mask as a means towards creativity. But they part company when Bakhtin argues that this is about avoiding convention in order to become an 'authentic human being'. (We will return to this distinction between the 'authentic human being' and 'stupid conventions' in the next chapter on Grotowski.)

A theatre without footlights

Theatrical space has been explored in terms of its plastic reality but not yet in terms of the relationship between the actor and the audience. Meyerhold argues that the 'beginnings of theatre are to be found in a ritualistic collective moment in which everyone participated'. He then turns to the split in the theatre space (mentioned above by Pushkin) which resulted in there being 'active and passive participants' and as 'theatre developed so the audience became progressively isolated'. And what marked that division between actor and audience?

> There arose that magic barrier which even today, in the form of footlights, divides the theatre into two opposed camps, the performers and the onlookers; no artery exists to unite these two separate bodies and preserve the unbroken circulation of creative energy.[138]

Meyerhold's observations on the popular theatre of Shakespeare and Molière focus on the unproductive separation of the audience from the actor.

> If we go to the heart of Molière's works, we find that he was trying to remove the footlights from the contemporary stage, since they were better suited to the heroic drama of Corneille than to plays with their origins in the popular theatre. […] How could Molière accept this segregation of actor and public?[139]

Meyerhold's alternative to footlights wasn't the 'cosmic populism' of Bakhtin's 'Carnival', but a dialogue with the audience informed by the traditions of sixteenth-century popular theatre. Where Bakhtin's streets are historical, Meyerhold's are actual with 'shop-windows piled high with all kinds of everyday wares and artful trifles' and 'cafes which line the pavements'. He creates theatre for these real people and warns that '[u]nless the theatre shouts as lustily as the streets, it won't attract an audience for love nor money'.[140] Bakhtin is in the realm of symbolic discourse. Meyerhold is talking about the material practice of theatre.

The destruction of the footlights was not simply a question of aesthetics, but was also about the purpose and meaning of the performance. We have already seen how Meyerhold's rehearsals were quite public affairs in which guests were asked for their opinion on what was happening on stage. This was even more so the case with his performances, as one of Meyerhold's actors explains:

> Naturally all theatres exist for the audience. All the concerns of the author, the director, the actors are centred on the audience. But for Meyerhold the audience occupied an exceptional position. The audience was his beacon, his compass, his thermometer without which he could not exist for a moment.[141]

This might suggest that Meyerhold was keen to woo and win over audiences – just like the actor that Stanislavsky sought to avoid at all costs. The opposite is true – he wanted to create an active debate within the audience, which meant provoking equal amounts of praise and criticism. Meyerhold describes the happy mean:

> If everyone praises your production, almost certainly it is rubbish. If everyone abuses it, then perhaps there is something in it. But if some praise and others abuse, if you can split your audience in half, then for sure it is a good production.[142]

Stanislavsky used the same quotation: 'Dumas said: When everyone abuses something, it doesn't mean that it is bad. When everyone praises something, it is probably banal. When some abuse and other praise something, it is a success.'[143] The political fission of Meyerhold's theatre was produced by him splitting the audience in this way.

Meyerhold writes about how his productions are left 'unfinished' in order to allow for their active participation in the event.

> We produce every play on the assumption that it will still be unfinished when it appears on the stage. We do this consciously because we realise that the crucial revision of a production is that which is made by the spectator. [...] The author and the director provide no more than a framework, and it must not cramp or hinder the actor and the spectator, but encourage them to work harmoniously together.[144]

Contrast Meyerhold's words with Bakhtin's:

> Footlights would destroy a carnival, as the absence of footlights would destroy a theatrical performance. Carnival is not a spectacle seen by the people; they live in it, and everyone participates because its very idea embraces all the people.[145]

How many times have we read Bakhtin writing about theatre being a closed art form? Here we see Meyerhold explaining how there can be a theatre without footlights, and that it is precisely because there is no separation between audience and actor that its meaning can be left open to the interpretation of each different audience member. Meyerhold demonstrates that by using the very same imagery, drawing on the same tradition of popular theatre, by invoking the same literary authorities (Gozzi, Pushkin) as Bakhtin, there is a theatre without footlights, a theatre which can participate in and reflect upon the social realities experienced by the audience and the actors. It was precisely this notion of a shared space between actor and audience that motivated Grotowski in his productions between 1957 and 1969.

Notes

1 Meyerhold in Hoover (1974) 77.
2 Hoover (1974) 109.
3 In Gladkov (1997) 167.
4 Gladkov (1997) 88.
5 In Law and Gordon (1996) 68.
6 In Rudnitsky (1981) 540.
7 Gladkov (1997) 87.
8 In Senelick (2014) 613.
9 Leach (1993) 5.
10 In Rudnitsky (1981) 201.
11 In Rudnitsky (1981) 202.
12 In Rudnitsky (1981) 198.
13 Rudnitsky (1981) 285.

14 In Rudnitsky (1981) 541.
15 In Rudnitsky (1981) 377.
16 In Rudnitsky (1981) 540.
17 *Life* (2008) 177.
18 *Life* (1967) 324.
19 Torpokov (1999) 77.
20 Leach (2003) 44.
21 In Senelick (2014) 203.
22 *Life* (2008) 264.
23 Senelick (2014) 159.
24 *Life* (2008) 248.
25 *Life* (2008) 248.
26 In Braun (1995) 38.
27 Braun (1991) 45.
28 E.g. Rudnitsky (1981), Picon-Vallin (1999).
29 *Life* (2008) 249.
30 Hoover (1974) 330.
31 In Hoover (1974) 40.
32 Whyman (2008) 212.
33 Meyerhold in Braun (1995) 38.
34 Leach (2003) 47.
35 Symons (1971) 32.
36 Meyerhold in Braun (1991) 298.
37 The title of Hoover's book of 1974.
38 *Formal Method* 7.
39 *Philosophy of Language* 102–103.
40 Medvedev (1985) 8.
41 Leach (1993) 11.
42 In Braun (1995) 28.
43 Braun (1995) 30.
44 Braun (1995) 31.
45 In Leach (1993) 9.
46 In Picon-Vallin (1999) 53 (my translation).
47 In Braun (1995) 38.
48 Braun (1991) 56.
49 In Schmidt (1981) 39.
50 In Law and Gordon (1996) 60.
51 Benedetti (1991) 284.
52 Benedetti (1991) 284.
53 Rudnitsky (1981) 222.
54 Braun (1991) 123–124.
55 Braun (1991) 124.
56 Braun (1991) 171.
57 *Dostoevsky* 217.
58 Braun (1991) 119.
59 Braun (1991) 120.
60 Braun (1991) 121.
61 Braun (1991) 122.
62 *Life* (1967) 324.
63 Braun (1991) 126.
64 Law and Gordon (1996) 60.
65 Meyerhold in Schmidt (1981) 130.
66 Rudnitsky (1981) 294–295.
67 In Leach (2003) 61.

68 Leach (2003) 61.
69 Meyerhold in Hoover (1974) 44.
70 Rudnitsky (1981) 293–294.
71 In Schmidt (1981) 38.
72 Picon-Vallin (1999) 204 (my translation).
73 Picon-Vallin (1999) 234 (my translation).
74 Leach (1993) 65.
75 Hoover (1974) 102.
76 Gladkov (1997) 103.
77 *Life* (2008) 104.
78 *Life* (2008) 9.
79 *Life* (2008) 10–11.
80 *Work* 11.
81 *Life* (2008) 248.
82 *Life* (2008) 243.
83 *Work* 330.
84 Meyerhold in Leach (1993) 54.
85 Rudnitsky (1981) 295.
86 Law and Gordon (1996) 36.
87 Hoover (1974) 101.
88 Constant-Benoit Coquelin wrote two short books on acting *L'art et le comedien* (1880) and *L'art du comedien* (1886).
89 In Braun (1995) 173.
90 Leach (1993) 53.
91 Leach (1993) 54.
92 Rudnitsky (1981) 294.
93 Rudnitsky (1981) 294.
94 Hoover (1974) 110.
95 Leach (1993) 52.
96 In Rudnitsky (1981) 296.
97 In Gladkov (1997) 104.
98 In Torpokov (1999) 155.
99 Leach (1993) 47.
100 In Sitkovetskaya, 20 October 1925.
101 In Hoover (1974) 251.
102 Senelick (2008) xix.
103 Meyerhold in Braun (1995) 62–63.
104 Mayakovsky in his *Mystery-Bouffe* (produced by Meyerhold in 1918 and 1922).
105 In Schmidt (1981) 47.
106 In Gladkov (1997) 132.
107 Benedetti (1988) 316.
108 Leach (2003) 38.
109 In Picon-Vallin (1999) 53 (my translation).
110 Rudnitsky (1981) 108.
111 In Hoover (1974) 38.
112 *Life* (2008) 5.
113 Hoover (1974) 38.
114 Braun (1995) 67.
115 Braun (1991) 137.
116 Picon-Vallin (1999) 21–23 (my translation).
117 In Symons (1971) 68 (Meyerhold's italics).
118 In Symons (1971) 68.
119 In Symons (1971) 67.
120 In Braun (1991) 137.

121 *Rabelais* 184.
122 Braun (1995) 182–183.
123 In Sitkovetskaya 9 October 1925.
124 *Rabelais* 46.
125 *Rabelais* 26.
126 *Rabelais* 44.
127 Braun (1995) 102–103.
128 Muza (1996) 4.
129 Braun (1991) 258.
130 In Hoover (1974) 44.
131 Braun (1995) 125.
132 Gladkov (1997) 115.
133 Sitkovetskaya in Anna Muza (2002).
134 In Hoover (1974) 299.
135 Muza (2002) 6.
136 Schmidt (1981) 112.
137 *Chronotope* 163.
138 Braun (1991) 59.
139 Braun (1991) 99.
140 Braun (1991) 263.
141 In Schmidt (1981) 46.
142 In Gladkov (1997) 165.
143 Stanislavsky in Senelick (2014) 215.
144 Braun (1991) 256.
145 *Rabelais* 7.

6 Grotowski: beyond theatre

Outline of a career

Grotowski was born in 1933 in Rzeszow, a small town east of Krakow. Raymonde Temkine notes that 'at the age of eighteen' Grotowski 'decided to become a director, but he felt the need for experience as an actor' and so in 1951 he began his studies at the Advanced School of Dramatic Art in Krakow, gaining his actor's certificate in June 1955.[1] Later that summer he went to Moscow to study direction at GITIS (Russian University of Theatre Arts). He returned to Poland in the autumn of 1956 after having made his first trip to South East Asia and took part in the political events that became known as the Warsaw October. His career falls into five distinct periods: between 1957 and 1969, the Theatre of Productions; between 1970 and 1976, the Theatre of Participation; between 1976 and 1982, the Theatre of Sources; and between 1983 and 1989, Objective Drama. His final project, Theatre as a Vehicle, began in 1989 in Pontedera, Italy, and ended with his death in 1999.

Grotowski was first known in Poland as a political firebrand rather than as a revolutionary of the theatre. As a 'national-level activist of a revisionist Communist youth organisation, the Union of Socialist Youth – Political Centre of the Academic Left' Grotowski wrote an article in 1955 calling for 'a young artists' club in Krakow' which elicited the following reply from playwright Slawomir Mrozek:

> Let's assume that Grotowski is really on fire. Unfortunately, nobody really knows what's burning there. Pray, Grotowski, why didn't you give us some specific examples? You signed yourself a theatre student but there's not even a small mention, for example, of what you're trying to accomplish in the theatre. Grotowski, you want to knock something over or go somewhere, you shake your fists at someone, but pray, tell us what, where, who.[2]

There is a strange prescience in Mrozek's question about what Grotowski 'was trying to accomplish in theatre'. Although his focus shifted from political to theatrical activity, he continued to search for a place – call it a club, a laboratory or a studio – where people could meet to pursue their interests and researches.

Grotowski's quest was equally ethical and aesthetic, which explains why he described the theatre as 'a place of provocation':

> In this struggle with one's own truth, this effort to peel off the life-mask, the theatre, with its full-fleshed perceptivity, has always seemed to me a place of provocation.[3]

This goes some way to answering Mrozek's question about 'what' he wished to accomplish in theatre. His work could be seen as a sustained negotiation with the falsity of much of the social regime in which he lived. Jan Kott observed that 'Grotowski's theatre developed at a historical moment of prolonged political unrest', continuing that

> [i]n conditions of arbitrary and unlimited political repression every public activity is a compromise. In the theatre compromise is always ultimately an artistic compromise. Grotowski made the heroic decision to be uncompromising. But under the conditions of repression, such a decision exacts the price of supplanting politics with metaphysics.[4]

Kott's phrase 'supplanting politics with metaphysics' very elegantly describes the shift from direct political engagement to a theatrical practice which proposed detaching the social, the 'mask', from the personal. In answer to Mrozek's last two questions, the 'who' became a small troupe of actors performing for small audiences, rarely numbering more than a hundred. The 'where', the theatre, with its 'full-fleshed perceptivity', became a place for research, experiment and performance (probably in that order).

Grotowski and Bakhtin

Grotowski admits to having been 'brought up on Stanislavski'. He admired 'his persistent study, his systematic renewal of the methods of observation, and his dialectical relationship to his own earlier work'. While agreeing that Stanislavsky 'asked key methodological questions', Grotowski's 'solutions however, differ widely' from his – 'sometimes we reach opposite conclusions'.[5] Like Stanislavsky he was keen to 'revolutionise the theatre itself'.[6] Grotowski certainly emulated Stanislavsky in his ceaseless, fearless questioning of the purpose of theatre. To return to the guiding theme of this book, theatre as a form and acting as an activity were permanently in question for Grotowski. They were endlessly productive problems rather than fixed and known entities. From the very outset theatre was always a 'vehicle' for Grotowski rather than an end in itself.

'Grotowski said that from Stanislavsky he learned how to work with actors, but it was from Meyerhold that he discovered the creative possibilities of the stage director's craft.'[7] When in Moscow

> Grotowski became interested in Meyerhold after reading the transcript of his *mise-en-scène* for *The Inspector General*.[8] It is through Meyerhold that Grotowski

understood that staging a play is but an answer to the play; not a submission but a reaction – this is the meaning of creation.[9]

Like Stanislavsky and Meyerhold he was creating a new kind of theatre and therefore required a new kind of actor to perform in his productions, thus explaining the symbiotic relationship between Grotowski the actor-trainer and Grotowski the director. Grotowski's training did not consist of a series of exercises set within a fixed system: it was not geared to giving his actors a theatrical toolkit. Rather than teach acting he wanted to work on the actor, with the actor, to help them to achieve the 'total act'. Lisa Wolford explains that while

> Grotowski's incorporation of codified physical training methods might owe more to Meyerhold's practice than Stanislavsky's, his emphasis on the 'total act' and on guiding the actor to develop the most subtle nuances of inner life within the framework of the role had little to do with the principles of constructivist theatre.[10]

Central to Grotowski's approach both to training and to performance is this tension between the form of an exercise and the inner life of the actor which can turn it into a 'total act'.

With his emphasis upon the person of the actor, it is not surprising to find connections between Grotowski and Bakhtin, particularly with those early writings that evoke so many resonances with Stanislavsky. Take the following statement which invokes Grotowski's 'total act':

> If the act takes place, then the actor, that is to say the human being, trans-cends the state of incompleteness to which we condemn ourselves in everyday life. The division between thought and feeling, body and soul, consciousness and the unconscious, seeing and instinct, sex and brain disappear; having fulfilled this, the actor achieves totality.[11]

Bakhtin writes about exactly the same sense of incompleteness that is experienced by an *I*. But where Bakhtin invokes and invites the intercessory figure of the observer-author, Grotowski argues that this can be achieved by the actor through the perfor-mance of the 'total act'. For Bakhtin the performance of an act transforms a possible ethical truth into an actual one, but it does not change his or her con-stitutive incompleteness. Thus, although Bakhtin and Grotowski start from the same image of incompleteness and both have the 'act' as a central concept, they then go in different directions. The double relation of *I* and *other* who become author and hero presents another level of relation between the two men. Although it is the actor who has to perform the total act, it is always for another. In the studio Grotowski's actors would work under his watchful eyes. The aesthetic work is undertaken by the actor and the director (a spectator who assists the actor in their process of authorship). In performance the act was performed for a small audience. These distinctions prompt the question as to whether

Grotowski's total act is ethical or aesthetic; or if the aesthetic work is a means of achieving an ethical end. Is the theatrical aesthetic, to return to an earlier phrase, a vehicle for ethical activity?

Grotowski's lack of completeness derives not from any constitutive lack within the self, but a division 'to which we condemned ourselves in everyday life'. Where in Bakhtin the *I* achieves an embodied understanding of an ethical truth through the performance of a once-only act, Grotowski's actor achieves self-realisation through a total act. This completeness is not that of a finished aesthetic image, but is the actor's experience of him- or herself as an undivided organism. With Bakhtin the body is instrumental in performing the activity; with Grotowski it is the organism where the initial division and the eventual totality are experienced. Completeness is not achieved aesthetically by another but organically within oneself. Grotowski argues that the inherent properties and potential of the body have been compromised by the social environment. This distinction between the social and personal informs Grotowski's account of the inner and outer body. The surface is the social mask, the life-mask that must be removed to reveal the truthful inner-ness beneath. It is as if the surface which has been in contact with the social environment is thereby corrupted, and it is only through lifting this away that one can get back to the original, natural truth of the body. This is the metaphysical dimension to Grotowski's thinking mentioned by Kott above.

Kumiega notes that 'it is the ethic, or attitude with which they [his 'training techniques'] are discovered, researched and performed, that is of primary sig-nificance if we are to attempt to penetrate the essence of Grotowski's approach and work'.[12] Grotowski's work on physical actions took him far from Stanislavsky's work on a role, and much closer to the actor's work on him- or herself. Like the other two directors he sought to situate his work in relation to art and life, but his project, firstly in the Theatre of Productions but more obviously in the Theatre of Parti-cipation, aimed to collapse these two categories. Aesthetic means are developed in order to work on oneself, which for Grotowski meant one's body. In Grotowski's own estimation of his career he admits

> [t]heatre has been a great adventure in my life, it has conditioned my way of thinking, my way of seeing people and looking at life. But I didn't look for theatre. In reality I always have been looking for something else. But I would say that my language has been formed by theatre.[13]

The aesthetic language of theatre has been a means of 'looking for something else' – an ethical quest for truthfulness?

Richard Schechner sees a common theme in the various projects in Grotowski's career:

> What unites all these periods, despite their diverse objectives, different styles, and fluctuations in the number of people participating, is Grotowski's insis-tence that what he has to offer can be acquired only through direct contact, person-to-person interaction, Martin Buber's '*ich und du*': the oral tradition.[14]

It would be wrong to say that in this sense Grotowski's approach was 'dialogical'. This is dialogue, but it is closer to the early Bakhtin of *Act* and *Hero* rather than his later sociological work. Bakhtin's *I* and *other* provides a good match for his intensely personal approach. Grotowski's interlocutor (either director or spectator) is not a person on the outside who grasps the other person as a visual image that can then be rendered as an aesthetically finished verbal image. Buber's *du* (thou) is very different to Bakhtin's *other*. It is an intimate addressee, not a person seen. Bakhtin's later analysis of dialogue moves even further from Grotowski, because although he writes of 'voices', they are the written not the spoken traces of other people's valuations and opinions. The outside position is Bakhtin's *sine qua non* for artistic creation, where Grotowski argues for proximity and intimacy. With Grotowski we have a model of dialogue based on closeness rather outside-ness, the familiar '*du*' rather than the *other*, the spoken rather than the written word.

For all Bakhtin's talk of dialogue, there is very little actual addressing of a person. But for all Grotowski's insistence upon the primacy of the spoken over the written, the personal over the collective, and the instant of the act, his practice was not about dialogue. The director's presence was often silent, a provocative witness rather than a Socratic midwife to the other's creative activity. Grotowski's stage montages were for public performance but were not directly addressed to the spectators. The collective presence of the spectators created the interpersonal space in which the actor could achieve the personal truth of a total act. It was an asymmetric dialogue in that the audience's active role amounted to being witness to the act of another. The heightened present moment of theatrical performance provided a model for a certain kind of interpersonal connection between actor and audience – a conflation of art and life. After 1969 Grotowski entered the first stage of his post-theatrical work, where art and life became one project.

Although Grotowski's ethical project has considerable resonance with Bakhtin's early manuscripts, there are also connections with the world of carnival and the grotesque. Grotowski's mature productions (*Kordian, Akropolis, Faustus, Constant Prince*) were very sophisticated montages that involved contradictory attitudes towards the values enshrined in the original plays: on the one hand, great respect and affection; on the other, parody and derision. In other words, precisely the grotesque that Bakhtin and Meyerhold wrote about. Grotowski went far beyond Meyerhold's banishing of the proscenium arch and extension of the thrust stage into the auditorium: he collapsed the boundary between audience and actor, both of whom shared the same space. This is the ultimate realisation of 'a theatre without footlights': for Bakhtin, the negation of the possibility of theatre, for Grotowski, its necessary condition. Grotowski's 1970 text 'Holiday' has echoes of Bakhtin's 'Carnival' but the space was neither the street nor the town square but forest, mountain and river. Where Bakhtin's milieu (like Dostoevsky's) was urban, Grotowski's was rural. The final connection comes through the body. Both Grotowski and Bakhtin had infirm bodies that generated constant medical concerns, and paradoxically, both conceived of communication and centred values in terms of the body.

Methodology

Grotowski's dialogues with the public

Although Grotowski was politically engaged in the events of the 'Warsaw October' in 1956 and wrote several articles for journals and newspapers, as he gradually found his artistic voice so the written gave way to the spoken word. He became celebrated for his talks for audiences, for radio, even for television. In his staged interviews he really did seem to engage in live dialogue.

> Grotowski has a special way of speaking, very much his own. He always improvises, inspired by questions. His books are simply transcripts of his public appearances. He is precise and logical, complementing his statements with metaphors, particularly when he wants to name something which defies definitions.[15]

For this reason Kolankiewicz warns that the

> printed word does not render, in the case of Grotowski's speech, all aspects of his message. In these circumstances, it is important that the reader remember that the author is constantly formulating his message in live speech before the participants of the meeting.[16]

What print misses is this sense of a thought unfolding live before an audience. We miss the process of him thinking. Kumiega further explains how the sense of his statements was conveyed 'not only in words, but often also in pauses, accents, tones of voice, gestures, enabl[ing] one to receive a deeper meaning from ordinary, everyday terms'.[17] Detailed analysis of Grotowski's approach to dialogue will reveal the significant differences between him and Bakhtin.

Grotowski's dialogue with actors

Eugenio Barba describes how '[s]ometimes Grotowski worked with only one participant in the presence of everybody'.

> For more than an hour we witnessed how he stimulated the actor with images, opening up the entire range of resonators and the regions of a secret and most profound voice. They were quite exceptional moments and the most moving thing of all was Grotowski's sense of delicacy and protection towards the actors who entrusted themselves totally to him.[18]

Schechner wrote about Grotowski's 'quality of attention which is like a luminous and pure consciousness, a consciousness devoid of all calculation, but at the same time attentive and generous'.[19] It was precisely this 'strong and direct relationship', Schechner continues, 'that enabled that actor to express something – something that right from the start could not belong to the actor, but which in time became truly his'.[20] We have seen how both Stanislavsky and Meyerhold worked with their actors, but neither achieved such a degree of intimacy and mutual purpose as Grotowski. Kumiega explains that Grotowski was proposing

> a total revaluation of the actor's art. He wanted the actor to be elevated from merely one of several factors in a theatrical event to the essence of theatre itself: simultaneously there should be a reduction of the artistic means of expression extraneous to the actor.[21]

Actor Zbigniew Cynkutis remembers that '[e]verything that we did that was any good was not even made by Grotowski but was *born between* me and Grotowski, Grotowski and me'. Adding that there was a 'strong direct relationship between Grotowski and each actor that enabled that actor to express something'.[22] Critic Jan Blonski argues that

> we may never be able to gauge to what extent the director in fact simply guides the actors to a discovery of the artistic forms that are already in them [...] and to what extent he imposes them on the actors.[23]

Once again, we are dealing with the degree to which it is the actor or the director who authors the character. Reflecting on his friend's career Flaszen explains that up until 1962

> the actor had been a man to be used during the performance, manipulated, his solutions suggested for him. [...] But during the work for *Dr Faustus* he began to listen to the actors. He was listening, watching, trying to fix something almost impossible to fix, points that may not have been aesthetically interesting, but were important as part of the process.[24]

Schechner was right to allude to Buber's book *I and Thou* where he distinguishes between two kinds of dialogue.[25] Addressing something or someone as an 'it' reduces them to an instrument which you use in your everyday life. By addressing someone as 'thou' you recognise their value. This describes the shift in the way Grotowski worked with his actors. From being a 'man to be used during the performance' the actor became a creative collaborator.

Possibly the most significant actor-director dialogue was that between Cieslak and Grotowski in the 1967 production *The Constant Prince*. Even though Grotowski had decided on the *cutting* of the text and on the staging (it resembled an old-fashioned operating theatre), there was clearly a great deal of creative latitude in his work with Cieslak on the role of Don Fernando. Thomas Richards describes their dialogue as a kind of merging (which in no way involved Bakhtin's notion of aesthetic outside-ness). '"Master Teacher" was a joint being, a Grotowski-in-Cieslak, designating the closest relationship, that of "transmission", from Grotowski to his disciple.'[26] Flaszen adds that '[s]omehow, Grotowski and Cieslak transcended the director-actor relationship [...] This was a departure from manipulation. It was a human relation transcending the professional relation'.[27] Once again, the human

and personal is opposed to the professional and institutional. The actor-director relationship changed again when the company entered into the devising process for their
final production, *Apocalypsis cum Figuris*. Flaszen explains that the 'basic method of his
activity was no longer the instruction of the actors, but rather expectation. He sat
silently, waiting, hour after hour. This was really a very great change, because previously he really was a dictator'.[28] Grotowski's intense and brief career as a director
followed the same contour as Stanislavsky's: from being a dictator to being a guide.

The development of Grotowski's actor training

Eugenio Barba's *The Land of Ashes and Diamonds* is a reflection upon his time as
Grotowski's assistant in the early 1960s. It is clear from Grotowski's letters just how
persistently he changed his own approach to actor training. As we move from 1962
through to 1964 we see his attempt to get away from the idea of a training exercise
being something fixed and generic. He explores how exercises can be used in such a
way that elicits a personal reaction from the actor. In a letter of September 1963 he
writes that he has 'put into effect a radical reform of the exercises' which is firstly
based on the 'individualisation of the exercises' such that '*[e]veryone becomes their own
instructor*' (his italics). In the section above we saw Grotowski moving from dictator
to guide, from giving instructions to following and encouraging the actor's own
creative process. The actors are no longer disciples in need of a master, but
autonomous learners and researchers. The *I* is no longer dependent on an *other*.

A year later in a letter of September 1964 Grotowski confirmed that this was
definitely the correct direction of travel: 'My tendency towards individuation
increases – almost every week it brings me a new illumination on the craft.' He
continues, '[s]trange experiences: I have changed the exercises and, to be frank, I
have reviewed the whole method. […] It seems to me to be such a vast change that
I will probably have to *relearn* the entire craft'.[29] Barba replied that he too was
changing the exercises, and in December Grotowski replied: 'You are right to revise
our exercises. There is no ideal model, as you well know, but everything has to be in
a state of continuous change.' He is constantly aware of a process of methodological
refinement: 'This does not mean a step back, rather that we are resolving the question of method at a higher level.'[30] Several themes arise from this letter. Grotowski
clearly considers training as an ongoing and potentially endless process of refinement
and relearning: its aim was not to arrive at a finished method, but the focus was
ever more closely upon the actor's creativity. Here he echoes Stanislavsky who
also insisted that training was a constant process within an actor's career.

We have seen both Stanislavsky and Meyerhold preferring to work in the
rehearsal studio. In a recorded interview Grotowski explains why he does:

> Performances were censored, but not rehearsals and the rehearsals have been
> for me the most important thing. There something happened between a
> human being and another human being, that is the actor and myself that
> touched this axis beyond any control from the outside. It means that the
> performance has always been less important than the work in the rehearsals.[31]

This last admission brings us back to the dialogue with the actor. At first he had a professional relationship with his actors, now it is 'between a human being and another human being'. Again, returning to Buber's opposition, we can see him shift from a more instrumental to a more personal dialogue with his actors. Training became less about the acquisition of techniques and skills and more about the search for exercises by means of which the actor could access their own creativity and humanity. Grotowski puts this in a wider context: 'The traditional European objective is to acquire a skill in order to vanquish the opponent/ enemy, whereas for the Oriental it was "a means to go out of one's self, to meet life; in fact it is life itself, a way of existence".[32] He will return to the theme of disarming in order to meet life in his later Theatre of Participation. Although the theme of art and life was theoretical for Bakhtin, Stanislavsky and Meyerhold, for Grotowski it became a practical concern to find how rehearsing and training can become a means of connecting with life, can become 'life itself'. The aesthetic and the ethical, form and experience, art and life become one.

In search of a method

The question of whether the approaches of Stanislavsky and Meyerhold were scientific has been discussed in earlier chapters. With the addition of the name 'laboratory' to Grotowski's theatre in 1962, and the title of one of his projects being Objective Theatre, we might imagine that he was quite scientific in his approach to actor training. We have already seen that Grotowski's actor training was in a constant state of evolution as he followed and developed the creative processes of his company. But we have also seen that his vigilance and rigour were used in search of an ever more personal revelation of meaning. He rejects as having 'no value' the idea that his statements and ideas about theatre add up to a system: 'That system would paralyse in the same way as all other systems.' He concludes,

> [i]f, in what I have said, there has been something that anyone listening was able to understand as a purely personal message, only for them and not for all the others, that has been the thing I wanted to express.[33]

In this carefully balanced response he reveals he was a skilful – even a wily – dialectician.

Was Grotowski's approach to actor training scientific? In a talk from 1970 Grotowski offers a typically nuanced response: 'We understood that we were dealing with a practical knowledge, and that it could not be identical to the knowledge of the scientist.' The reason for this is that their work involved 'the interpenetration of conscious and unconscious', and when assuming 'a scientific attitude' only the conscious acted. He concludes that 'everything I have spoken of was a practical question; it was pragmatic'.[34]

In *Towards a Poor Theatre* Grotowski says that he took the Bohr Institute as a model for his own laboratory precisely because he was interested in it as a centre for the discussion and practice of methodologically rigorous research (the type

Bakhtin and Medvedev demanded above). Temkine explains the way in which Grotowski considered it 'scientific': 'Without a doubt, he has been careful to reject all definitions of the theatre as a scientific discipline, especially as relates to the actor's technique, which has become his primordial concern.'[35] Grotowski admitted that the two to three hours devoted daily to exercises 'is also something like a scientific investigation. We try to discover certain objective laws governing man's expression.'[36] In a talk in 1970 he explains, 'In the beginning it was theatre. Later a laboratory. And now it is the place where I hope to be faithful to myself.'[37]

From 1965 Grotowski's theatre was funded as 'a research institute for the actor's craft', which, Temkine noted, was a 'new and unprecedented type of institute, at present unique in Poland'.[38] She also notes that it was funded by the Communist authorities. In a letter to Barba, Grotowski notes that this 'official status of institute of theatre research' was partially defined in relation to the other conventional theatres in Poland, but he continues,

> how are we to define ourselves to ourselves? And how should the actors see themselves? As artists like any other? As artists different to the others? Scientists? Guinea pigs? Apostles? Or something else altogether? And these are only half of the questions.[39]

For all these questions, Grotowski did have a definable approach even if it resisted calcifying into a method or system. In his recorded interviews he is remarkably consistent in his terminology and concerns. His approach to actor training is characterised by two expressions in Latin: the *via negativa* and the *conjunctio oppositorum*. Rather than adding to the actor's skill-set he proposed taking away those blocks that prevented them from acting personally and truthfully:

> We are not after the recipes, the stereotypes which are the prerogatives of professionals. [...] Instead, one must ask the actor: 'What are the obstacles blocking you on your way towards the total act which must engage all your psycho-physical resources, from the most instinctive to the most rational?' We must find out what it is that hinders him in the way of respiration, movement and – most important of all – human contact.[40]

He returns again and again to this paradox of training: 'it is not a matter of learning new things, but rather of ridding oneself of old habits.' Grotowski's role was to identify

> what it is that blocks his intimate associations, thus causing his lack of decision, the chaos of his expression and his lack of discipline, what prevents him from experiencing the feeling of his own freedom, that his own organism is completely free and powerful, and that nothing is beyond his capabilities.[41]

This explains why Grotowski's approach to training became so focused on the individual, because each person will have their own unique set of blocks and resistances. The words he uses to describe his approach are 'distil', 'subtract' and 'eliminate': 'Ours then is a *via negativa* – not a collection of skills but an eradication of blocks.'[42] Barba explains how the Buddhist concept of *Sunyata* can explain Grotowski's approach.

> It is a practice which stands midway between affirmation and negation, between action and renunciation of action. […] In *Towards a Poor Theatre* Grotowski applied this vision to the actor: 'The requisite state of mind is a passive readiness to realise an active role, a state in which one does not *want to do something* but rather *cannot help not doing it.*' […] One can see how *Sunyata* inspired his *via negativa* to describe the essence of theatre: the relationship between actor and spectator.[43]

With his feeling for paradox and dialectic, Grotowski conceived of the actor's creativity as a negotiation between form and experience.

> Creativity, especially where acting is concerned, is boundless sincerity, yet disciplined: i.e. articulated through signs. The creator should not therefore find his material a barrier in this respect. And as the actor's material is his own body, it should be trained to obey, to be pliable, to respond passively to psychic impulses as if it did not exist during the moment of creation – by which we mean it does not offer any resistance. Spontaneity and discipline are the basic aspects of an actor's work and they require a methodical key.[44]

Throughout his pronouncements about theatre he repeats this opposition between discipline, structure, form, repeatability and the unrepeatable, spontaneous moment of the actor's personal experience. Thus in his training exercises 'we looked for a conjunction between the structure of an element and the associations which transform it into the mode of each particular actor'. It is a tension between 'the objective elements' and 'purely subjective work. This is the contradiction of acting. It is the kernel of training'.[45] To describe this contradiction he uses the image of a glass cowl protecting a flame, or river-banks containing the flow of a river: the actor places him- or herself 'as far away from mechanics as from chaos: between the two shores of my precision, I allow this river, which comes out of the authenticity of my experience, to advance, slowly or rapidly'.[46]

When Grotowski writes about the actor relying upon their feeling rather than thinking or even looking, he again echoes Stanislavsky, and distances himself from Meyerhold's conscious actor. He warns that if you look for solutions 'you will block the natural creative process', because in looking 'only the brain works; the mind imposes solutions it already knows and you begin juggling known things. That is why we must look without fixing our attention on the result'.[47] He advises that to act (or react) truthfully one must not 'conduct the process but refer it to personal experiences and to be conducted. At these moments one must be internally passive but externally active'.[48] Grotowski recounts that his friend 'and very close colla- borator' Ludwig Flaszen 'was the first one to point out to me – rather bluntly – by showing me that what I did spontaneously, by merely following the demands of my metier, often led me to new perspectives'. In other words 'they were not the product of a firmly established theory. My productions led me to artistic awareness and were elucidated after they had taken place'.[49] Grotowski is methodologically rigorous in finding a vocabulary and forms of experimentation that reveal what for him is the truth about acting.

The way towards a Poor Theatre

Grotowski's *via negativa* applies equally to his theatre productions. The very title of his book *Towards a Poor Theatre* indicates that these are indications of a direction of travel rather than descriptions of an existent theatre aesthetic. Grotowski's methodological restlessness and rigour is fuelled by his constant questioning of theatre. What is it, and how can we achieve it? Stanislavsky and Meyerhold both asked and answered these questions, which created what Bakhtin would call a dialogising background for Grotowski's own research.[50] Grotowski's background included both Meyerhold and Stanislavsky, but he also addressed the developing world of recorded media, and this informs his definition and defence of theatre.

> Since film and TV excel in the area of mechanical functions (montage, instantaneous change of place, etc.), the Rich Theatre countered with a blatantly compensatory call for 'total theatre'. The integration of borrowed mechanisms (movie screens onstage, for example) means a sophisticated technical plant permitting great mobility and dynamism.[51]

If Grotowski's *via negativa* was about taking away what prevented an actor from responding spontaneously and sincerely to an impulse, then his Poor Theatre was about stripping away whatever detracted from the relation between actor and audience. He concludes that theatre 'cannot exist without the actor-spectator relationship of perceptual, direct, "live" communion'.[52] Grotowski's theatre goes back to the roots of the genre.

> I am trying to create a theatre of participation, to re-discover factors which characterise the origins of theatre. Place actors and spectators close together, in a new scenic space which embraces the entire room, and you may create a living collaboration. Thanks to physical contact, the spark can cross between them.[53]

Kumiega compared Grotowski's desire for physical union with the audience to the Romantics

> who attached the greatest importance to audience involvement in a performance: it was a dream of art penetrating into the reality of life. [...] It strove in its highest achievement towards mystery, to a union with the viewers, if not in ritual, then in a common sacrifice, in a gesture which would shake the world.[54]

Overview of Grotowski's Theatre of Productions (1957–1969)

In the first years (1957–1962) Grotowski's stagings were relatively conventional, but individual productions after 1962 became 'detailed investigations of the actor-audience relationship. That is, we consider the personal and scenic technique of the actor as the core of theatre art'.[55] Elsewhere he noted that 'for each new production, a new space is designed for the actors and spectators'.[56] Richard Schechner noted that not only was Grotowski a stage director and deviser of a training method, but – following Meyerhold – a stage-author (in the sense that some film directors are called 'auteurs' or authors) creating unique performance texts through the montage of images and actions drawn from dramatic literature.[57]

Staging the dialogue between actor and audience

Poor Theatre was not a fixed idea which was then applied to a series of productions; rather it was a question about theatre, whose implications were explored through practical experiments. Grotowski's four productions made between 1962 and 1967 were particular stagings of this dialogue between actor and audience. Rather than a theatre, his productions required an adaptable space that could accommodate the cast and an audience of between 40 and 120. Stanislavsky and Meyerhold had used the studio as a place of training, experiment and research, while their performances took place in larger theatres; Grotowski made it the place for theatrical performance.

> The division into stage and auditorium was abolished and substituted by a uniform theatre space which was both the stage and the auditorium. The whole room was the place of action. Chairs were placed on different levels and in many varied patterns, so that the spectators would be mutually surprised by each other's presence.[58]

Grotowski didn't create 'sets'

> in the usual sense of the word. They have been reduced to the objects which are indispensable to the *dramatic action*. Each object must contribute not to the meaning but to the *dynamics of the play*; its value resides in its various uses.[59]

He explains that 'spatial relations are only important if they form an integral part of the *structure of the production*'.[60] The phrases in italics indicate his insistence upon this being drama rather than discourse. Grotowski went beyond the stage-auditorium dichotomy and created different set-ups in the way one might create a laboratory experiment to explore a particular problem. The terms he uses – 'structure', 'dynamics' – suggest an objective approach to the spatial set-up between actor and audience. One of the questions that drove his researches was the nature of this relationship with the audience: were they passive spectators, witnesses or participants? Grotowski explains how he and the architect Gurawski, his collaborator in scenography, 'studied this problem over many years'. He concludes that

> [a]fter so many explorations, experiences, and reflections, I still doubt the possibility of direct participation in today's theatre, in an age when neither a communal faith exists, nor any liturgy rooted in the collective psyche as an axis for ritual.[61]

This seems the perfect articulation of a post-modern sensibility and explains the underpinning motor of his ceaseless search for a theatre of participation. We might compare this lost vision of a single, communal faith with Bakhtin's vision of a society which teems with conflicting and contradictory voices. Bakhtin's preoccupation with singularity and wholeness came early in his career, after which he embraced plurality.

The theatre space Gurawski and Grotowski used was what one could call an architectural metaphor drawn from the play. For example, there is a scene in *Kordian* where the eponymous hero is taken to a lunatic asylum. This prompted Grotowski to set the whole play in a lunatic asylum, with the audience as fellow patients. In his production of Marlowe's *Doctor Faustus* the audience are guests at Faustus's last dinner during which he reviews his life. In this dinner setting he 'found a direct word-for-word situation. The dramatic function of the spectator and the function of the spectator as spectator were the same'.[62] In *Acropolis* the audience sit on bunk beds in an accommodation hut in Auschwitz; in *The Constant Prince* they peer down into the pit of an old operating theatre as the central character is tortured and abused. In each case Grotowski has taken a place and made this the space for the entire production.

Christopher Baugh describes the set of *The Constant Prince*, which he saw in Manchester in 1968, and emphasises the fact that Gurawski and Grotowski had created 'a "place" rather than a "scene"':

> Even during the pact of performance, it remained a place; it did not take on any of the locational qualities of the dramatic space of the action. The palisade never *became* the walls of a room or dungeon; the rostrum never *became* a potential platform in the castle nor stood in for a piece of furniture. It seems that Grotowski's 'place' was speaking to its audience in its own voice […].[63]

Baugh makes a crucial distinction between the realistic and non-realistic scenography. Here the built-space speaks to the audience 'in its own voice'. He goes on to explain that even the way that the audience was ushered into the space enhanced the sense of 'encounter' that Grotowski has written about:

> The entering people were made aware of the particularity and precision of its arrangement, and the purposeful way in which Grotowski's assistants directed the audience. The accuracy of the audience placement and their relationship with the top of the palisade was precise: an encounter was being constructed in which a significant thing would be enacted; it could not be otherwise because of the deep sense of purpose, the silence and the bareness of the light.[64]

It is precisely this attention to detail which helps to create the encounter between actor and audience from the moment they enter the space.

Baugh's description helps us to understand how Grotowski developed Meyerhold's notion of theatrical time as the present moment and scenographic space as a place of action. We should not confound the purely ethical act of Bakhtin's act-performing *I* with Grotowski's total act, but there is a connection in the sense of once-only time and specificity of place. The ethical impact of theatre resides precisely in its being 'an act carried out *here and now* in the actors' organisms, in front of other men', 'theatrical reality is instantaneous, not an illustration of life'.[65] He describes the 'actor's act' as being 'an invitation to the spectator' which could be compared 'to an act of the most deeply rooted, genuine love between two human beings – this is just a comparison since we can only refer to this "emergence of oneself" through analogy'.[66] It is this sense of intimate contact which distinguishes his theatre of the total act from Meyerhold's Total Theatre. Grotowski stresses the necessity for a completing *other*, stating that 'the actor's performance must be motivated by an impulse to communicate with something, some witness, outside the self, otherwise the work degenerates into self-indulgence'.[67] While the relationship between audience and actor is paramount, this is not to say that the actor strives to *please* or flatter them. Grotowski would stress that the actor 'is under an obligation to make his/her work clear and comprehensible to the spectator', but that this did not mean 'that the actor should court the spectator of the marketplace, far from it'.[68]

A dialogue with plays from the past

As early as 1959 Grotowski was warning that '[t]he creative theatre […] does not want merely to illustrate the dramatic text mechanically and slavishly'.[69] In his production of Cocteau's *Orphée* he 'treated the text as material for a discussion with the author, and above all, with the spectator'.[70] This non-illustrative approach should not suggest that Grotowski considered himself in any way 'anti-literary': 'How could I separate theatre from literature? For me, as for any self-respecting European, the relationship between theatre and literature is an extremely strong one.'[71] This sense of literary heritage is borne out in his choice of repertoire. Flaszen explained that '[t]he repertoire of the Thirteen Rows […] is based at present on Polish romantic drama, from Mickiewicz to Wyspianski'. He continued that

> [i]n the romantic drama, the collective complexes of the Poles, their inner struggles, truths and follies, have been voiced most fully. What Dostoevsky is for the Russians, Polish romantic literature is for the Poles.[72]

The importance lay in the shared cultural meaning these works had – it was 'in their blood', something shared and understood. For all this, Grotowski was merciless in his creation of his performance montages. In a programme note he quotes Meyerhold: 'To choose a play does not necessarily mean to share the playwright's views.'[73] Flaszen adds that 'the company of the Thirteen Rows was very much for the autonomy of theatre'.[74] For theatre to be 'creative' it has to assert itself as an art form in its own right, which meant not acting as a visual illustration of a play.

In what way did his productions of these plays constitute a meeting between actor and audience? The answer lies in the nature of the space he created: sitting in a mental institution we wonder whether our hero Kordian was or was not mad to attempt to assassinate the Czar of the Russian Empire; sitting at a dinner table we listen to the self-accounting of Faustus; or we peer down into sunken space and watch the attempts of his detractors to test the constancy of Don Fernando in his beliefs. Grotowski has cut away the greater part of the plays to leave one central concern that is examined in one space – there is no change of scene. One could call this central concern the guiding 'myth' of the play. Grotowski declared that he was interested in the myths underlying a work and which 'are not an invention of the mind but are, so to speak, inherited through one's blood, religion, culture and climate'.[75] Such myths are found in 'either a classical text to which, through a sort of profanation, we simultaneously restore its truth, or a modern text which may well be banal and stereotyped in its content, but nevertheless rooted in the psyche of society'.[76] Barba explains that Grotowski 'approached the classics with the stubborn conviction that they contained an archetype, a situation which was fundamental to the human condition'. And, as explained above, he then 'constructed scenic equivalents', what I have called architectural metaphors, for these archetypes.[77]

Grotowski wanted to get at the ethical kernel of the play, and was less pre-occupied with the aesthetic considerations: props, costumes and furniture weren't on stage to be beautiful but to serve his analysis of the play's central myth. His productions brought about a confrontation between the world presented by the actors and the present reality of the audience:

> Only confrontation is possible. […] A confrontation is a 'trying out,' a testing of whatever is a traditional value. A performance which, like an electrical transformer, adjusts our experience to those of past generations (and vice versa), a performance conceived as a combat against traditional and contemporary values (whence transgression) – this seems to me the only real chance for myth to work in the theatre.[78]

He makes a categorical distinction between illustration and confrontation. In an illustration of a play, the scenic element provides a background for the world of the play, it does not comment upon the meaning of the play. The words, the lines, are what convey the meaning of the play. Grotowski's 'scenic equivalents' for the archetypes of the play are central to the meaning of his productions. For all that Grotowski might insist his approach was not anti-literary, it did invert the usual hierarchy where the word is the privileged conveyor of meaning in the theatre. The medium for the dialogue between the worlds of the play and its production is not verbal but plastic, not words but movements and sounds in a particular space and in a particular relation to the spectators.

Grotowski's language reflects if not a scientific at the very least a methodologically rigorous approach to his work. His stage montages 'test' the myths and values of a text against the present audience's experience. 'To confront the text means to test it, to struggle with it, to come to grips with its meaning in terms of our own modern experience, and then to give our own answers.'[79] Put more forcefully: 'To put two opposite views on the stage, to create brutal confrontations in order to see if these past dreams are concrete and strong, or only abstractions.'[80] Where Barker wrote about theatre-time being double – the represented (historical) and the representing (performance) – here there is a single time where the past is tested against the present. Where Stanislavsky demanded an identification with the world and values of the play, Grotowski insisted upon 'confrontation'. He uses the image of putting on the 'ill-fitting skin' of old myths 'to perceive the relativity of our problems, their connection to the "roots," and the relativity of the "roots" in the light of today's experience'.[81] He takes James Joyce's *Ulysses* as an example of testing ancient myth against contemporary experience:

> *Ulysses* is not an illustration or travesty. I am conscious of Joyce in his work, and his work is part of our world. At the same time something archaic exists in the book and in that sense it is eternal.[82]

Grotowski's engagement with the literary text brings him unexpectedly close to Bakhtin in what one critic called his dialectic between 'apotheosis and derision'.[83] A scene from Part III of Mickiewicz's *Dziady* offers a good example of this dialectical engagement:

> The performance was ruled by the principle of counterpoint, a sharp interplay of contradictory elements. The key scene was that of the Great Improvisation where the monologue by Konrad was rendered in the form of a way of the cross. Konrad – in iconographic postures of Christ on the way to Golgotha – walked round the room, swaying and falling under the weight of the cross, whose function was performed here by a broom.[84]

Grotowski notes that '[i]t was not by chance that the Middle Ages produced the idea of "sacral parody"'.[85] Rather than a dialectic that resolves into a synthesis, Grotowski is echoing the carnivalesque doubleness of Bakhtin's Rabelais study. Burzynski and Osinski note that in his productions there is an alternation 'of grotesque sequences' with 'serious moments which then reverted again to grotesque' and the 'eagerness to break the recognized canon of "beauty" by mixing up the aesthetic categories.[86] This found its expression in the unity of tragedy and grotesque, of the sublime and the trivial, of the "high" and the "low", of the "ugly" and the "beautiful"'.[87]

Grotowski's production of Wyspianski's *Akropolis* is possibly the most challenging of his confrontations of the modern and Romantic culture. Where the original was a celebration of the rich heritage of European culture, his production was set in a bunk house in Auschwitz concentration camp, an approach he describes tersely: 'We did not want to write a new play; we wanted to *confront*.'[88] His attitude towards the original is nuanced: Temkine argues that 'Grotowski does not betray the spirit of the work of Wyspianski. What he rejects, because today it is a lie, is its optimism'.[89] Once again, it is about a certain attitude, an archetype within the text and not the specifics of its literary construction. He defines the 'acting score' as 'the elements of contact' with the old text, and while there was a 'script of sorts' it 'made no sense as drama'.[90,91] However, even though the performance event was organised 'according to the logic of our cues' he insists that the 'essential parts of the text – those which carry the sense of the literary work – remain intact and are treated with great respect. Otherwise there could be no meeting'.[92] Grotowski's argument is constructed on this opposition between illustration and meeting, between previously held meanings and the present situation.

Self and character

I have already referred to Stanislavsky's distinction between two aspects of the actor's work: work on the self and work on the role. In a typical conflation, Grotowski considers the role as a means by which actors worked on themselves. He notes that when playing King Lear: 'the difference between myself and Lear is big enough for me to be aware that I am playing someone else.' But Grotowski's interest is precisely in the identity of the actor him- or herself. This prompts the terrifying question 'which self? The one known to my friends? The one known to my enemies? The one that I would like others to know? The one I dream about? The one I do not like?'[93] Grotowski proposes that through a dialogue with the character as something *other* to themselves an actor can thereby identify their own *I*. Certainly Grotowski does not approach a character as another human as do Bakhtin and Stanislavsky. Grotowski's character is neither an intimate addressee (the *du* of Buber) nor an enabling *other* in Bakhtin's sense: it is simply an image of a human from a different time (but within the same Polish culture) against whose difference the present-day actor can gauge him- or herself. In Buber's terms, the character is an *es* or 'it', an instrument to help the actor achieve self-discovery.

Just as the director takes the classic text as a point of departure for a confrontation or meeting, so must the actor confront or meet the character. Grotowski explains that the actor must not 'illustrate Hamlet, he must meet Hamlet'.[94] He notes that while the actor has a text, 'an encounter is necessary'. The role as given in the text 'is an instrument for making a cross-section of oneself, analysing oneself and thereby re-establishing contact with others'.[95] Quite *how* this helps to re-establish contact with others is never really explained. Just as Grotowski proposed that the audience must try on the ill-fitting skin of a play's central myth or archetype in order to experience its difference from their present day life, so actors must test themselves against their roles. This approach is that of neither Stanislavsky nor Brecht: 'It is not a question of portraying himself under certain given circumstances, or of "living" a part; nor does it entail the distant sort of acting common to epic theatre and based on cold calculation.' Grotowski argues that the actor must 'use the role as a trampoline, an instrument with which to study what is hidden behind our everyday mask – the innermost core of our personality – in order to sacrifice it, expose it'. His most radical image is that the actor must 'use his role as if it were a surgeon's scalpel, to dissect himself'.[96] If this seems like an evocation of Artaud, Grotowski notes that actors work on their characters not to 'torture them', but 'to find out who they really are'.[97]

Grotowski is clearly more interested in the identity of the actor than that of the character. In the chapters on Bakhtin and Stanislavsky a character was that which could be understood and narrated about a person. Grotowski seems uninterested in this narrative or autobiographical self. He rejects fiction, the social and anything beyond the personal and physical zone. Indeed, he demonstrates a profound mistrust of anything that cannot be touched and felt. Grotowski rejects the entire zone of the social, fictional and imaginary. Nick Worrall noticed that Stanislavsky had an

> interest in types who stand above the crowd, who are defined by a proud, even tragic, isolation and separateness. The type usually takes the form of the artist, the philosopher, the outcast or, most often a combination of the three, the 'superman'.[98]

Kumiega makes a similar point about how Grotowski's mature productions (excepting *Akropolis*) all dealt 'with the image of one individual, isolated from the surrounding environment and social milieu because of a particular set of ethics or principles adhered to'.[99] The theme of the individual who is isolated from or opposed to society has a deep resonance in Grotowski's attitude towards truth. The truth of an actor's work derives from them stripping away their social selves – Grotowski referred to the 'life-mask' – to reveal their 'real' selves beneath.[100] The social is associated with superficiality and falsehood.

Even though the accent is on the self of the actor, we still have to remember that this exploration takes place in front of an audience. Acting becomes therefore not a transformation of the actor into the character, but 'simply an act of total self-revelation', a 'laying bare of the body', it is an act 'of tearing off the mask of daily life, of exteriorising oneself. Not in order to "show oneself off", for that would be exhibitionism. It is a solemn act of revelation'.[101] Grotowski's aesthetics were subject to his ethical demand that the actor should shake off inauthentic socially imposed masks through a public act of self-revelation. In his essay on the chronotope Bakhtin offers an opposite strategy – putting on rather than taking off masks – in response to the same situation: 'In the struggle against the inadequacy of all available life-slots to fit an authentic human being, these masks take on an extraordinary significance.'[102] Bakhtin then goes further. What they say cannot be grasped in 'a direct and unmediated way'. They are masks, not real people, 'their being coincides with their role, and outside this role they simply do not exist'. They insist on their right to be 'other' in this world:

> the right not to make common cause with any single one of the existing categories that life makes available; none of these categories quite suits them, they see the underside and the falseness of every situation.[103]

Although Bakhtin and Grotowski both agree that there is a primordial mismatch between the social mask and one's own personal life-slot, they come to profoundly different conclusions. Where Bakhtin advises a constant play of masking, Grotowski argues for a complete removal and laying bare of the true, underlying self. Is the audience an enabling *other* in their role as witness of the actor's act of unmasking? 'Take other people, confront them with oneself, one's own experiences and thoughts and give a reply. In these somewhat intimate human encounters there is always this element of "give and take".'[104] Even if this is Grotowski's model for a kind of dialogue, it is a one-way exchange that neither asks for nor expects a response from the other.

The actor's body

Both Bakhtin and Grotowski were plagued with ill-health throughout their lives: one had osteomyelitis which resulted in a leg being amputated in 1938, the other suffered from a recurring kidney complaint. Temkine recounts that when Grotowski was sixteen he

> fell gravely ill, and was virtually given up by the doctors. […] For an entire year he was in the hospital, in the communal ward, where he was surrounded by terminal patients. He felt deeply what dying meant, and he came out of the experience transformed.[105]

Grotowski explains that because of this 'physical weakness I needed the body, I was craving organicity'. He needed to arrive at something that would give him

> the ground, the support – the confirmation from my 'source'. I am sure that inside me was some hidden fear of life, of my own weakness, some need for a powerful weapon, a need for some strong basis for my ego.[106]

This personal situation affected his notion of the actor's body and authentic acting. To be divided into 'me' and 'my body' indicates 'a lack of trust in the body which is, in fact, a lack of trust in one's self. That's what divides the being'.[107] Bakhtin, stoic to the last, makes no connection between his experience of his own body and how he used the body in his theory. Grotowski is quite frank about the connection. The organicity he craved is also described as undividedness: a self which is 'you-unrepeatable, individual, you in the totality of your nature: you in the flesh, you naked. And, at the same time, it is you who embodies all the others, all beings, all of history'.[108] He points out that the 'etymological meaning of "individuality" is "indivisibility" which means complete existence in something'.[109] Where Grotowski sees wholeness in bodily terms, the early Bakhtin sees the *other*'s body as a visually apprehended whole which leads on to the creation of an aesthetic image. History and culture for Grotowski is something embodied, in the flesh and blood.

Kolankiewicz makes a connection between Grotowski's conception of the whole man and the lectures Adam Mickiewicz gave at the College de France (where Grotowski was to lecture in the 1990s).

> He talked there about 'the complete human' transformed from the banal man. He meant a concrete existence (not divided into body and psyche), using the organ of 'feeling' as the basic instrument of direct perception. Such

existence was characterised, according to Mickiewicz, by free immediacy of reactions, continuous movement and action, and, above all, through deed. Deed was in that image the calling of the 'complete man'.[110]

This focus on the deed brings us back to Stanislavsky's physical actions, which Grotowski made his own. In Grotowski's theatre the principle sources of semiotic material are movements and sound produced by the actor's body.

In his quest for organicity Grotowski rejects the socially constructed self, which is often taken as the thinking self, the self as articulated in language. He argues that the 'social' should be discarded as inessential, as 'unreal': 'if one is investigating "who am I?", then this question will send you somewhere back and your limited "I" will disappear, and you will find something else, *real*.'[111] He realised that it 'was not a mental investigation' but something 'printed' within the flesh.[112] For Grotowski the body is the self, thus to lack self-confidence (confidence in one's body) results in the actor not being able to create. Grotowski trusts the self's knowledge of the body and profoundly mistrusts the images of the self furnished by the *other*'s eye: 'all psychic states observed are no longer lived because emotion observed is no longer emotion.'[113] When Grotowski worked with his actors, his focus was on their inner sensation – he rejected Brecht's approach to acting precisely because it was based on watching. 'Certainly Brecht did study the technique of the actor in great detail, but always from the standpoint of the producer observing the actor.'[114] Grotowski avoided intellectual analysis and external description; his was a dialogue of co-experience not aesthetic distance. He doesn't compare his status as a spectator of actors to that of Brecht.

Echoing the anti-intellectualism of Stanislavsky, Grotowski insists upon the truth of feeling over thinking, body over mind.

> I know what it is I feel. I cannot define it but I know what it is. It is nothing to do with the mind; it affects other associations, other parts of the body. But if I perceive, it means that there was a sign. The test of a true impulse is whether I believe in it or not.[115]

An actor's (affective) association 'is something that springs not only from the mind but also from the body. It is a return towards a precise memory. Do not analyse this intellectually. Memories are always physical reactions'.[116] He gives as an example a movement of the hand and finger which could recall 'an experience where we touched someone, maybe a lover', and thus how this could relate 'to an important experience which *was* or which *could have been*. That [is] how the *body memory/body-life* reveals itself'.[117] However neurologically inaccurate, Grotowski's argument is that memories – not just individual, but cultural – are held locked in the body and released through these physical actions. This leads him to conclude in his text 'Exercises': 'It is thought that the memory is something independent from the rest of the body. In truth, at least for actors – it's something different. The body does not *have* memory, it *is* memory.'[118] This may make little sense either physiologically or neurologically but it underlines his belief in the centrality of the body.

The actor's score – in search of true signs

The body was not just a value in itself but also the means by which the actor generates signs. Grotowski's quest for a language of theatrical signs began in earnest when working on his 1961 production of *Shakuntala*. The company harboured a 'hidden intention – a desire to discover a system of signs applicable in theatre, in our civilisation. This is what we did: the performance was in fact constructed out of little gestures and vocal signals'.[119] One question that preoccupied him in the early 1960s was whether 'a system of signs' exists for the actor. 'We asked questions above all about signs' and identified that the 'elements of expressions' were 'movement, impulse, sound, intonation'.[120] This early attempt at finding a form adequate to the actor's personal experience was unsuccessful: the actor 'could not reveal himself as an individual' because it was the director who had built the 'structure of signs', which Grotowski describes as an 'intrusion'.[121] Only an actor can create these signs because it is they who are moving and making sounds and then feeling the internal resonances generated by them.

Grotowski's attitude towards signs is extremely complex. To say that it is completely opposed to the sociological approach of Voloshinov and Medvedev or Bakhtin's dialogical approach is true but shines little light on his notion of the actor's sign. Grotowski's notion of the *conjunctio oppositorum* emphasises the need for form to contain, to channel, to protect experience. Presumably this is a personal experience that the actor can refind through the performance of a specific action. In a similar way to Stanislavsky, an actor's whole performance can be understood as a score of these actions. The formal aspect of his score is not to do with meaning but with the repetition of those actions such that they can always generate the same personal experience within the actor. This experience is rooted in the actor's past (and, he would argue, body) even though it is re-experienced in the present moment of the performance (through the body).

It would be a mistake to argue that Grotowski was principally interested in the spiritual and inner dimension of acting. In 1965 he wrote that actors in their daily work

> do not concentrate on the spiritual technique but on the composition of the role, on the construction of form, on the expression of signs – i.e., on artifice. There is no contradiction between inner technique and artifice (articulation of a role by signs).[122]

Where Medvedev has argued that all 'ideological creation' must be realised 'in some definite semiotic material' which in turn 'is part of the practical reality that surrounds man', Grotowski roots the sign in the physical work of the actor.[123] Both the creator and the process are entirely individual. He is interested in what is significant within the walls of a theatre, not within the much broader sphere of society. He uses the term 'sign' without there being a signifier and a signified; it is semiotic only in the medical sense of the word. A sign is no longer something recognised and thereby confirmed in its status as a sign by another. It is not social, but personal – a creation of the actor's. This explains why when Barba writes of Grotowski's vision 'of an actor capable of creating "signs", they are subject to a 'theatrical logic', are 'rooted in organic coherence' and presuppose a 'physical and psychic discipline'.[124] The guarantee of the truth of the sign lies in the individual actor's body rather than the body politic. Quite what the audience is meant to experience or how this score becomes a means of intimate relation or meeting between actor and audience is left unclear. Grotowski's is more a theory of expression than communication.

Kott chose the word 'metaphysics' to describe Grotowski's approach to working under the Communist authorities. A further quotation from his article explains why he chose this word:

> Grotowski brought a Method and metaphysics to the West. His Method is precise and verifiable; his metaphysics is obscure and ambiguous. [...] The corporality of the Laboratory Theatre, the ultimate precision of gesture, faces transformed into masks by a simple contraction of muscle, the sounds as language – these can only be compared with Japanese Noh, in which the actor's art is handed down from generation to generation. Even Kabuki, in comparison with the Laboratory Theatre, seems to be too loose.[125]

The body is at the core of this dilemma between method and metaphysics. On the one hand there is the admirable discipline of the actor's body; on the other hand there is an ambiguity, even an obscurity, as to what these bodily signs mean. What is it that constitutes Grotowski's sign? Is it that a given movement or sound evokes an affective resonance within the actor's body? By virtue of it being seen by the audience this sign is an image, but it is not a symbolic representation of anything. The actor's body is not an image of a character in the way described by Stanislavsky, Bakhtin or even Meyerhold. Grotowski rejects any mental symbolisation, indeed any mental transcendence and argues only for an embodied knowledge.

Another way of trying to grasp the nature of Grotowski's conception of a sign is to compare it to that of his contemporary, Joseph Chaikin who asks:

> Do you think there exists a universal grammar of emotions and does one have to look for it? For me, a matter of ambition, of what I would like to achieve most, a guiding principle, is to search for such a vocabulary of emotions that would be common to all human nature, above culture.[126]

Grotowski does not believe such a 'grammar of emotions' exists, and sees it as the actor's personal responsibility to create signs. Grotowski is closer to Meyerhold who writes that 'every movement is a hieroglyph with its own peculiar meaning. The theatre should employ only those movements which are immediately decipherable; anything else is superfluous'.[127] As ever, this quest for a system of signs was subject to a *via negativa*:

> we do not work by proliferation of signs, or by accumulation of signs (as in the formal repetitions of oriental theatre). Rather, we subtract, seeking

distillation of signs by eliminating those elements of 'natural' behaviour which obscure pure impulse.[128]

Although Grotowski took much inspiration from the theatre of India and South East Asia, he rejected what he called an 'alphabetic theatre' where '[e]ach gesture, each little motion is an ideogram which *writes out* the story and can be understood only if its conventional meaning is known'. To understand the actor's work the spectator 'must learn the language, or rather the alphabet of the language'.[129] Throughout his writings Grotowski rejects the alphabetic sign because it 'does not reveal the human personality, I mean, the actor as being', because 'there's no confession' in such theatre.[130] This argument brings us back to the total act of self-revelation that the actor makes before the audience.

Holiday, carnival, meeting – beyond theatre

When the company began work on *Apocalypsis*, it became clear that this production would not be a response to one individual text. Gone was the dialectical negotiation with a particular text, the scenic metaphor and costume: the actors wore their own clothes and performed in a room lit by two large floodlights with the audience seated or standing. The performance was a meeting between actor and audience as human beings. This was the apotheosis of a theatre without footlights: as Flaszen explains, 'it was no longer necessary to establish a wall in relation to others by being an "artist" behind an objective structure. A factor of *direct* human communication appeared'.[131] Once again, one comes up against the problem of the means of signification. Is it possible to have just direct human communication without some specific form?

Apocalypsis was performed during the transition to post-theatre (the first public performance was in February 1969, the last in March 1980). Flaszen describes how the performances reflected Grotowski's move into the second phase of his work – Theatre of Participation.

> In the course of the years, what in *Apocalypsis* is theatre form became more and more marginal, and the degree of opening out the performance became so considerable that cases of spontaneous audience participation in the action began to happen; the majority of the audience, however, no matter how ready they were for it, felt the existence of a borderline which in the theatre divides even emotionally united persons into active and passive participants.[132]

Apocalypsis was the logical conclusion to a line that had begun with Stanislavsky's rejection of theatricality in a search for a more truthful theatre and was a logical extension of Grotowski's *via negativa*. He too wanted a living response, but not through the artistic mediation of a theatre production but rather an immediate, unmediated reaction to the world and to the people in it. Although his approach may have few of the characteristics of Bakhtin's early philosophy, there are two structural similarities: both men rejected theatre and both took their field of activity as the dialogue between self and other. Both men began from the assumption that humans are incomplete: Grotowski's quest was for meaning and he knew that in some way this was to be achieved through some form of inter-action with another person. After some thirteen years in professional theatre, Grotowski felt he needed another means by which the actor-person could dis-cover a meaningful dialogue with others. His theatrical work had relied on a negotiation with the written word conducted through the establishment of a score of physical actions, now he sought to establish a connection with others simply through actions.

From acting to action

Even in his formal farewell to theatre Grotowski refers back to Stanislavsky (he admits 'I considered him once to be my father') to help orientate himself in his post-theatrical career.

> Do you want me to say that I have transcended him? I have too much respect for Stanislavsky to say this; for the theatre, he was a great man – but I am not interested in the theatre any more, only in what I can do leaving theatre behind. [...] I needed years to realise that I must leave this behind.[133]

He singles out the damaging doubleness of the actor's work: on the one hand having to think 'what it will give the spectator', on the other 'what the character he creates is doing and thinking'.[134] It is precisely this kind of split consciousness that Grotowski wished to avoid. 'This is the split condition, the maimed condition, where everything is done by halves and where everything acts separately – thoughts, concepts, movement, feelings; partly I suppose to avoid acting with one's entire human presence, not to be oneself, whole.'[135] Now even acting is being described in terms of the divided self.

Just as Grotowski insisted that the actor learn how to perform a total act, so now he demands total presence in these post-theatrical actions. 'For us the ques-tion is: what do you want to do with your life; and then – do you want to hide, or to reveal yourself, do you want to discover yourself, in both senses of the word: discover – uncover?'[136] Grotowski is still using the metaphor of unmasking, but the means has changed, there is no longer the 'instrument' of the character. He had reached the point at which 'one discovers that it is possible to reduce oneself to the man-as-he-is; not to his mask, not to the role he plays', adding that this 'reduction to the man is possible only in relation to an existence other than him-self'.[137] Like Bakhtin, he poses the question of identity in terms of a relation to another: 'What are man's capacities in action, when confronted face to face with another man? What is creative in man in the face of the living presence of others, in a mutual communion?'[138] Where before the actor performed for an audience, now it is one person meeting another.

From theatre to meeting

Grotowski gave a series of talks in the United States in May and December 1970 excerpts from which were edited into two texts entitled 'That Which Was' and 'Holiday'. In the first he reflects on the theatre he had left behind, in the second he looked forward to a new kind of practice, what would be later called a Theatre of Participation. In 'Holiday' he notes how the words 'show, performance, theatre, spectator'[139] are now 'dead' for him. In another version of 'Holiday' he notes how one 'must not look for the audience's acceptance' but accept oneself, indeed the 'very word audience, for that matter, is "theatrical," dead. It excludes meeting, it excludes the relation: man-man [*clzowiek-clzowiek*]'.[140] He argues that '[i]t is not theatre that is indispensable but: to cross the frontiers between you and me; to come forward to meet you'.[141] The person-who-was-the-actor walks across the frontier of the footlights and meets another person.

> In this meeting, man does not refuse himself and does not impose himself. He lets himself be touched and does not push with his presence. He comes forward and is not afraid of somebody's eyes, whole. It is as if one spoke with one's self; you are, so I am; and also: I am being born so that you are born, so that you become; and also: do not be afraid, I am going with you.[142]

Grotowski's friend, actor and director, André Gregory, echoes this post-theatrical vocabulary. He argues that it is no longer important to create art 'which is then presented to people', more important is that 'people are involved in the creative process', and concludes that 'the barriers are simply disappearing between those who are the audience and those who are the artists'.[143] In the film *My Dinner with André* he describes the experience of being in one of Grotowski's post-theatrical gatherings. He is in a forest with a group of foreigners who do not speak English: 'What do you do, that has any kind of meaning or importance?'[144] This was like no theatre workshop he had ever led, most of which had been based around character-work. 'Except that in the improvisations in these workshops, the theme is oneself [...] in this case *you're* the character, so you have no imaginary situation to hide behind, and you have no other person to hide behind.' The questions that

> Stanislavski said that the actor should constantly ask himself as a character – Who am I? Why am I here? Where do I come from? and Where am I going? – but instead of applying them to a role, you apply them to yourself.[145]

When he poses the question of what the whole thing was about, he doesn't know – '[b]ut it was something to do with living'. Once again, like Grotowski, Gregory formulates his argument around Stanislavsky, work on a role and questions of identity.

Grotowski argues that '[i]f one does not possess that meaning, one lives in constant fear'. This is a fear that 'flows from ourselves. It is our own weakness, and the weakness is the lack of meaning'.[146] But rather than arming oneself against this fear, in the spirit of the *via negativa* he argues one must disarm: 'We arm ourselves in order to conceal ourselves; sincerity begins where we are defenceless. Sincerity is not possible if we are hiding ourselves behind clothes, ideas, signs, productions, effects.'[147] We have already seen how Grotowski was unimpressed by verbal discourse, and now he even more emphatically rejects 'the chatter of forms'.[148] Kolankiewicz recalls a moment in one of these meetings when, 'after a time, we stopped talking. Verbal communication became almost superfluous. It turns out that there are other possibilities of transmitting to someone one's emotions, of sharing joy'.[149]

In both 'That Which Was' and 'Holiday' he describes how an exercise only had value when it was still a physical challenge for the actor, rather than a confirmation of their technique. Gregory describes a vivid moment in his meeting where Grotowski held his hand over a naked candle flame. It was a purely physical challenge. In the quest for a nonverbal, physical communion, Grotowski seems to be seeking something like the intercorporeal dialogue of Bakhtin's carnival.

Emerson offers a much wider definition of carnival as 'an attitude, a holiday attitude – and by "holiday" [*prazdnik*] is meant any peak point or threshold that is […] valued for the aspect of "change and renewal in it, its striving toward the future"'. She continues,

> [i]t is simply a name given to that moment of enablement – inevitably transitory – during which the self feels itself to be an agent in the world, that moment when a human being no longer feels helpless, nor prays, nor begs.[150]

Later in the book she seems to echo Grotowski:

> The suspension of everyday anxieties during 'holiday time' and 'carnival space' – the specific locus being the vulnerable, yet superbly shame-free, grotesque body – rids both me and my most proximate neighbour of the excessive self-consciousness that keeps both of us lonely, our words insipid, and our outreaching gestures timid.[151]

Although Grotowski's means might be very distant from those of Bakhtin, isn't this open vulnerability, this reaching-out to another, precisely what the post-theatrical work was all about?

Summary

Informing every aspect of Grotowski's practice – as a director, actor-trainer and auteur of montages – was the question, what is theatre? In the spirit of his *via negativa* Grotowski defined theatre by what it was *not*. Unable to compete with the technological sophistication and capability of film or television, he argued that theatre should focus on the relation between actor and audience, which prompted the second aspect of his *via negativa* – clearing the stage of everything that he felt impeded this relation. Thus every aspect of scenic representation and animation devolved to the actor. In contrast to Meyerhold's Total Theatre he proposed a theatre of the total act. As a creator of performance montages Grotowski acknowledged the influence of Meyerhold but went far further in creating a unique performance space and text. When it came to his work as actor-trainer and director he was much more collaborative, and like both Stanislavsky and Meyerhold moved progressively towards an actor's theatre. Whether or not one can say that Grotowski reached his goal of creating a Poor Theatre, he certainly created a direction of travel which involved him having an ever closer relation with and placing ever more creative responsibility upon the actor. There is freedom for the actor but only within the clearly defined parameters set by Grotowski.

Several questions follow from Grotowski's approach to making theatre and to his abandonment of theatre. Many of these stem from his definition of theatre as the relation between the actor and the audience. His theatre developed from a complex of three relations: the actor who worked with the director on their relation with the character, and then the actor and the audience. Bakhtin and Stanislavsky both considered that a character had a relation to a human being; this relation between the actor/author and the character included degrees of empathetic identification and aesthetic distance. Meyerhold considered the character in almost sculptural terms: the *emploi* of an actor – their physicality, voice and way of moving – would recommend them for a certain range of roles. In all three cases the character has a certain content, certain definable features which would be recognised by the audience. For Grotowski the character was a means by which the actor could work on him/herself and thus created a score of actions by means of which they could reveal themselves to the audience. With no setting, no historical situation, and no characters, this was an act of revelation of the actor in the here and now.

Although Grotowski might have rejected the notion that he had a system in his approach to theatre, his two key concepts – *via negativa* and *conjunctio oppositorum* – gave a definable contour to his conceptual development. On the one hand he pursued a merciless *ascesis*, shedding anything that could impede the meeting between audience and actor, on the other he insisted that the actor's experience had to be shaped and channelled by a recognisable and repeatable form: a score of signs. Any pre-existing form, be it the codified gestures of Noh, Kathakali or Beijing Opera, is rejected as being 'alphabetic' – by which we can understand 'codified' – and thus unable to assist the actor in their personal confession. 'Selves' and 'roles' we construct through our social development are rejected as inauthentic masks that have to be removed to access the underlying, true self. Grotowski rejects the possibility or value of understanding oneself as a character.

In this period of Grotowski's career (1957–1975) we have seen four major changes in his approach theatre: from 'experimental' productions to very detailed montages of plays, to a devised piece, to a post-theatrical engagement with the audience. The question he asks of theatre leads him to reject it as a genre in favour of a new kind of interaction with people. At each stage of his development there is a progressive shedding of theatrical means and conventions, until there is the simple fact of co-existence and the performance of actions.

By 1970 he was proposing a mode of communion – rather than communication – which neither acknowledges nor engages in a wider cultural debate. There is no reflection upon the actions performed, no narrative frame within which they can be understood. There is no image of these actions. As the quotations from André Gregory suggest, Grotowski wasn't alone in this retreat from the forms and conventions of (Western) theatre. His 1975 project in Wroclaw was attended by some luminary figures, for example theatre directors Peter Brook and Luca Ronconi. His approach was not simply a response to the cultural stultification under the Polish Communist regime, but part of a wider examination of the role of works of art in contemporary life. His rejection of all social discourse as being inauthentic leaves a massive question as to the possible content of this relation between the actor and the audience. His theatre takes place in a present that acknowledges neither a social nor a historical dimension; it is a radical now, set apart from the world outside. He began with a small theatre and ended up creating post-theatrical communities that were apart from rather than a part of the greater community. If it was a monastery then it was certainly unlike Friar Jean's Thelema in *Gargantua and Pantagruel* whose motto was *fais que voudra* ('do what you will'). Grotowski rejects the optimistic social discourse envisaged by Medvedev and Voloshinov, as well as Bakhtin's notion of dialogism. His point of connection with Bakhtin was in rooting his ideas in the body, but one that neither rejoices in nor acknowledges the material bodily lower stratum. It is a carnival of sorts, but without the laughter. For all that, the doors of his centre in Pontedera, Italy, were open and over the years his visitors could be numbered in their thousands.

Notes

1 Temkine (1972) 48.
2 In Kumiega (1985) 82.
3 Grotowski (1991) 21.
4 In Kumiega (1985) 82–83.
5 Grotowski (1991) 15–16.
6 In Kumiega (1985) 83.
7 Slowiak and Cuesta (2007) 7.
8 This must surely be Sitkovetskaya's edition of *Meyerhold Repetiruet* (Meyerhold Rehearses).
9 Temkine (1972) 50.
10 In Hodge (2000) 193.
11 In Kumiega (1985) 128–129.
12 Kumiega (1985) 112.
13 In Daly (n.d.).
14 Schechner and Wolford (1997) 464.
15 Burzynski and Osinski (1979) 108.
16 In Kumiega (1985) 224.
17 Kumiega (1985) 216–217.
18 Barba (1999) 96.
19 In Schechner and Wolford (1997) 109.
20 In Schechner and Wolford (1997) 192.
21 Kumiega (1985) 12.

22 In Kumiega (1985) 51.
23 In Kumiega (1985) 51.
24 In Kumiega (1985) 131.
25 Buber (1958).
26 In Schechner and Wolford (1997) 468.
27 In Kumiega (1985) 153.
28 In Kumiega (1985) 91.
29 Barba (1999) 131.
30 Barba (1999) 138–139.
31 In Daly (n.d.).
32 In Kumiega (1985) 115.
33 In Kumiega (1985) 238.
34 'That Which Was' (n.p.).
35 Temkine (1972) 59.
36 In Burzynski and Osinski (1979) 35–36.
37 'That Which Was' (n.p.).
38 Temkine (1972) 53.
39 Barba (1999) 140.
40 Grotowski (1991) 177.
41 Grotowski (1991) 96–97.
42 Grotowski (1991) 17.
43 Barba (1999) 49.
44 Grotowski (1991) 217.
45 In Schechner and Wolford (1997) 43.
46 In Schechner and Wolford (1997) 107.
47 In Schechner and Wolford (1997) 37.
48 In Schechner and Wolford (1997) 40.
49 In Temkine (1972) 71.
50 For example, in *Discourse* 281, 358, 397, 414.
51 Grotowski (1991) 19.
52 Grotowski (1991) 19.
53 In Kumiega (1985) 146.
54 Kumiega (1985) 35.
55 Grotowski (1991) 15.
56 Grotowski (1991) 33.
57 Schechner and Wolford (1997) 24.
58 Burzynski and Osinski (1979) 20.
59 In Kumiega (1985) 67.
60 Schechner and Wolford (1997) 110.
61 In Schechner and Wolford (1997) 111.
62 Schechner and Wolford (1997) 50.
63 Baugh (2005) 195.
64 Baugh (2005) 196.
65 Grotowski (1991) 86–87.
66 Grotowski (1991) 212.
67 Schechner and Wolford (1997) 339.
68 Schechner and Wolford (1997) 339.
69 In Schechner and Wolford (1997) 21–22.
70 In Burzynski and Osinski (1979) 15.
71 Wolford (1996) 198.
72 In Burzynski and Osinski (1979) 61.
73 In Cioffi (1996) 87.
74 In Burzynski and Osinski (1979) 13.
75 Grotowski (1991) 42.

76 Grotowski (1991) 43.
77 Barba (1999) 39.
78 Grotowski (1991) 89–90.
79 In Schechner and Wolford (1997) 81–82.
80 In Schechner and Wolford (1997) 82.
81 Grotowski (1991) 23.
82 In Schechner and Wolford (1997) 51.
83 Kumiega (1985) 38.
84 Burzynski and Osinski (1979) 21.
85 Grotowski (1991) 22–23.
86 Burzynski and Osinski (1979) 15.
87 Burzynski and Osinski (1979) 14.
88 In Schechner and Wolford (1997) 52.
89 Temkine (1972) 122.
90 In Schechner and Wolford (1997) 52.
91 Kumiega (1985) 60.
92 In Kumiega (1985) 132.
93 In Kumiega (1985) 225.
94 Grotowski in Slowiak and Cuesta (2007) 91.
95 Grotowski (1991) 180.
96 Grotowski (1991) 37.
97 Grotowski (1991) 88.
98 Worrall (1996) 103.
99 Kumiega (1985) 54.
100 For example, Grotowski (1991) 17, 21, 23, 37.
101 Grotowski (1991) 178.
102 *Chronotope* 163.
103 *Chronotope* 159.
104 Grotowski (1991) 180.
105 Temkine (1972) 48.
106 Schechner and Wolford (1997) 254–255.
107 'Exercises' (n.p.).
108 'Exercises' (n.p.).
109 Grotowski (1991) 217.
110 Kolankiewicz (1979) 115–116.
111 Schechner and Wolford (1997) 252.
112 In Kumiega (1985) 231–235.
113 Grotowski (1991) 202.
114 Grotowski (1991) 173.
115 Grotowski (1991) 193.
116 In Kumiega (1985) 120.
117 'Exercises' (n.p.).
118 'Exercises' (n.p.).
119 In Burzynski and Osinski (1979) 19.
120 In Kumiega (1985) 152.
121 In Kumiega (1985) 152.
122 Grotowski (1991) 17.
123 Medvedev (1985) 7.
124 Barba (1999) 40.
125 In Schechner and Wolford (1997) 135.
126 Kolankiewicz (1979) 40.
127 Leach (1993) 56.
128 Grotowski (1991) 18.
129 In Kumiega (1985) 116.

130 'Exercises' (n.p.).
131 In Kumiega (1985) 103.
132 Burzynski and Osinski (1979) 107.
133 Grotowski (1973) 21.
134 Grotowski (1973) 21.
135 Grotowski (1973) 21.
136 Grotowski (1973) 22.
137 Burzynski and Osinski (1979) 109.
138 Burzynski and Osinski (1979) 109.
139 Grotowski (1973) 19.
140 In Schechner and Wolford (1997) 220.
141 In Schechner and Wolford (1997) 221.
142 Grotowski (1973) 24.
143 In Kumiega (1985) 179–180.
144 Gregory and Shawn (1981) 24.
145 Gregory and Shawn (1981) 26.
146 Grotowski (1973) 20.
147 In Schechner and Wolford (1997) 221.
148 In Schechner and Wolford (1997) 221.
149 In Burzynski and Osinski (1979) 124.
150 Emerson (1997) 103.
151 Emerson (1997) 163.

Conclusion

The field of reference throughout this book has been narrowly focused on a small number of books by the subjects of my study. In this conclusion I will widen the focus of reference and application to include very brief discussions of other thinkers and practitioners. In the Introduction I borrowed the title of Roland Barthes's collection of essays, *L'obvie et l'obtus* (*The Obvious and the Obtuse*). I wanted to ask questions that might seem to require no discussion since they were so obvious. Other questions and ideas (particularly those of Bakhtin) I did not want to examine directly. In many respects I am following Bakhtin's lead in taking both approaches. His early phenomenological approach asks very basic questions about our attempts to make sense of the world and our place in it. Were it not for his fundamental level of enquiry it might seem too obtuse to ask questions like, what is a character? What does it mean to know something? Bakhtin's consistent references to theatre only to insist upon the superiority of the novel demands that we ask the seemingly ridiculous question: what is the difference between a novel and theatre?

Bakhtin's argument in *Toward a Philosophy of the Act* was that the truth of a philosophical principle comes from a person doing something about it, from it being put into practice. It is surely this insistence that theory be made real through embodied practice that recommends Bakhtin's early way of doing philosophy to the student of theatre. However this book has not been an attempt to write a book call *Toward a Philosophy of Acting*. Its aim has been to show that questions about acting, and more broadly about theatre, touch upon themes and processes which are central to our understanding of both ourselves and other people. Might the actor's ability to reproduce forms of human behaviour itself be a form of understanding how humans behave?

Novel and theatre

There is one very basic similarity in the reading of a novel and the reading of a playscript: with both the reader creates mental images from written signs. For example, these may be mental images of how a character looks, speaks or moves. Bakhtin dwells very little on the creative processes of the reader, being more interested in the interaction of author and character. From one perspective it is all too obvious to point out the difference between a character in a novel and on the stage. But it is a question which reveals much about the nature of theatre. Unlike the novelistic image, a character on stage is a physically material presence. A character has to be there the moment the actor walks on stage whether speaking lines or not. That is why performing a role involves more than remembering the lines. The actor's creative work is to give body and voice to a character – to make a literary image into a material reality.

Although Stanislavsky adapted prose fiction for the stage – notably Dostoevsky's *The Village of Stepanchikovo* – he does not dwell upon the process by which the novelistic image transfers to the stage. Did he feel that he *was* the Uncle in *The Village of Stepanchikovo* precisely because it was a short novel? A novel furnishes a great deal more information about the character than a playscript where there is little back-story and no description of how they look, talk and walk. Probably for this reason Mladen Materic argued that character is a concept taken from the nineteenth-century realist novel. Compared to a novel, a playscript is much less complete. It cannot offer the detail of description that one finds in a novel because it takes place in real time and space, both of which are limited. Theatre has therefore to be far more economic in its use of visual means and of spoken dialogue. For this reason it centres upon image, metaphor and action. It has to be suggestive and appeal to the audience's imagination. This incompleteness of the playscript explains why Stanislavsky felt the need to fill it out with background detail and why I have described his production notes as novelisations of the playscript. As it were, he is restoring the playscript to the complete status of a novel.

In *Author and Hero* Bakhtin argued against the possibility of adapting Dostoevsky for the stage because one cannot stage voices. Even though he wrote this before he had developed his theory of novelistic discourse, already he was proposing an alternative notion of the character – as a voice, rather than an image. In moving away from the phenomenological and the visual to the verbal and acoustic, he opened the way for his later sophisticated analysis of dialogue in the novel. In the section below on time and space we will see the same shift from a phenomenological account of physical position and duration, to an analysis of the genres by which time and space are represented in literature.

It is precisely because Bakhtin's early writings take a phenomenological approach to character that they can illuminate the creative process of the actor – we are still in the realm of the material world as a place of observed action. The specificity of theatre is that its means of representing the actions of humans in the world are material: everything on stage has its own colour, texture, weight, dimension and scale. We have seen in Chapter 5 that it was precisely this materiality that made theatre inimical to Symbolists as an artistic form. They sought a more spiritual mode of representation. We will return to a more full discussion of this materiality in the section below.

Bakhtin's central criticism of dramatic dialogue was that it was less capable of reflecting the divided mind of a character. Dramatic dialogue provided Bakhtin with a foil to demonstrate the greater sophistication of novelistic dialogue where two voices could sound simultaneously in the same word or line. In theatre the dialogue is spoken by the actor/character. It is physically impossible to be double-voiced in the sense that Bakhtin intends. While this is true of realist theatre, in many of the theatrical genres mentioned by Bakhtin, there is another kind of dialogism taking place. Before the auditorium was darkened and separated from the stage by the proscenium arch, the actor would address their public which was visibly and audibly present. This is true of Shakespeare's stage, of the pageant wagons of mystery cycles, or the portable booth and trestle stages of miracle plays and the touring troupes of the Commedia dell'Arte. Is there not a double-voicing in the asides of an actor to the audience, or in their soliloquies? There is much subtle metadramatic reference in Shakespeare's plays where the audience is reminded that the characters on stage are acting like actors in a play. There is a very productive 'doubling' of the world represented and the means of representation. Or take the example of the metadrama in *Hamlet* which is a reflection upon how politics resembles theatre, both in Elsinore and more generally. This dialogue was possible because of the acknowledged presence of the audience. Of course this dramatic dialogism disappeared once actors were instructed not to deliver their lines directly to the audience but to address the other actors, and to believe in the world pictured behind the proscenium arch. It was precisely the shift to greater theatrical realism that robbed the stage of its own form of double-voicing. A great deal of Bakhtin's problem with theatre is simply that its dialogue, spoken as it is by one actor at a time, cannot do what novelistic dialogue can do. But this is like criticising ceramics for not being woodwork.

Acting and act-performing

Hamlet's major problem is not that he cannot act, but that he cannot find the right moment to act. His reflections on the propitious moment of action again folds the representing time of the performance with represented time of the story, *mimesis* and *diegesis*. In this study the terms 'action', 'character' and 'story' have been interlinked in complex ways: Stanislavsky develops a method of physical action that is taken up and transformed by Grotowski. When Stanislavsky traces drama back to the ancient Greek verb *dran* (to do), he is probably also thinking of Aristotle's definition of tragedy as the imitation of an action.

We have seen how Bakhtin's early *Toward a Philosophy of the Act* has been so useful in offering an actor a model for the world view of the act-performer. Both he and Stanislavsky demanded a form of behaviour that was an unmediated and non-transferable response to the immediate environment. In Stanislavsky's case this in turn demanded a total revolution in the notion of staging and the role of the actor. It is an irony that while Bakhtin's ideas about the experience of the act-performer illuminate Stanislavsky's ideas about truthful acting, they have nothing to do with Bakhtin's own notion of character, which requires the intercessory figure of the *other*. Ethics is the preserve of the act-performing *I* and aesthetics the realm of the authoring *other*. While the act is the endpoint of his account of ethical activity it is both the beginning and the very form of the stage actor's creative activity. Through performing the physical actions given in a playscript the actor can enter into the emotional life of the character. It is a process of empathetic identification.

When we turn to Meyerhold and Grotowski the act becomes something different again. It is no longer a representation of an action, but an enaction which draws attention to its very mode of enactment. We return to a metadramatic form of theatre. Meyerhold's theatricality means that both audience and actor take pleasure from how the action is performed. The sets are abstract in that they represent nothing, but they are dynamic structures, generating a kind of excitement that one finds in a circus. A delight in the material processes of theatre. Grotowski was much more concerned with the ethical dialogue between audience and actor, and aesthetics played a secondary role in his theatre. The play was reduced to the performance of a set of physical actions whose performance was scored in meticulous detail. With Grotowski's account of acting we almost return to a Bakhtinian notion of ethical commitment. It is ethical because the actor's engagement with the character is a means by which he or she can tackle moral questions. To put this in more general terms, I suggested in Chapter 6 that theatre, or the 'aesthetic', is a vehicle by means of which the actor can work on him- or herself.

Time and space in the novel and in theatre

The early Bakhtin offers two accounts of time and space: the first is a phenomenological description of the experience of being an embodied self, that is, of being in time and space. Later he would offer an account of the genres or forms of time and space in written narratives. I have argued that the first is directly useful to the actor while the second is more useful in understanding the history of theatre. Although theoretically dense his phenomenological description of first-person consciousness provides what Clifford Geertz calls a 'thick' description of human experience. Bakhtin describes what meaning feels like; when something matters so much you are compelled to act upon this feeling. I have argued that this is precisely the feeling-state that an actor has to develop when playing a character (in realistic dramas). Much of the vividness of Bakhtin's early philosophy stems from the fact that he situates the body of the act-performer in lived time and space. This may well stem from a desire to 'de-transcendentalise' Kant's categories of time and space (a philosophical project that falls outside the interests of this present study), but the result is that they are presented as a person's experience of a lived environment and horizon rather than as impersonal categories of thinking.

> Here we employ the Kantian evaluation of the importance of these forms in the cognitive process, but differ from Kant in taking them not as 'transcendental' but as forms of the most immediate reality. We shall attempt to show the role these forms play in the process of concrete artistic cognition [artistic visualisation] under conditions obtaining in the genre of the novel.[1]

It is precisely this casting of time and space as things to be physically experienced – 'forms of the most immediate reality' – rather than thought about that helps

Bakhtin's theory of the novel to translate to the realm of theatre. However, for all that Bakhtin wrote about the unrepeatable moment of an action, and the untransferable position of the act-performer, it is hardly a literal description of place and time. He writes about space rather than a specific place. There is a degree to which he is writing both literally *and* metaphorically. We use spatial metaphor to describe our evaluative attitude towards things in the world: thus to take a position on a matter is to put oneself in a particular relation to it. The place of answerability is quite as much topological where relations are expressed spatially, or diagrammatically, as it is topographic where the actual features of a place are described. Bakhtin is discussing a sense of being in a particular relation to an object or person or event.

The superscription to Chapter 2 – 'Jesus help me find my proper place' – suggests that we have a moral obligation to move in order to find our proper place, rather than accepting our given place. Possibly Bakhtin's inability to move with ease led to his stoic acceptance of his position, of his place from which he felt compelled to answer. It is precisely because Bakhtin thinks topologically rather than topographically that leads to confusion about his notion of time and space. This is an example of what Holquist described as Bakhtin's habit of generalising about specifics. Without wishing to diminish the philosophical pungency of his account of ethical commitment, Bakhtin's description of situatedness, of the feeling of being answerable, can be of huge use to an actor. The master-distinction between horizon and environment is similarly a mix of phenomenological description and spatial metaphor. Once something is on my horizon I have marked it as an object of specific attention. Although Bakhtin's early phenomenological works are about time and space they are figurative, topological, rather than topographic.

The discussion thus far has been about the situatedness of a perceiving subject. Bakhtin's concept of outside-ness brings the other person into play, and more particularly the interrelation between author and hero, actor and character. The very notion of the incompleteness of one's vision/knowledge of oneself is predicated on a topological relationship. There is a strong connection between this aspect of Bakhtin's thinking and the work of George Lakoff and Mark Johnson, particularly *Metaphors We Live by* (1980). One way for the actor to 'get into the mind' of a character is to recreate the spatial orientation in the world of an act-performing *I*.

Now let us deal with his later account of time and space in *Forms of Time and of the Chronotope*. In this conclusion I have been following the implications of Bakhtin's categorical distinction between the novel and theatre. His early manuscripts are about 'verbal creation' and the only extended literary treatment in both *Author and Hero* and *Act* is Pushkin's poem 'The Parting', not a novel. This returns us to the difference between 'verbal creation', be it novel or poem, and theatre. Space and time in a work of literature are imagined categories, created by the reader. Theatre space is both real and not real, representing and represented. Performance time flows irreversibly forward in rhythmic pulses, each with its own unrepeatable patterning. With the concept of the chronotope Bakhtin introduced the notion that one could identify characteristic 'forms of time' in literature (in fact he was writing about forms of time *and* space, as is suggested by the Greek title). I have suggested that the chronotope could be very productively adapted to a discussion of theatre production which is even more palpably about forms of time and space. Plasticity is the sculptural form of space; rhythm and duration are forms of time. Both the actor's and the director's work involves the development of a sensitivity to these felt aspects of time and space. Theatre is inescapably an art form based in time and space. The dramatic text lives on as literature; theatrical performance exists in an unrepeatable present.

Bakhtin did relate the chronotope to theatre. He wrote about the chronotope 'of the entr'acte, the chronotope of theatrical space, the right to act life as a comedy and to treat others as actors, to rip off masks'.[2] He explains that

> [a]t the heart of *Tristram Shandy* lies the intervallic chronotope of the puppet theatre, in disguised form. Sterneanism is the style of a wooden puppet directed and commented upon by the author himself.'[3]

As ever, Bakhtin is drawing on theatre as a metaphor, firstly for an attitude to living one's life and secondly for the author's relation to his own writing. But why not follow Bakhtin's line of argument and state that any recognised form of communication that is undertaken for a length of time is going to acquire generic features and become aware of itself as a medium of expression? This is the central message of Bakhtin's arguments in the 1930s, which are themselves a development of ideas articulated by Voloshinov and Medvedev in the 1920s. Every utterance bears a trace of its speaking community, and its recognisable features will be obvious to other speaking communities. This might help the reader to follow Bakhtin's more complicated account below:

> Cultural and literary traditions (including the most ancient) are preserved and continue to live not in the individual subjective memory of a single individual and not in some kind of collective 'psyche', but rather in the objective forms that culture itself assumes (including the forms of language and spoken speech), and in this sense they are inter-subjective and inter-individual (and consequently social); from there they enter literary works, sometimes completely by-passing the subjective individual memory of their creators.[4]

Culture as a recognisable phenomenon is the result of the communicative activity of its members over time. Literature is, as it were, the memory of this communicative activity. Everyday genres of speech become taken on in literature and thus acquire a degree of historical permanence. On this point of cultural transmission Grotowski is ambivalent. On the one hand he protests that, as a European, of course he respects his literary heritage. On the other he argues that it is only the body that remembers.

Let us pursue the argument about generic memory. I would suggest that Marvin Carlson's *Haunted Stage* (2003) is a chronotopic study, arguing as it does that theatres, stages, designs, indeed all aspects of theatrical production, are haunted by memories of earlier forms. Part of an audience's enjoyment of a production is based on its ability to recognise certain rules and stylistic features. The most obvious example is in pantomime, where an audience is expected to shout 'he's behind you' when the baddie enters behind the hero. Each genre in theatre is a certain game with the audience, a game with its own rules which assigns roles to audience and actor. Bakhtin was right to argue that there is no such thing as an 'Adamic' language that is purely denotative. Theatre, like any other regularly practiced communicative act develops its own iterative memory.

Bakhtin's essay on the chronotope charted the twin development of the representation of historical time and individual consciousness in the novel. In Chapter 2 I offered a history of the late nineteenth-century stage from Charles Kean and the Saxe Meiningen troupe through to Stanislavsky's early experiments. Kean's use of authentic period costume and props inspired Chronegk to develop this sense of historical period, though it also prompted critics to question whether this was theatre or archaeology. Chronegk went further than Kean in keeping his actors within the frame of the proscenium arch and in no longer addressing the audience directly. With Stanislavsky period detail soon gave way to a theatrical reality that was not created by stage setting and costume but through the actor's work on character. He rejected the excessive detail of the historical line, but also of naturalism. Let us recall the anecdote of Stanislavsky building a house on stage 'real to the last detail' which nevertheless remained 'theatre' because 'no real house would ever be built inside a house'.[5] The real in theatre doesn't lie in the object *per se* but in how it is brought into play by the actors. Part of the pleasure in the theatrical sign is its suggestibility, its need to be completed by the audience's imagination. Because it cannot be a photographic reproduction of the real the stage picture or scene is necessarily a selection of details from the possible whole. The theatrical sign is synecdochic. Part of an object can be used to suggest the whole, as when a sail, or even something like a sail (a handkerchief), is taken as the ship. Stanislavsky admitted that in early productions his actors needed to be supported by rather gross external detail, but as his training developed they achieved this reality through their ability to believe in (or is it imagine?) the reality of the stage world. Training exercises such as 'circles of attention' helped them to maintain their focus on the stage world rather than becoming distracted by the audience beyond.

Meyerhold's Symbolist productions already demonstrated a feeling for the sculptural and musical form of the actor's movement on the stage. This feeling for musicality can already be detected in his criticism of Stanislavsky's productions of Chekhov's *The Seagull*. He lamented the use of sound effects to create atmosphere rather than attending to the 'sheer musicality of the actors who grasped the rhythm of Chekhov's poetry and succeeded in casting a sheen of moonlight over their creations'.[6] This isn't a symbolic form of time but a feeling for its musicality and explains why he wrote to Chekhov: 'Your play is abstract, like a Tchaikovsky symphony. Before all else, the director must get the "sound" of it.'[7] Where Stanislavsky held a belief in a more spiritual union between actor and character, character and audience, Meyerhold developed a more material approach to questions of acting, characterisation and audience address. Stanislavsky experimented with Symbolist drama and famously collaborated with Craig on a production of *Hamlet* (who characteristically insisted upon total artistic control). But while Meyerhold's staging led seamlessly into modernist and finally to constructivist productions, Stanislavsky's stage remained the representation of the space and time of the play. The thread that led Meyerhold from Symbolism through *commedia*-inspired productions to his collaborations with the constructivist designers Popova and Stepanova was his vision of theatre as an autonomous art. Even though both he and Stanislavsky saw the possibility of collaboration in the late 1930s, one cannot ignore the differences in their aesthetics and political outlooks. Like Craig and Appia, Meyerhold dispensed with the picture-frame proscenium arch and approached the three-dimensional stage as a space for the actor's movement. But where Craig and Appia used lighting, screens and rostra to create three-dimensional volumes of space, his constructivist collaborators created dynamic structures like chutes and treadmills.

What do Meyerhold and Grotowski mean when talking about the 'autonomy' of theatre? Answering this question returns us to the theme of time and space. Bakhtin writes about novelistic discourse being both represented and representing. It was precisely this 'double' space that Clive Barker was discussing in Chapter 2: on the one hand the physical dimensions of the stage space, on the other the suggested space of a play's different settings. There are two times and places. Barker also mentioned a third space – the auditorium, that 'ominous blackness beyond the picture-frame'[8] that Stanislavsky writes about in *An Actor's Work*.

In very different ways Meyerhold and Grotowski created a unified space and time of performance, one shared by both audience and actor. This was a material unity, and not the narrative unity of time and space that Aristotle wrote of. Meyerhold was among those artists who returned to the reality of the materials of their art, rather than using these materials to represent some other reality.

> Words alone cannot say everything. Hence there must be a *pattern of movement* on the stage to transform the spectator into a vigilant observer, to furnish him with that material which the two people in conversation yielded to the third, the material which helps him grasp the true feelings of the characters. Words catch the ear, plasticity – the eye.[9]

For this reason he declares that '[w]e have only to talk to the latest followers of Picasso and Tatlin to know at once that we are dealing with kindred spirits' and concludes that what the '*modern* spectator wants is the placard, the juxtaposition of the surfaces and shapes of *tangible materials!*'[10] Even at the height of his constructivist phase, he argues that the actor's material consists 'of plastic forms in space' – bodily movements which are 'subject to constant laws of mechanics'.[11] Meyerhold's approach to space and to time is unflinchingly modernist. Plasticity and rhythm are materials from which he creates his productions. His notion of *emploi* is a typology of the physiological shapes of actors and their corresponding styles of movement and speech. In this way he develops Appia's notion of the human figure as *Massgebend* (the measure of spatial scale for the stage) into something much more dynamic. The human figure is both the material and the manipulator of performance materials. Theatre lies in the relation between the moving figure and its stage environment. Above Meyerhold described Chekhov's plays as abstract, in that they were musical and not representational. The same could be said of his own productions. Unlike Bakhtin's representational notion of narrative rhythm, the organising principle of Meyerhold's performance time is neither the logic nor the psychology of narrative, but the logic of music. Accordingly his compositional method was the montage of scenes, putting them together according to their rhythmical suitability rather than a logic of story-telling.

As the 1930s drew on so pressure from the Soviet authorities saw Meyerhold returning to more realistic productions, for example his 1934 production of Dumas's *Dame aux Camélias*. As realism became official policy so its opposite, 'formalism', became a term of official opprobrium. Meyerhold's theatre was closed in January 1938 and he was executed in February 1940.

Grotowski's productions of the 1960s demonstrated continuity with Meyerhold's bold formal experiments. His approach to time and space in theatrical production owed more to Meyerhold than to Stanislavsky: he created montages and included the audience in his single theatrical space. There were significant differences from Meyerhold: he performed in a studio space so that he could experiment with different actor-audience configurations, meaning that the spectator took on different roles. The more important difference was in the nature and significance of the stage image and the sense of the time of performance. Rather than choosing to set his productions in a variety of scenes, his mature productions selected one single situation by means of which the audience could judge the gap between the values of that play and those of the present day. Grotowski argued that without the possibility of a shared set of beliefs uniting past and present, audience and actor, the space and time of the theatre had to become one of forensic investigation of those beliefs. This was not a verbal dialogue about or between values, but a physical situation experienced by the audience. The means of communication were entirely theatrical, but lacking any of the exuberance or provocation of Meyerhold's productions. This was a Poor Theatre that brought together the actor and audience into close physical proximity, so that the movements and sounds of the one would have maximum and direct impact upon the bodies of the others. If the use of non-realistic staging and montage composition owed a debt to Meyerhold, then the physical actions of the actors owed an equal debt to Stanislavsky. Grotowski's stage metaphors were a complex hybrid of the here and now of performance and the other time and place of a play: they were not past narratives played in the present, but viscerally embodied now.

Bakhtin's ideas about time and space are useful because they oblige a student of theatre to realise the very different ways in which this live medium creates and conveys its meaning as distinct from the novel. I would argue that it is not productive to apply Bakhtin's theories directly to theatre, even when he himself has written about acting (as in *Author and Hero*) or theatre styles, or even theatre architecture. Bakhtin took theatre for granted. It was a repertory of fixed images that helped him to describe the operations and dynamics of the novel and its discourses. In my argument I have subjected theatrical practices to the very unusual questions that Bakhtin asked of the novel. He has thereby unwittingly proposed a very unfamiliar way of looking at and understanding the shifts in thinking about theatre and the practice of theatre that took place in his lifetime.

The actor's body and the image of the character

Bakhtin's early philosophy is, very literally, complex. He creates conceptual vortices where one concept draws in another and thus creates an ever-widening spiral of thought. Unfortunately, written arguments have to be linear and deal with things in order. Thus, in the section about time and space I had to bracket out a consideration of the body. And yet Bakhtin makes the very obvious point that a body is in time and space. Ineluctably. However he also points out that we can also transcend our bodily situation through thought. Bakhtin's career as a writer and teacher is such an act of transcendence: undistracted by the inconvenience and pain of his own bodily condition he wrote about bodies from his early phenomenological manuscripts to *Rabelais and His World*, his paean to the material body.

Bakhtin's early ideas about the body have immense application to the Stanislavsky tradition of acting where the central question is about how an actor can embody a character. Bakhtin's description of first- and third-person experience of the body is at one level thuddingly obvious. Given that our eyes are in the front and centre of our face of course we cannot see ourselves in the round. We can only grasp the image of another's body in the round. Bakhtin's vivid descriptions of these two experiences of the human body can help an actor to make the leap from their given body to the one they are tasked to create. To embody a character an actor has to be able to feel space gaining 'body as the possible horizon of mortal man and as his possible environment' and time possessing 'valuative weight and heaviness as the progress of mortal man's life'.[12] Note the use of the terms 'environment' and 'horizon' in his description. In this equation between physical weight and meaning lies the key to embodying a character. By this means the 'flesh' of the character creates 'an incarnation of meaning in existence rather than a validation and demonstration of meaning in existence'.[13] This is the difference between a thought that is the subject of a theoretical discussion, and one that is embodied as a motive for action. Simply put, this is the difference between embodied and abstract knowledge.

The same phenomenological theory of first- and third-person experience leads to an account of how the observation of a real person can result in the creation of their literary image. Bakhtin starts with a spectator who is drawn to observe another person and ultimately create a verbal image of them. I have pointed out that the work of the actor is the complete opposite: starting with a written script, the actor, with the assistance of the director, has to embody that character. In Chapter 3 I explored how an understanding of Stanislavsky's actor training reveals substantial gaps in Bakhtin's theory both of the body and of characterisation. Neither in Bakhtin's notion of time and space, nor of the body, does he include the notion of movement. Is it that there is still an element of the Kantian philosopher in him, as he attempts to establish an architectonics, a set of spatial relations that are, as in any building, set in stone? In his writings from early to late, the body is always an image (no matter how fantastical). The term image (Russian *obraz*) is both actual (a visual image) and metaphorical (a literary image). In his early philosophy he writes about verbal images of the hero, and in later writings about images of language. An image is both a thing seen from somewhere, the result of a perceptual act, and a totality of understanding, a conceptual act. An image is therefore both given (to the senses) and created (by the intellect). According to Bakhtin, to grasp something as an image is to understand it as a totality and in its totality. It is that light bulb moment of understanding that makes one exclaim: 'Oh, I see.' Once again, this is a phenomenological rather than an epistemological account of understanding: Bakhtin describes the experience of a moment of understanding. This question of whether an image is perceptual or conceptual could be extended in the light of Merleau-Ponty's phenomenology and more recent neurophysiological research. For example, we do not actually 'see' a face as a finished image, as much as recognise a selection of distinctive facial features which we take together as that person's face. People with the condition of prosopagnosia cannot arrive at such recognition. A face is not a given image but one constructed in an act of recognition and understanding.

The aesthetic theories of both Bakhtin and Stanislavsky rely on the ability of one person to enter into the experience of another. Neither offers an account of how this process of empathetic transposition might take place. The process surely begins with a recognition of signs for inner mental or affective states. Bakhtin very tellingly describes what another looks like when in pain (he had enough experience of this himself). We can judge the emotional state of a person from their facial expressions (Paul Ekman's *Emotions Revealed*, 2007, is a significant study in the area) and their accompanying vocal sounds, rhythms and intonations. Bakhtin is right that we know these as signs of emotions in others, but can only imagine how we ourselves look in such emotional states. To recognise the emotional state of another is one degree of fellow feeling, but what of full-blown empathy? Is it a process of imagining the bodily sensations of another? Are actors particularly gifted in this process of bodily imagining? Although they deserve much more space, I shall very briefly touch on how Evgeni Vakhtangov and Michael Chekhov, two of Stanislavsky's most talented students, developed this aspect of acting.

Chekhov and Vakhtangov are playing pool together very badly.

> Suddenly, Vakhtangov announced, 'Watch this!' Changing his entire physical stance and attitude, Vakhtangov sank ball after ball while Chekhov watched in amazement. After Vakhtangov finally missed a shot, a startled Chekhov asked how such prowess was possible. Vakhtangov replied that he decided to imagine that he was the greatest pool player ever, taking on his posture, movements, and way of thinking. Vakhtangov explained that he himself could never play billiards as brilliantly.[14]

Where Stanislavsky demands that the actor imagine themselves in the situation of the character, Vakhtangov imagines the figure and the actions of the character. His sense of justification comes from believing in the acting and not necessarily the content of the action. Chekhov criticised Stanislavsky's early creative method because he stressed 'that everything was from inside and we must forget how we looked'. Chekhov argued that you must have both this inner richness, and you must 'know how you look from the outside'.[15] The early Bakhtin, as ever more on the side of Stanislavsky, argued that imagining one's body is a cognitive activity and is thus unconvincing. He contends that 'in the act of thinking I first of all abstract myself from that unique place which I – as this unique human being – occupy in being'.[16] Vakhtangov and Chekhov (and Meyerhold too) counter that it is not cognitive but part of our kinaesthetic feeling of ourselves. The intuitions of these theatre practitioners are now being confirmed by such neurophysiologists as Alain Berthoz, who argues that an important aspect of the brain is to simulate movement.[17]

A central feature of Chekhov's approach is that an actor uses their imagination. His approach is both visual *and* physical. First you see the character in your mind's eye and then you have to embody this image of the character. It is therefore a highly sophisticated relay between our visual and our kinaesthetic senses.

> By imagining *Romeo and Juliet*, and especially your own part in it, you have to try to develop in more and more detail everything you are going to perform. The more details the better. That means that you have to *act* in your imagi- nation, your own part, and also act other parts as much as you need in order to clarify your own part, your own character, etc.[18]

He then goes on to describe how the actor needs to exercise the imagination, after which 'you will find that almost at once your physical body will become like the imaginary one'.[19] In other words, if you work on your imagination, you will find that the process of transferring the imaginary to the physical becomes easier. Chekhov is asking us to use our *kinaesthetic imagination* to feel movement without actually moving physically.

The theme of the image has highlighted differences between all the figures in this study. In Stanislavsky's early career he had to resist imitating the image of actors whom he admired, and the notion became associated with an external and superficial acting. Stanislavsky and Bakhtin both agreed on the priority of feeling over thinking, but Stanislavsky went further by prioritising internal feeling over seeing. Many of Grotowski's metaphors concern a rejection of the superficial in favour of the internal. The outside is associated with insincerity and affectation, whereas truth is found within the body – under the skin. Grotowski's speeches and interviews are littered with injunctions to tear off the life-mask to reveal the underlying person beneath. In one interview he asks whether he has managed to throw 'off this accursed image'.[20] The mask is something put over the face to disguise one's true identity. Grotowski associates mask and image as examples of habits that have been acquired for purposes of social deception. They are false because they come from outside and not inside. Concerning the actor's work

Grotowski would declare '[o]nly a description "from within" is possible here'.[21] His ethics and his aesthetics are both driven by a set of oppositions that resolve down to a profound mistrust of the social sphere. The only place of truth is the individual body and its 'natural' responses to the sounds and movements of other bodies that have been freed themselves from social imposture. He describes such forms as the Indian *Kathakali* and the Japanese *Noh* as 'alphabetic' theatre and rejects them as models for either acting or actor training precisely because their meanings have been codified over years of practice.

Just as Grotowski declared that there is no common set of beliefs that unify an audience, so he rejects any formal rules or protocols by which there could be a shared language between actors and audience. If this position seems at the opposite pole to members of the Bakhtin Circle, who were fascinated by the generic shaping of social speech, there is an interview conducted late in his life where Bakhtin gloomily states that '[e]verything that was created during the past half century on this graceless soil, beneath this unfree sky, all of it is to some degree morally flawed'.[22] However Bakhtin might have felt towards the end of his life, this does not diminish the theoretical force of his ideas about the social dynamics of discourse.

Taking a completely opposite attitude towards body, mask and image is Meyerhold. His, as Marjorie Hoover has stated, is a conscious art of theatre. Where Stanislavsky relies on the unknowable creative processes of the subconscious, and Grotowski relies on the instinctive promptings of the body, Meyerhold demands his actors be aware of every nuance of rhythm and movement on stage. There is a key passage in Chapter 5 which lists concepts like *risunok* and *raccourci* whereby the actor judges their own outline or shape in performance. Not only did Meyerhold demand a conscious art of acting, he considered it 'essential that the actor find pleasure for himself in executing a given movement or action pattern [*risunok*]. If you find that pleasure, then everything will work out'.[23]

In Bakhtin's early theory the character is the aesthetic image of a living body; in the practice of Stanislavsky, Meyerhold, Chekhov and Vakhtangov it is the actor's body that has to be transformed into the image of a character. The actor's body is at once instrument, material and artist.

I have already made some conclusions about the body in this study: Bakhtin's neither moves nor learns from its experiences of act-performing; it is not a body that develops or comes together as a whole. His body is given a position and answers from there. His fruitful distinction between given and created has no application to the body. He also makes a categorical division between the external body (which is seen by me) and the internal body (which is felt by me). Stanislavsky's given body was stiff and had to be gradually transformed through training. Moreover he insists that because sustained use generates bad habits the actor's body must be constantly renewed through training. Meyerhold's image of the human body was profoundly different to that of either Stanislavsky or Grotowski. The actor's body is grasped in its spatio-temporal materiality and it is bodily movement that generates affect and meaning through assuming particular shapes and performing certain movements. Behind this 'image' of the actor's body is a notion of the human body as a moving being.

The spatial metaphor of 'inside' and 'outside' has been critical to understanding how a character is created. This division corresponds to two contrasting approaches to characterisation: one that begins inside and then is manifested externally; the other focuses on the body's external activity that is monitored internally. Bakhtin argued that while the body could be felt from the inside, it could only be understood *as an image* from the outside. Meyerhold argues almost exactly the opposite. Appealing to the behaviourist theories of Ivan Pavlov he argued that by moving in a certain way an actor will generate a specific emotion, both within him/herself and in the audience. Stanislavsky and Grotowski value an inner body from which issues truthful movement. We must conclude by underlining that 'inside' and 'outside' are *only* metaphors, and that the more important fact to grasp is that the body and the brain, the motor and sensory nerves, are intricately, intimately and functionally connected. An essential part of an actor's training is to develop this sensitivity towards both one's own movement and that of others, to create an image of both oneself and others moving in space and time.

Character

So far we have arrived at some conclusions about concepts of time and space, of body and image. Scarcely detachable from these concepts is the equally contested notion of character. In Bakhtin's early theory he suggests that the image of a character is the only form in which we only understand ourselves as act-performing people. When interpreting this notion we have to remember that his phenomenological thinking shifts between the literal and the figural. Thus while he might describe the character as the embodiment of the meaning of a person's life, the whole being the body of the character, this is a figure. Above I discussed the fact that a face is both a percept and concept, a whole that is the result of both seeing and interpreting what is seen. Is a character, like a face, just such a whole? Is character a gestalt, a form in which and by which we understand ourselves as meaningful beings? Possibly a workable definition of a gestalt is that it is a form of understanding. This is an argument borrowed from Merleau-Ponty's *Phenomenology of Perception*. Because we make sense in wholes, we assume that they are in fact things existing rather than things constructed. As we shall see in a few paragraphs ahead, we have to remember the fact that they are *constructions* and not naturally occurring things in the world.

Bakhtin certainly proposes the whole of a character as an aesthetic construct and not an organic whole. It is precisely this organic wholeness of the body which is the ultimate arbiter of truth for Grotowski. For all the directors in this study but Grotowski, the task of the actor is to incorporate the character. What separates them is their approach to how this incorporation takes place and what is being incorporated. The character for Stanislavsky is some kind of essence of humanity shared by the actor. It is an essential part of human nature. According to Stanislavsky theatre must look for 'the grain of eternally pure human feelings and thoughts […] and is understood by everybody in every age and in every language […] only that which can never under any circumstances lose its sense of beauty'.[24] Every stage in the creative process from first reading to last performance, from playwright to actor to audience, is guided by an identity with the character.

Brecht challenged this notion of the unchangeable truth about human beings which leaves them with a closed and inevitable fate rather than with a moral choice that is open to them. There is no space to pursue the detail of Brecht's ideas about character and acting, but we can at least put forth a brief critique of Stanislavsky's ideas about character. When discussing 'psychological realism' I suggested that the term 'psychological' was being used as a descriptor for what goes on inside our heads: it is the logic of our psyches. Two things follow from this definition: firstly, that a character has a mind like any other human; secondly, that a character's thoughts can be pieced together logically. The actor's work is to provide a logic for a character's given actions in a play. In order to be understandable as a character, it has to have this logic. Narrative and character are thus inextricably linked. Stanislavsky sees the notion of character as an unalterable truth of nature. We have seen two challenges to this notion: firstly that as a gestalt it is perceived as whole, but one that is constructed; furthermore, Barthes argues that this construct is to the advantage of a particular class, and it disguises this cultural particularity by claiming to be nature.

In Roland Barthes's *Mythologies* he defines a myth as a socially constructed sign that pretends to be natural. One of the articles in this collection is about the trial of a small land-owner Dominici, who was accused of the murder of members of a wealthy family.[25] Although no direct evidence implicated Dominici, the judge asked the jury to consider what kind of man this was and convict him. Barthes argues that this is a trial by literature – in other words by precisely the same logic that Stanislavsky had been using in his analysis of character. Barthes is pointing to a grotesque reversal of the claim of realism, where the truth of fiction is that it resembles life. In the Dominici trial real life is interpreted according to the logic of fiction. Twenty years later Barthes would describe the operation of these fictional codes: 'Although entirely derived from books, these codes, by a swivel characteristic of bourgeois ideology, which turns culture into nature, appear to establish reality, "Life".'[26] I have already quoted Nick Worrall who commented on 'narrow versions of "realism"' which tended 'to underwrite the "status quo" and reinscribe the contours of a "given" reality within the consciousness of the perceiver, rather than to awaken new ways of seeing and interpreting social reality, or challenge accepted orthodoxies'.[27]

Meyerhold also held to the notion of a character as a whole, but it was a physical rather than a psychological entity. Casting was a process of matching the physical and vocal characteristics of the actor – their *emploi* – with those of the character. Implicit in the *emploi* is the notion that there is a range of characters which any actor is suited to play. I have referred to the typology of *emplois* that are listed in the back of Hoover's book. Even though it took the form of a plastic reality Meyerhold still held to the idea of character as something pre-existing, indeed with a generic history – one that Bakhtin had also traced. The actor does not so much create as bring to life, to animate the already existing features of this character.

Grotowski showed at best an ambivalent attitude towards character. Consider his concept of the mask. The roles and genres of social interaction described in such intricate detail by Bakhtin and Voloshinov are reduced to and dismissed as nothing more than masks. What for Bakhtin and Meyerhold was regarded as an essential tool for understanding human interaction is rejected as being superficial. One has to ask whether he rejects the very notion of character precisely because it is an external means of understanding the self. According to Grotowski a character is an instrument for the actor to work on him- or herself. This very instrumentality consists in the character having a certain content against which actors can measure themselves. Grotowski doesn't expand on this question, but insists that whatever the character might mean or evoke within the actor's psyche is a private matter. Moreover, whatever the actor's score of actions evokes in the imaginations of the audience is their construction, and a thing separate from the actor's experience. Now we are left with a less structured notion of character – it is something that one creates because as humans we develop these patterns to make sense of the world. Grotowski argues that there is no longer that shared covenant of meaning offered by realism and his productions invited neither the actor nor the audience to identify with the character.

Other, I and thou

To conclude this reflection on character let us return for one last time to Bakhtin's early notion of *I* and *other*. One can only wonder at what led him to leave a phenomenological analysis of types of experience for one that dealt with a more sociological analysis of types of discourse, but it yielded a series of fundamental questions about acting, both local and general. One problem with a theory including the word *other* is that it can be confused with Lacan's *Other* (what he calls the big Other, *le grand Autre*) which is a category of irreducible alterity, a difference with which we cannot identify. Todorov's 1984 book on Bakhtin uses the word alterity in connection with Bakhtin's *other*. This is to make an unjustified connection with Freudian psychology and to ignore Bakhtin's insistence upon 'a human being's absolute need for the other, for the other's seeing, remembering, gathering, and unifying self-activity – the only self-activity capable of producing his outwardly finished personality'.[28] Bakhtin's *other* is much more about altruism than alterity. The *other* is both an agent of authorship, one who can redeem the meaninglessness of my own life, and the form in which *I* see other people (*I* can only experience my own subjectivity). When I wrote about 'character' as a form of understanding, as a gestalt, it was written with Bakhtin's early writings in mind.

One of the biggest questions about Bakhtin's early theory of character is whether he is writing about a creative process or an interpersonal dialogue where a loving *other* offers an *I* the existential solace and solidity of a finished image invested with meaning. This rests on the assumption that the *I* exists solely in the realm of thought and as such cannot have the embodied meaning of something in the natural world as all *others* and images are.[29] However framed, Bakhtin's categorical oppositions and definitions result in a set of very limited notions: of character (or image of *other*), of embodied existence and of the thinking self. Why is it that Bakhtin cannot accept the validity of the autobiographical self – that continually updated story that we tell about ourselves? Bakhtin's phenomenology is limited to finished images which can never be parts of an ongoing dynamic process, such as the development of a self. However, in the notion of the *I*'s temporal loophole, the fact that there is always an unpredictable future ahead of oneself, lay the seeds of Bakhtin's later notion of a character as a voice, a consciousness that answers for itself and by itself. Our open-ended existence is thus a positive and negative: a source of incompleteness but also hope.

Another way of understanding Bakhtin's *I* and *other* is to compare it to Buber's *I* and *thou* (*ich und du*). According to Holquist 'Bakhtin had read Buber by the time he came to write these early essays'.[30] This may be so, but the comparison only highlights the very significant differences between their ways of thinking, the most fundamental of which is that Buber is talking about questions of address. Bakhtin uses *other* as a general pronominal category for that which is not experienced as *I*. Buber's entire framework is based on the distinction between two different attitudes towards an addressee. When I address someone or something as *thou*, it is in a consciousness that is free of any narrow personal interests. The experience of a *thou* is a moment of co-presence outside the locational logic of time and space. He calls this address a 'primary' word, but warns that this form disappears

> [a]s soon as the relation has been worked out or has been permeated with a means, the *Thou* becomes an object among objects – perhaps the chief, but still one of them, fixed in its size and its limits.[31]

When the person or thing becomes an 'object among objects' then the dialogue has taken on the instrumental form of *I* and *it* (*ich und es*). Buber warns that all *I–thou* dialogues are destined to degenerate in this manner as we cannot remain long from our worldly interests.

Bakhtin's *other* is neither a substitute for the pronouns 'he', 'she' or 'it', nor the subject of an address ('thou') but an image: the other person grasped visually or transformed into a verbal image. Thus, while Buber's dialogue can be directly understood in terms of theatrical practice, Bakhtin's requires a much less direct path.

The irreducible essence of theatre for Grotowski was an intimate dialogue between actor and audience which prompts Schechner to ask whether he was familiar with Buber.

> Without referring to Martin Buber's 'ich und du' (I and you) directly, Grotowski spoke a great deal, and with commitment and passion, about finding a 'secure partner', a being – not necessarily another human person – with whom one could communicate.[32]

Later Schechner goes so far as to argue that constant throughout the different phases of Grotowski's career is his 'insistence that what he has to offer can be acquired only through direct contact, person-to-person interaction, Martin

Buber's "ich und du": the oral tradition'.[33] Is Schechner referring to his public discussions and interviews, his dialogue as a director with his actors, or the actor's dialogues with the public? Certainly his work with core members of his ensemble fit into the category of *I* and *thou*, and one could argue that his theatre aimed for a similar intimacy of connection with the audience. His insistence on the lack of a shared set of beliefs in the mid-twentieth century makes it more likely he would consider the audience as a collection of individual 'thou's rather than a collective 'we'. But can one talk of an *I–thou* dialogue when the flow of address is one-way? Even if 'thou' is the most appropriate pronoun for Grotowski, this was not a genuine dialogue since the audience had nothing to say. This despite the fact that he was constantly experimenting with putting the audience in a different place and thus giving them a different role. Even if the audience's role was non-speaking it was not creatively passive since the creation of the character was left to the audience. In this respect there is a similarity between Grotowski's and Bakhtin's spectator: both are authors of the character. The difference being that the act of authorship is private in one, public in the other. Grotowski recounts that when he was asked his profession by a customs officer he answered that he 'was a professional spectator – that is what the official noted down. It is evident to me that the work of the director is to be a professional spectator'.[34]

Quite how one would characterise the dialogue in his paratheatrical meetings is an interesting question. In Buber's sense it was *I–thou*, but without the supporting belief system. Grotowski was a scientific sceptic who was motivated by the desire for genuine dialogue. He accepted he lived in a post-religious age and rejected what he regarded as the sham of Communist society. He finally rejected theatre as a form and opted for a non-verbal dialogue. But a dialogue about what? Without the verbally revealed content of another person's life what can one discuss?

How would this discussion of pronouns illuminate the work of Stanislavsky and Meyerhold? The actor's relation to the audience and their character can be expressed as a gain/loss ratio with Stanislavsky: the less present the audience, the greater connection between the actor and the character. His actor seeks not 'the sound of vulgar bursts of applause' but to have the work received in 'heartfelt silence, in great intimacy'.[35] While the silence and intimacy clearly influenced Grotowski, the difference between them lay in the invisibility of Stanislavsky's auditorium. Theatre for Stanislavsky was the actor's work, with the audience being, ideally, an invisible and silent 'they'. Another difference from Grotowski was in how Stanislavsky figured the relation between the actor, the character and the audience. Stanislavsky assumed that the actor and the audience experienced the same character as that written by the author, a continuity of experience that was guaranteed because all great theatre deals with constants of human nature. Some thirty years later Grotowski rejected this notion of universal values and invited both the actor and the audience to gauge themselves against the actions and decisions of a character, who being the product of a different historical period with its own values, was necessarily something other. Only with Grotowski can one begin to talk about otherness in the post-modern sense of being not-me.

Meyerhold had a different form of audience address to both Grotowski and Stanislavsky. Spectators were treated very much as a collection of 'thou's who were actively encouraged to disagree, and thus resist the consensus of a 'we'. As for the relation between actor and character, it was more instrumental than transcendental. The actor was *both* the sculptor *and* the plastic material from which the kinetic image of the character was constructed. But when we get to Meyerhold's behaviourist account of movement we encounter a contradiction. On the one hand he argues that a particular movement will excite a corresponding emotion or reaction in the audience. But on the other he wants each member of the audience to make up their own mind as to the meaning of the play. How is this possible if they are all biomechanically determined to respond to the actor's movements in different ways?

What conclusions can we reach about the ethics and aesthetics of character? Bakhtin argues that a character can only be authored by another, and this through an act of aesthetic altruism. I have argued against his categorical prohibition of an *I* being able to construct a convincing image of him- or herself. At the heart of the actor's work for Vakhtangov, Chekhov and Meyerhold is this capacity for constructing a self-image. If this is possible for the actor might it not be something of which non-actors are capable? Moreover the images provided by Bakhtin's author are time-limited, therefore progressively less accurate. Contemporary psychological theories propose that we have an autobiographical memory by means of which we create a constantly updated narrative of one's past and one's future plans and possibilities. Just as we construct ourselves as a character using the other as a model, so we construct others as characters. Some major questions remain to be answered: do we use the same logic to make sense of our lives as Stanislavsky recommends that the actor employ to create a credible character? Do we understand other people as characters? Barthes argues that this is not simply a question of aesthetics but of ethics. Dominici the person was not tried. It was Dominici the character portrayed by the judge who was tried and found guilty (only many years later did the person receive a pardon). In *Mythologies* Barthes points to how aesthetic constructs, that is, products of bourgeois culture, are presented as being real, as *nature*. That is the very same nature which for Stanislavsky is the source and guarantee of truth and authenticity.

However, it is premature to announce the 'death of character' (the title of a book by Elinor Fuchs, published in 1996). While the fate of 'character' might have been decided in academic debate, the same is not true in the wider cultural debate where actors will be invited to explain how they 'got into' a certain character, and commentators in print and other media will still discuss whether that characterisation, or even that character, was convincing or not. The reason for this continued existence may lie in the double status of the character. Just as psychologists and academics know that characters are not real, so do actors, audiences and cultural commentators: they are constructs in which we agree to believe because, however provisional, they help us to make sense of human behaviour.

Bakhtin moved away from a character conceived as an image in the author/observer's eyes, to being a voice, a responsive subject: in short, from being a 'he' or 'she' to an 'I'. Even though this new conception of character is not an image, it is still a literary representation. In just the same way, however much Stanislavsky may claim that a character is 'like me', it cannot ever be completely 'me'. If the actor completely identified with the character he or she would be dealing with either psychosis or possession. However the alternative to this over-identification is not to play at being the character. Playing is anathema for both Stanislavsky and the early Bakhtin. Both agree that you have to answer for yourself with yourself. With his categorical distinction between ethical act-performing and aesthetic authorship, Bakhtin excluded the possibility of acting as an art. He could grasp the act of authorship as being creative but not the act of performance. It was precisely the conscious awareness of playing that appealed to Meyerhold's notion of acting. And this sense of play informed the later Bakhtin's approach to the relationship between the voices of characters and the author. Only with Grotowski could one say that the notion of character as a shared whole of meaning was finished. The actor's *I* is revealed and yet not represented, the aesthetic form here is the actor's score by means of which a certain affective state can be revisited in each performance. The score is a logic of performance and not a logic of psychology. What the audience sees and gleans from the performance is their own business.

Science: ways of knowing, kinds of meaning

The theme of science has threaded through this study. Stanislavsky argues that his method is not scientific but more about feeling. Meyerhold seemed to be much closer to science in his biomechanical training. Grotowski added a new twist to the theme by describing his studio as the Laboratory Theatre. To broaden this discussion let us return to the etymology of the word science. *Scientia* in Latin is the knowledge of a fact or situation and is characterised by certainty rather than belief. It is associated with expert knowledge. Introducing his revised study of Dostoevsky, Bakhtin declares that he is interested in neither his thinking nor specific works but the aesthetic theory at its heart, this 'completely new type of artistic thinking' whose 'significance extends far beyond the limits of the novel alone and touches upon several basic principles of European aesthetics'. It was 'something like a new artistic model of the world'.[36] Can the same claim be made for theatre practice?

Stanislavsky pointed out the difficulty he had in bringing to life the meaning of his lines. I have argued that both Bakhtin and members of his Circle defined very accurately two kinds of meaning. One is a meaning that is unattributable and general, the other is a meaning for somebody. Expressed in philosophical terms, this is the difference between epistemological and axiological meaning. An actor has to speak lines that are true for the character, that seem to come from a lived context. When the early Bakhtin described meaning as having 'weight', he was referring to this sense of context. Lev Vygotsky's name has been mentioned earlier, but a brief excursion into his account of meaning and sense will demonstrate the connection between his thinking and Bakhtin's (one made by many other commentators).[37] Alex Kozulin explains how Vygotsky distinguishes between the meaning and the sense of a word.

He made a distinction between word meaning (*znachenie*), which reflects a generalised concept, and word sense (*smysl*), which depends on the context of speech. The sense of a word is the sum of all the psychological events aroused in a person's consciousness by the word. […] A word acquires its sense from the context in which it appears; in different contexts, it changes its sense.[38]

We see how existing word meanings (*znachenie*) are oxygenated by new idiosyncratic senses that have been generated by local dialogues. A similar process of approximation takes place when we look up an unfamiliar word in a dictionary. Even though we have helpful citations which show how it has been used in context, we still have to try it out a few times before we feel that it fits, and we can start to lend it our own idiosyncratic sense. Vygotsky is describing a constant dialectical engagement between the individual and society. His writings provide a bridge between Bakhtin's early phenomenology and the later sociological writings. While both agree on this distinction between a generalised, lexical meaning and a less-established, context-specific meaning, Vygotsky is the one who emphasises the importance of both. Bakhtin assumes but never emphasises the existence of the generalised meaning: he is far more interested in the spoken life of the word. Both men are working in the field of what Saussure would call *parole* (speech) as opposed to *langue* (language as a system). Bakhtin's perspective is literary and sociological, Vygotsky's is sociological and developmental. Vygotsky focuses upon the interaction between an individual and a speaking community and this is how he provides a bridge between the early and late Bakhtin. The late Bakhtin argues for an accumulation of meaning through social use, Vygotsky for an accumulation of meaning through individual experiment.

Given that Vygotsky deals with everyday and not literary utterance, it is not surprising that his analysis also comes close to that of Voloshinov. In the section on the writings of the Bakhtin Circle in Chapter 1 of this study there is an analysis of the one-word utterance 'well'. Vygotsky notes that this kind of dialogue between partners always presupposes 'sufficient knowledge of the subject to permit abbreviated speech'.[39] In a rather uncanny echo, Vygotsky then uses the same excerpt from Dostoevsky's diary as Voloshinov where six drunk artisans argue, each one using the same swear-word to express a completely different theme. For example, the second drunk repeats the 'very same noun in response to the first fellow, but now in an altogether different tone and sense – to wit, in the sense that he fully doubted the veracity of the first fellow's denial'.[40] The example demonstrates how the meaning of a spoken word is dependent not only on context but the manner in which it is delivered.

Vygotsky's 'context' is really what Stanislavsky would call the given circumstances of the utterance. He also points to the fact that meaning is not simply conveyed through the lexical content of the word but also the evaluative intonation (as Bakhtin had also noted). It is this feeling of interaction between word and world that the actor has to reproduce – the word as a spontaneous reaction to an event in a world. Vygotsky's writings provide another important bridge in this study because he was also interested in theatre. He had, for example, written a long chapter about *Hamlet* in his *Psychology of Art* (1925). In a later book he connects the problem of theatre with a central problem in acting – how to reconcile thought and language.

> The theater faced the problem of the thought behind the words before psychology did. In teaching his system of acting, Konstantin Stanislavsky required the actors to uncover the 'subtext' of their lines in a play.[41]

Vygotksy argues that thought, unlike speech, 'does not consist of separate units'. For example when he calls to mind the image of a 'barefoot boy in a blue shirt running down the street', he doesn't enumerate each separate feature: 'I conceive of all this in one thought, but I put it into separate words.'[42] Language is inevitably linear, putting one thing after another; thought is experienced in wholes. Vygotsky puts his finger very precisely on the actor's problem which is to reconstitute the 'one thought' from the 'separate words' of a script.

In his classic *The Interpersonal World of the Infant*, Daniel Stern returns to this dialectical negotiation between the linearity of language and the multi-levelled nature of embodied experience. He describes language as 'a double-edged sword'. While language makes it possible to share experiences with others, '[i]t also makes some parts of our experience less shareable with ourselves and with others. It drives a wedge between two forms of interpersonal experience: as it is lived and as it is verbally represented'.[43] All of this is to say that the actor deals with a problem that is not specific to theatre but common to all negotiation with language: one begins with the 'abstract level intrinsic to language' and has to recreate 'the personal, immediate level'.[44]

There isn't sufficient space to explore his notion of how an individual develops intellectually, or how language develops through individual acts of thought, but there is a very strong link with the sociological approach of Voloshinov and with my argument in Chapter 3 about actor training. In the final pages of *Thought and Language* Vygotsky explains that he has 'tried only to give a general conception of the infinite complexity of this dynamic structure'.[45] Any kind of training or education is both dynamic and infinitely complex, a process of feeding forward what is already known to test how it can resolve novel problems. New knowledge is thereby generated which will in turn be fed forward when faced with the next novel problem. It is both pragmatic and dialectical. It is precisely this dynamism that was lacking in Bakhtin's phenomenological thinking. His notion of the image was too limiting because it was too static.

In the light of this discussion about learning and development let us return to an argument opened in the introduction to Part II where Sharon Carnicke discussed the thinking of Stephen North on the relationship between scholars and practitioners. He quite rightly questions the 'usual relationship' where scholars 'make knowledge' and practitioners 'apply it' and argues that practice itself generates 'new and legitimate knowledge'.[46] After the arguments in the preceding six chapters I would now conclude that practice cannot be undertaken without an informing and guiding knowledge. Furthermore, practice is only pursued with the aim of generating new knowledge. This generative dimension marks the difference between creative practice and repetitive exercise. However, the knowledge behind practice is not organised into a system. It is not architectonically structured, but organised in a way that it can be generative. Practice should not simply apply theory, it should question and expand existing theory.

The above argument prompts us to question the very opposition between practice and theory. How can this opposition be sustained after we have read so many thoughts and reflections written by practitioners? Or are we to understand that these thoughts do not constitute theory? In a letter already quoted Stanislavsky explains the process of creating his system to Elizabeth Hapgood:

> What does it mean, writing a book about the system? It does not mean writing down something that is already cut and dried. The system lives in me but it has no form. It is only when you try to find a form for it that the real system is created and defined. In other words, the system is created in the very process of being written down.[47]

This is an incredibly sophisticated account of how a theory is elaborated. Stanislavsky echoes the tension between thought and language. But there is also the problem that once theory has been systematised, either it is reproduced in repeated applications (the 'usual relationship' North noted above), or it is gradually changed through continued practice. Vygotsky described the development of meaning as a constant, complex and dynamic process of renegotiation through use. Can we therefore distinguish between two kinds of practice: one which is a slavish repetition of the already known, the other being heuristic practice, where previous knowledge has the status of a hypothesis which is tested against the novel situation?

We have seen all three directors in this study constantly changing their approach to training in the light of new challenges. One could define the actor's work as using their score as a means of generating performances which are always a spontaneous response to the given circumstances of that particular audience but within the fixed parameters of a structure, the actor's performance score. 'Heuristic' means finding out, and if in any practice, be it a public performance or a training session, nothing new is found out, then this process is simply a mechanical repetition. Which returns us to the doubleness of performance (and more generally of practice). There must always be a margin of outside awareness which monitors the contours of time and energy of that performance. Theory in this case is an intellectual margin which transcends the immediate situation of practice both to regulate a performance and to see new possibilities for that practice. It is precisely this 'loophole' that saves practice from becoming endless repetition.

So what is an actor's knowledge? Is it a body-based skill, the ability to do something that an untrained member of the public cannot? Director Peter Brook argued that '[w]hen one does exercises, it isn't to make people more powerfully skilful, it's to make everybody from the start quite simply more sensitive'.[48] The distinction between skill and sensitivity echoes Grotowski's demand that his training was about taking away rather than adding. Because Grotowski proposed a practice based on the removal of blocks rather than the teaching of skills he resisted at every point elaborating any system of rules. Is the empathy that both Bakhtin and Stanislavsky write about a kind of interpersonal skill? A kind of emotional intelligence by means of which the practised actor can 'get into' a character more effectively than one less practised? Is the practised actor more sensitive to changes in rhythms, in the dynamic contours of energy, in the feel of an audience? Is this what Artaud means by the actor being an acrobat of the heart?

Even if there are some necessary skills (as there certainly are in Meyerhold's training), there is a contradiction in this form of knowledge. Embodied knowledge has to be invisible. Like a cricketer or a racing driver, the actor cannot consciously think of their options: they have to react spontaneously with speed and accuracy. This is an informed spontaneity. Through training the actor and sportsperson have learned and remembered hundreds of possible choices upon which they can call. But the choice is not arrived at through conscious reflection: thinking is too slow. And yet as Stanislavsky pointed out, because this knowledge has become second nature, the actor has to submit to regular retraining since unconsciously acquired habits can impair the actor's skills. Skills get rusty. The status of an actor's knowledge is one of constant renegotiation.

And what of the responsibility of the scholar to the 'practitioner'? This study has also been an exercise in exploring the relation between theory and practice and understanding how the two can engage in an inter-illumination which changes both. It is not simply seeing each thing in a different light but seeing hitherto undetected potentials and problems and therefore and thereby areas for development or change. Even less is it about applying or super-imposing theory upon a practice. It has been about identifying gaps and absences in two areas of thinking and testing how each can complete the other. A dialogue.

Notes

1 *Chronotope* 85.
2 *Chronotope* 163.
3 *Chronotope* 166.
4 *Chronotope* n.17, 249.
5 In Hoover (1974) 38.
6 Braun (1991) 32.
7 Braun (1991) 33.
8 *Work* 10–11.
9 Braun (1991) 56.
10 Braun (1991) 173.
11 In Braun (1995) 173.
12 *Act* 65.
13 *Hero* 10.
14 In Gordon (1987) 77.
15 Chekhov (1985) 152.
16 *Hero* 31.
17 Berthoz (2000).
18 Chekhov (1985) 53–54.
19 Chekhov (1985) 152.

20 Kumiega (1985) 228.
21 Kumiega (1985) 186.
22 Bocharov (1994) 1012.
23 Gladkov (1997) 103.
24 *Life* (2008) 105–106.
25 Barthes (1973) 43–47.
26 Barthes (1974) 206.
27 Worrall (1996) 6.
28 *Hero* 35–36.
29 *Hero* 110.
30 Holquist (1990b) xxxv.
31 Buber (1958) 31.
32 In Schechner and Wolford (1997) 112.
33 In Schechner and Wolford (1997) 464.
34 'The Director as Professional Spectator'.
35 *Work* 55.
36 *Dostoevsky* 3.
37 For example: Holquist (1990b) 80–83, Morson and Emerson (1990) 211, Brandist (2002) 60, 182.
38 Kozulin (1986) xxxvii.
39 Vygotsky (1986) 240.
40 *Philosophy of Language* 103.
41 Vygotsky (1986) 250.
42 Vygotsky (1986) 251.
43 Stern (1998) 162.
44 Stern (1998) 163.
45 Vygotsky (1986) 254.
46 In Carnicke (1998) 66.
47 *Work* 687.
48 Brook (1994) 7.

Select bibliography

Allain, Paul, *Gardzienice – Polish Theatre in Transition*. Amsterdam: Harwood Academic Publishers, 1997.

Autant-Mathieu, M.C., 'Stalin and the Moscow Art Theatre', in *Slavic and East European Performance*. New York: City University of New York. Vol 23, No.3, 2003, pp.70–83.

Avsey, Ignat, Introduction to *The Village of Stepanchikovo*. London: Penguin, 1983, pp.ix–xxi.

Bakhtin, M.M., *The Dialogic Imagination*, Ed. Michael Holquist, Tr. Caryl Emerson and Michael Holquist. Austin: University of Texas Press, 1981.

——, *Problems of Dostoevsky's Poetics*, Ed. and Tr. Caryl Emerson. Manchester: Manchester University Press, 1984a.

——, *Rabelais and His World*, Tr. Helen Iswolsky. Bloomington: Indiana University Press, 1984b.

——, *Speech Genres and Other Late Essays*, Ed. Caryl Emerson and Michael Holquist, Tr. Vern McGee. Austin: University of Texas Press, 1986.

——, 'Prefaces to Tolstoy's Dramas and Resurrection', in Morson and Emerson 1989, pp.227–242.

——, *Author and Hero in Aesthetic Activity* in *Aesthetics of Answerability* Tr. Vadim Liapunov, Ed. Vadim Liapunov and Michael Holquist. Austin: University of Texas Press, 1990.

——, 'Contemporary Vitalism', Tr. C. Byrd in F. Burwick and P. Douglass (Eds) *The Crisis in Modernism: Bergson and the Vitalist Controversy*. Cambridge: Cambridge University Press, 1992, pp.76–96.

——, *Toward a Philosophy of the Act*, Tr. Vadim Liapunov, Ed. Vadim Liapunov and Michael Holquist. Austin: University of Texas Press, 1993.

——, 'Additions and Changes to Rabelais', Tr. Sergei Sandler, in *PMLA* Vol 129 No.3, 2014, pp.522–537.

Balukhaty, S.D., *The Seagull Produced by Stanislavsky*, Tr. David Magarshack. London: Dennis Dobson, 1952.

Barba, Eugenio, *The Land of Ashes and Diamonds*. Aberystwyth: Black Mountain Press, 1991.

Barker, Clive, *Theatre Games*. London: Methuen, 2010 (2nd Ed.).

Barthes, Roland, *Mythologies*, Tr. Annette Lavers. London: Granada Publishing, 1973.

——, *S/Z*, Tr. Richard Miller. New York: Farrar, Strauss and Giroux, 1974.

——, *L'obvie et l'obtus*. Paris: Editions du Seuil, 1982, Many of these essays are translated in Stephen Heath's collection *Image, Music, Text*, first published in 1977.

Beacham, Richard, *Adolphe Appia*. London: Harwood Academic Publishers, 1994.

Benedetti, Jean, *Stanislavski, a Biography*. London: Methuen, 1988.

——, (Ed. & Tr.) *The Moscow Art Theatre Letters*. London: Methuen, 1991.

——, Translator's Foreword to *An Actor's Work*. Abingdon: Routledge, 2008, pp.x–xxiv.

Bentley, Eric (Ed.), *The Theory of the Modern Stage*. London: Penguin, 1968.

Bertensson, Sergei, 'The Brothers Karamazov at the Moscow Art Theater', in *American Slavic and East European Review*, Vol 16, No.1, Feb. 1957, pp.74–8.

Berthoz, Alain, *The Brain's Sense of Movement*. Cambridge Mass. and London: Harvard University Press, 2000.

Beumers, B., *Yuri Lyubimov at the Taganka Theatre (1964–1994)*. London: Routledge, 1997.

Bevington, David (Ed.), *Medieval Drama*. Boston: Houghton Mifflin Company, 1975.

Bocharov, S.G., 'Conversations with Bakhtin', in *PMLA* Vol 105, October 1994, pp.1009–1024.

Bochert, Donald M. (Ed.), *Encyclopaedia of Philosophy*. Farmington Hills, Mich: Thomson Gale, 2006 (2nd Ed.).

Boleslavsky, Richard, *The First Six Lessons*. New York: Routledge, 2003.

Borovsky, Victor and Leach, Robert (Eds), *A History of Russian Theatre*. Cambridge: Cambridge University Press, 1999.

Bradshaw, Martha (Ed.), *Soviet Theatres 1917–1941*. Ann Arbor, Mich.: Edwards Brothers Inc., 1954.

Brandist, Craig, *The Bakhtin Circle*. London: Pluto, 2002.

Brandist, Craig, Shepherd, David and Tihanov, Galin (Eds), *The Bakhtin Circle: In the Master's Absence*. Manchester: Manchester University Press, 2004.

Braun, E. (Ed.), *Meyerhold: A Revolution in Theatre*. London: Methuen, 1991 (2nd Ed.).

——, (Ed. and Tr.), *Meyerhold on Theatre*. London: Methuen 1995 (2nd Ed.).

Brewster, Ben, 'From Shklovsky to Brecht: A Reply', in *Screen* Vol xv No.3, 1974, pp.82–102.

Bristol, M., *Carnival and Theater*. London: Methuen, 1985.

Brook, Peter, *There Are No Secrets*. London: Methuen, 1993.

——, *Platform Papers* No.6. London: National Theatre, 1994.

Buber, Martin, *I and Thou*, Tr. Ronald Gregor Smith. Edinburgh: T&T Clark, 1958 (1923).

Burzynski, Zbigniew, and Osinski, Tadeusz, *Grotowski's Laboratory*. Tr. unknown. Warsaw: Impress Publishers, 1979.

Carlson, Marvin, 'Theatre and Dialogism', in *Critical Theory and Performance*, Eds Janelle Reinelt and Joseph Roach. Ann Arbor: University of Michigan Press, 1992.

——, *Performance – A Critical Introduction*. London: Routledge, 1996.

——, *The Haunted Stage*. Ann Arbor: University of Michigan Press, 2003.

Carnicke, Sharon M., *Stanislavsky in Focus*. Amsterdam: Harwood Academic Publishers, 1998.

Chekhov, Michael, *Lessons for the Professional Actor*. New York: PAJ, 1985.

Cioffi, Kathleen, *Alternative Theatre in Poland 1954–1989*. Amsterdam: Harwood Academic Publishers, 1996.

Clark, Katerina, and Holquist, Michael, *Mikhail Bakhtin, A Biography*. Cambridge, Mass.: Harvard University Press, 1984.

Cooper, Simon and Mackey, Sally, *Drama and Theatre Studies*. London: Stanley Thornes, 2000.

Craig, Edward Gordon, *On the Art of the Theatre*. London: Heinemann, 1968.

Damasio, Antonio, 'The Hidden Gifts of Memory', in *Memory*, Eds Antonia Byatt, Harriet Harvey Wood. London: Vintage, 2006.

Diderot, Dennis, *Selected Writings on Art and Literature*, Tr. Geoffrey Bremner. London: Penguin, 1994.

Donnellan, Declan, Introduction to Stanislavsky's *An Actor's Work*, 2008 pp.ix–xi.

Ekman, Paul, *Emotions Revealed: Understanding Faces and Feelings*. New York: Henry Holt and Co, Owl Books, 2007.

Emerson, Caryl and Morson, G.S., *Mikhail Bakhtin, Creation of a Prosaics*, Redwood City, Calif.: Stanford University Press, 1990.

Emerson, Caryl, *The First Hundred Years of Mikhail Bakhtin*. Princeton: Princeton University Press, 1997.

Frank, J., *Exile's Return*, Vol III of a Biography of Dostoevsky. London: Robson Books, 1987.

Gladkov, A., *Meyerhold Speaks, Meyerhold Rehearses*, Tr. Alma Law. London: Harwood Academic Publishers, 1997.

Gorchakov, Nikolai, *Stanislavsky Directs*, Tr. Miriam Goldina. New York: Funk and Wagnalls, 1954.

——, *The Theatre in Soviet Russia*. London: Oxford University Press, 1957.

Gordon, Mel, *Stanislavsky in Russia*. New York: Applause, 1987.

Gregory, André and Shawn, Wallace, *My Dinner with André*. New York, Grove Press, 1981.

Grotowski, Jerzy, 'Holiday', in *New Theatre Quarterly* Vol III No.10. Cambridge: Cambridge University Press, 1973. pp.19–24.

——, *Towards a Poor Theatre*. London: Methuen, 1991.

——, *Interview* in http://owendaly.com/jeff/grotowski – accessed 16 October 2014.

Harvey Wood, Harriet and Byatt, A.S., *Memory*. London: Chatto & Windus, 2008.

Hirschkop, Ken, *Mikhail Bakhtin: An Aesthetic for Democracy*. Oxford: Oxford University Press, 1999.

Hirschkop, K. and Shepherd, D. (Eds), *Bakhtin and Cultural Theory*. Manchester: Manchester University Press, 1989 (1st Ed.), 2001 (2nd & Revised Ed.).

Hodge, Alison (Ed.), *Twentieth Century Actor Training*. London: Routledge, 2000.

——, Introduction to *Author and Hero in Aesthetic Activity*. Austin: University of Texas Press, 1990a, pp.ix–xlix.

——, *Dialogism*. London: Routledge, 1990b.

——, Preface to Bakhtin's *Toward a Philosophy of the Act* (1993) pp.vii–xv.

Hoover, Marjorie, *Meyerhold: The Art of Conscious Theatre*, Amherst: University of Massachusetts Press, 1974.

Houghton, Norris, *Moscow Rehearsals*. New York: Grove Press, 1962.

Kolankiewicz, Lezek, *On the Road to Active Culture*. Wroclaw: Grotowski Centre, 1979.

Komissarzhevsky, Victor, *Moscow Theatres*. Moscow: Foreign Languages Publishing House, 1959.

Kozulin, Alex, *Vygotsky's Psychology: A Biography of Ideas*. Cambridge, Mass: Harvard University Press, 1990.

Kumiega, J., *The Theatre of Grotowski*. London: Methuen, 1985.

Law, Alma and Gordon, Mel, *Meyerhold, Eisenstein and Biomechanics*. Jefferson, N.C. and London: McFarland & Co, 1996.

Leach, Robert, *Vsevelod Meyerhold*. Cambridge: Cambridge University Press, 1993.

——, *Stanislavsky and Meyerhold*. Oxford: Peter Lang, 2003.

Lemon, L. and Reis, M. (Eds.) *Russian Formalist Criticism*. Lincoln: University of Nebraska Press, 1965.

Magarshack, David, *Stanislavsky, A Life*. London: Faber and Faber, 1950.

——, Introduction to *On the Art of the Stage*. London: Faber and Faber, 1967, pp.11–87.

McCaw, Dick, *The Laban Sourcebook*. Abingdon: Routledge, 2011.

Medvedev, P.N., 'The Formal Method', in Shukman (1983a) pp.51–66.

——, 'Sociologism', in Shukman (1983b) pp.67–74.

——, 'The Immediate Tasks facing Literary-Historical Science', in Shukman (1983c), pp.75–92.

——, *The Formal Method*, Tr. Albert Wehrle. Cambridge, Mass.: Harvard University Press, 1985.

Merleau-Ponty, M., *Phenomenology of Perception*, Tr. Colin Smith, London: Routledge, 1992.

Meyerhold, Vsevlod, *Meyerhold on Theatre*, Ed. and Tr. Edward Braun, London: Methuen, 1991.
——, *Meyerhold Repetiruet*, Vol 1, Eds O.M. Feldman and M.M. Sitkovetskaya, Tr. William Galinski, Moscow: 1993, unpublished typescript, 54pp.
Mitchell, Stanley, 'Some preliminary remarks towards a history of the politicisation of Russian Formalism', *Screen* Vol. xv, No.4, 1974, pp.74–81.
Moore, Sonia, 'The Method of Physical Actions', in *Tulane Drama Review* No.9, 1965, pp.91–94.
Moran, Dermot, *An Introduction to Phenomenology*. London: Routledge, 2000.
Morson, G.S. and Emerson, Caryl (Eds), *Rethinking Bakhtin: Extensions and Challenges*. Evanston, Ill: Northwestern University Press, 1989.
Muza, A., 'Meyerhold at Rehearsal: New Materials on Meyerhold's Work with Actors', 1996, Johns Hopkins University Press on the WWW, http://muse.jhu.edu.
Osborne, John, *The Meiningen Court Theatre*. Cambridge: Cambridge University Press, 1988.
Picon-Vallin, B., *Meyerhold*. Paris: CNRS, 1999 (2nd Rev. Ed.).
Poole, Brian, 'From Phenomenology to Dialogue', in Hirschkop and Shepherd (2001), pp.109–135.
Richards, T., *At Work with Grotowski on the Physical Actions*. London: Routledge, 1995.
Rowell, George, *The Victorian Theatre 1792–1914*. Cambridge: Cambridge University Press, 1978 (2nd Ed.).
——, *Theatre in the Age of Irving*. Oxford: Blackwell, 1981.
Rudnitsky, Konstantin, *Meyerhold the Director*, Ed. S. Schultze, Tr. G. Petrov. Ann Arbor: Ardis, 1981.
Schechner, R. and Wolford, L. (Eds) *A Grotowski Sourcebook*. London: Routledge, 1997.
Schmidt, P. (Ed.), *Meyerhold at Work*. Manchester: Carcanet Press, 1981.
Sekirin, P. (Ed. and Tr.), *The Dostoevsky Archive*. Jefferson, N.C.: McFarland, 1997.
Senelick, Laurence, 'Stanislavsky's Double Life on Art', in Benedetti (2008) pp.xiii–xxv.
——, *Stanislavsky: A Life in Letters*. Abingdon: Routledge, 2014.
Sheets-Johnstone, Maxine, *The Primacy of Movement*. Amsterdam: John Benjamins Publishing Company, 2011 (2nd Ed.).
Shepherd, David (Ed.), *The Contexts of Bakhtin*. London: Harwood Academic Press, 1998.
Shukman, A. (Ed.), *Bakhtin School Papers*, Oxford: RPT Publications, 1983.
Simsonson, Lee, 'The Ideas of Adolphe Appia', in *The Theory of the Modern Stage*, Ed. Eric Bentley. London: Penguin, 1968, pp.25–50.
Slowiak, James and Cuesta, Jairo, *Jerzy Grotowski*. London and New York: Routledge, 2007.
Smeliansky, Anatoly, Afterword to *An Actor's Work*. Abingdon, Routledge, 2008.
Stanislavsky, K., *On the Art of the Stage*, Tr. David Magarshack. London and Boston: Faber and Faber, 1967a (2nd Ed.).
——, *My Life in Art*, Tr. James Robbins. London: Methuen, 1967b.
——, *Building a Character*, Tr. E.R. Hapgood. London: Methuen, 1979.
——, *An Actor Prepares*, Tr. E.R. Hapgood. London: Methuen, 1980.
——, *Stanislavsky's Legacy*, Tr. & Ed. E.R. Hapgood. London, Routledge, 1999.
——, *My Life in Art*, Tr. & Ed. Jean Benedetti. Abingdon: Routledge, 2008a.
——, *An Actor's Work*, Tr. & Ed. Jean Benedetti. Abingdon: Routledge, 2008b.
——, *An Actor's Work on a Role*, Tr. & Ed. Jean Benedetti. Abingdon: Routledge, 2010.
Stanislavsky, K. and Rumyantsev, Pavel. *Stanislavski on Opera*, Tr. & Ed. Elizabeth Reynolds Hapgood. New York and London: Theatre Arts Books, Routledge, 1998.
Stern, Daniel, *The Interpersonal World of the Infant*. London and New York: Karnac, 1998 (Revised Edition).

Stout, Rowland, 'Twentieth-Century Moral Philosophy', in *The Routledge Companion to Twentieth Century Philosophy*, Ed. Dermot Moran. Abingdon: Routledge, 2008, pp.851–882.

Symons, P., *Meyerhold and the Grotesque*. Coral Gables, Fla.: University of Miami Press, 1971.

Temkine, Raymonde, *Grotowski*. Tr. Alex Szogyi. New York: Avon Books, 1972.

Todorov, Tzvetan, *Mikhail Bakhtin, The Dialogical Principle*. Manchester: Manchester University Press, 1984.

——, 'I, Thou, Russia', in *Times Literary Supplement*, 13 March 1998, pp.7–8.

Torpokov, Vasily, *Stanislavsky in Rehearsal*. New York and London: Routledge, 1999.

Vakhtangov, Evgeni, *Ecrits sur le theatre*. Lausanne: Editions L'Age d'Homme, 2000.

Voloshinov, Valentin, *Freudianism: A Critical Sketch*, Tr. I.R.Titunik. Bloomington: Indiana University Press, 1976a.

——, 'Discourse in Life and Discourse in Art', in *Freudianism* (1976b) pp.93–116.

——, 'The Latest Trends in Linguistic Thought in the West', in *Shukman* (1983a) pp.31–50.

——, 'Literary Stylistics', in *Shukman* (1983b) pp.93–152.

——, *Marxism and the Philosophy of Language*, Tr. L. Matejka and I.R. Titunik. Cambridge, Mass: Harvard University Press, 1986a.

Vygotsky, Lev, *Thought and Language*, Tr., Rev. and Ed. Alex Kozulin. Cambridge, Mass: The MIT Press, 1986b (9th ed.).

Whyman, Rose, *The Stanislavsky System of Acting*. Cambridge: Cambridge University Press, 2008.

Wölfflin, Heinrich, *Principles of Art History*, Tr. M.D. Hottinger. New York: Dover Publications, 1932 [First German edition in 1915].

Wolford, Lisa, *Grotowski's Objective Drama*. Jackson: University Press of Mississippi, 1996.

Worrall, Nick, *Moscow Art Theatre*. Abingdon: Routledge, 1996.

Index

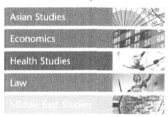
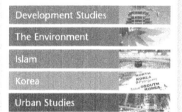

*9 7 8 1 1 3 8 8 9 1 4 4 9 *

An environmentally friendly book printed and bound in England by www.printondemand-worldwide.com

PEFC Certified

This product is
from sustainably
managed forests
and controlled
sources

www.pefc.org

PEFC
PEFC/16-33-415

This book is made of chain-of-custody materials; FSC materials for the cover and PEFC materials for the text pages.

#0028 - 050216 - C0 - 234/156/14 [16] - CB - 9781138891449